FRESH & FAST
VEGETARIAN

FRESH & FAST

VEGETARIAN

RECIPES THAT MAKE A MEAL

Marie Simmons

Photographs by Luca Trovato

 HOUGHTON MIFFLIN HARCOURT BOSTON NEW YORK 2011

Copyright © 2011 by Marie Simmons

Photographs © 2011 by Luca Trovato

For information about permission to reproduce selections from this book,
write to Permissions, Houghton Mifflin Harcourt Publishing Company,
215 Park Avenue South, New York, New York 10003.

www.hmhbooks.com

Library of Congress Cataloging-in-Publication Data
Simmons, Marie.
Fresh & fast vegetarian : recipes that make a meal / Marie Simmons ;
    photographs by Luca Trovato.
p. cm.
Summary: "Approximately 150 simple vegetarian dinners" — Provided by publisher.
ISBN 978-0-547-36891-7 (pbk.)
1. Vegetarian cooking. 2. Cookbooks. I. Title. II. Title: Fresh and fast vegetarian.
TX837.S4868 2011
641.5'636 — dc22   2010049779

Book design by Melissa Lotfy
Food styling by Rori Trovato / Prop styling by Dani Fisher

Printed in the United States of America

DOC 10 9 8 7 6 5 4 3 2 1

2047

To my friends at La Cocina Que Canta
and Rancho Tres Estrellas

Acknowledgments

One writes a cookbook recipe by recipe, cooking for days and days, pausing between bites to shop the markets and restock, compare notes with fellow cooks and feed friends and neighbors. Finally, the pages multiply, the deadline is near and the book is done. It's hard work, but because I am blessed with a sweet husband who encourages me each and every day and a coterie of generous, caring friends, colleagues and neighbors who share my passion and curiosity for food and are always happy to be volunteer tasters, the process is a pleasure.

The seed for this book was planted at La Cocina Que Canta, the cooking school at Rancho La Puerta in Tecate, Mexico, where I often teach. I am deeply grateful to Antonia Allegra for inviting me to be guest instructor, and to the fabulous staff—some of the most charming human beings on the face of the earth—who make their beautiful kitchen sing and ensure that each of my visits is inspiring and memorable.

Food and eating are so central to my circle of humanity that it is difficult to list everyone who has helped to bring this book to fruition. Those who grace my life on a regular basis are Debbie and Peter Rugh, Kathleen de Wilbur and Perry Dexter, Kathleen O'Neill, Brooke Jackson, Richard Clark, Paula and Edward Hamilton, Wendy Beers, Caryl Levine and Ken Lee, Linda Romanelli Leahy and Rob Leahy, Marvin and Maral Angus, Tracy West and Kathryn Johnson; my yoga teacher Vicki Bell; my long-time New York food editor friends Babs Chernetz, Susan Westmoreland, Michele Scicolone and Tamara Holt; my close neighbors on Rosalind Avenue, Emory and Josephine Menefee, Chere Douglas, Roger, Jools and Ryan Hand and Ruth and Mike Peretz, who are always happy to taste and offer their comments; and my book club pals Sue Ewing, Patricia Flynn, Susan Heller, Alice Johnson and Elizabeth Tilson, who all love to cook and eat as much as they love books.

This book wouldn't exist without my amazing agent, Carole Bidnick, or Rux Martin, a fabulous editor, who said, "Let's do it," without hesitation when she heard I wanted to write a vegetarian cookbook. Thank you also to Luca and Rori Trovato and Houghton Mifflin Harcourt's designer Melissa Lotfy for the beautiful photographs and the fresh, clean look. I'm also grateful to Houghton's managing editor for cookbooks, Rebecca Springer, and Jacinta Monniere for her painstakingly accurate typing.

Finally, a loving nod to my precious family: John, Stephanie, Seraphina, Shawn and Joseph—you are the reason I continue to cook.

Contents

Introduction

My transition from omnivore to mostly vegetarian was gradual enough to register as a nonevent. I only wish I had a dramatic revelation to share. Although I care deeply about the health of the planet, the treatment of the animals we eat and how our food is grown, there was nothing sudden or militant about my choosing vegetarian meals. The simple fact is I eat plant-based foods because they taste good and they make me feel better.

I come to the vegetarian table as a person who loves food, loves to cook and loves big, bold imaginative flavors. As my repertoire of ingredients and techniques and my knowledge of cooking grow, I find myself cooking meat less and less often. My mantra is fast, great-tasting recipes that use the freshest ingredients possible.

I grew up in New York's Hudson Valley, surrounded by farms. It wasn't unusual to come home after school on a September afternoon to bags of freshly harvested tomatoes, eggplant, zucchini (and their glorious blossoms, which Mom fried and we ate like potato chips) or just-picked corn lined up on the back steps. These were gifts from neighbors and relatives, happy to share the bounty of their gardens.

My mother, a schoolteacher and an excellent Italian cook who often quoted her grandmother's saying, "I'd rather spend money on good food than on the doctor," believed that food was the medicine we needed. And to Mom, that meant lots of vegetables. Vegetables, she claimed, had magical powers that would make us big and strong, give us bright eyes and shining hair and ward off that dreaded visit to the doctor. I believed her.

Another major reason for the vegetarian shift at my table must be credited to the growth in the glorious farmers' market movement. Growing up in an agrarian region, I took the local farm stand bounty and the produce from neighbors for granted. Later, as a young adult, I made my way to the big city. It was a time of change. The Union Square Market in the middle of Lower Manhattan opened. Saturday mornings, without fail, my husband, John, and I hopped on our bikes and pedaled over the Brooklyn Bridge to stock up. We must have been quite a sight, with ears of corn bungeed over our back wheels and backpacks bulging with peaches, tomatoes, green beans and, of course, a bouquet of flowers sticking out of the top. This adventure was simply an extension of my childhood. Some of the same farmers who supplied the local farm stands I visited with Mom as a kid were even there.

But no matter how experienced a cook you are, getting a vegetarian meal on the table day after day can be a challenge. One solution is to move the starch—whole grains or beans—to the center of the plate and surround it with ample servings of vegetables. One of my favorite meals is creamy white cannellini beans topped with blistered cherry tomatoes and salty black olives, served with a side dish of broccoli florets stir-fried with crunchy walnuts and red onion slivers. The comforting meatiness of the beans, the tanginess of the tomatoes, the saltiness of the olives and the exciting mix of flavors and textures in the broccoli give the plate contrasts in taste, color and texture—all the elements I look for in a meal.

In this book, "fast" means a meal that takes between 30 and 45 minutes to cook. Since prep times vary according to your skill and style in the kitchen, it's difficult to estimate them reliably, but most of the recipes in this book can be made in half to three-quarters of an hour. If a recipe does take longer than 45 minutes, it is marked "When You Have More Time." All the recipes include menu ideas for combining two or three dishes—suggestions intended to help you pull together a hearty, satisfying and delicious meal. Use them as a spring-board, but feel free to mix and match the recipes throughout the book to create your own favorite combinations.

Recently, a friend who was attempting to transition into cooking more vege-tarian meals complained, "Gosh, I spend a lot of time chopping." It's true that when you're dealing with fresh produce, there can be a lot of trimming, rinsing and chopping, but over the years, I've discovered ways to reduce prep and cook times. For instance, potatoes, beets and winter squash cook in half the time when the pieces are sliced or cubed. Searing food in a heavy skillet is quicker than oven-roasting. Although I prefer vegetables fresh from the farmers' market, I keep bagged, trimmed supermarket vegetables on hand for emergencies. The quickest-cooking members of the grains-and-beans clan—quinoa, bulgur, farro, white rice and lentils—are always in the pantry, and I keep a batch of brown rice soaking in water, refrigerated, overnight, which cuts the cooking time almost by half.

To help you avoid the frustration of not having a specific ingredient, I've in-cluded user-friendly substitutions at the end of many of the recipes. And for those who prefer no dairy or eggs, more than half of the recipes in this book are labeled "Vegan." Quick Hits—short recipes that encourage you to add a simple embellishment to a basic food—appear at the beginning of each chapter. For example, jazz up a batch of cooked bulgur or quinoa with garlic and almonds tossed in warm olive oil or add crumbled feta cheese, dried fruit and pistachios to a salad of mixed greens.

Whether it's a bowl of fancy lettuces garnished with cheese curls, dried fruits and nuts or a simple soup or hearty stew laced with exotic spices, a vegetarian meal need not be a challenge or a cause of frustration. As my mother and grand-mother knew, the ultimate goal of the cook is to be certain everyone has some-thing good to eat.

FAST TECHNIQUES

I'm always looking for ways to cook the foods I love quickly without sacrificing taste and quality. Here are a few of my solutions.

Give vegetables a good soaking.

Freshly harvested vegetables are higher in moisture and cook more quickly because their moisture converts to steam, cooking them from the inside out. Because we don't always have access to freshly harvested vegetables and often depend on bagged precut vegetables from our supermarkets, I use this technique to replace some of the moisture that has dissipated. Place the vegetable in a large bowl, cover with cold water, add a handful of ice cubes and soak for 10 to 20 minutes while you prep the other ingredients. This method is most effective with carrots, cauliflower, broccoli, greens, bell peppers and celery.

Don't peel.

Potato skins add flavor, as do beet skins, squash skins and carrot peels. Rinse the vegetables in a bowl of water and keep a stiff brush handy for scrubbing off surface dirt.

Cut vegetables into smaller pieces.

Cutting up vegetables shortens their cooking time. A shredded beet cooks faster than a beet the size of a golf ball, and sliced and diced potatoes and winter squash cook faster than large pieces.

Grate garlic, don't chop it.

I hate to chop garlic. I'm too rushed and resent the time it takes, and I find garlic presses cumbersome. Enter my trusty Microplane rasp grater (see Favorite Tools, page 7). Two strokes of a peeled garlic clove along this sharp grater, and you get soft, fine garlic every time. A small marble mortar and pestle makes quick work of mashing garlic with coarse salt. Also, beware of out-of-season or winter garlic, which is strong-tasting. In winter, I halve the amount of garlic in most recipes.

Cut onions into thin lengthwise slices.

This is the fastest, easiest way to cut them. First, halve the onion from stem to blossom end, then peel. Place it cut side down on the cutting board and cut lengthwise into thin slices. They will separate into thin crescent-moon-shaped pieces. You can vary the thickness depending on what you need, cutting them into ¼-inch-thick slices for salads, ⅛-inch-thick slices for sautés and ¼- to ½-inch-thick slices for roasting. A bonus of cutting them this way is that they will often match the shape of your other ingredients, so everything cooks evenly.

Pan-searing gives fast, flavorful results.

Heat a cast-iron skillet or other heavy skillet (not nonstick) until it is hot enough to sizzle and evaporate a drop of water, drizzle the pan with a little olive oil and add the vegetable. I use this method mostly for cherry tomatoes and mini bell peppers. The vegetables blister and blacken in a couple of minutes, the juices caramelize and the cooking time is cut in half. Direct-heat pan-searing at a slightly lower temperature also works with thick slices of beet, carrot and winter squash.

Use high heat for roasting vegetables.

Don't be afraid to crank the oven up to 450°F. I preheat the oven and a heavy-gauge baking sheet at the same time. When the food hits the pan, it immediately begins to sear. For even browning, spread the oiled and seasoned vegetables on the pan; don't crowd. This technique cuts about 20 minutes from most vegetable roasting times.

FAVORITE TOOLS

Baking sheets

I prefer rimmed sheet pans, sometimes called jelly roll pans. They are a godsend for high-temperature oven-roasting. To avoid buckling, buy only heavy-gauge metal pans with a high, rolled rim. The best size is approximately 16½ by 11¾ by 1 inch. For easy cleanup, line with a sheet of aluminum foil.

Cheese plane

A stubby V-shaped spatula with a sharp-edged horizontal opening in the middle, a plane makes thin curls of cheese, which are good for portion control. Cut from a wedge, pressing down hard and drawing the plane toward you across the surface. If you don't have a cheese plane, you can use a vegetable peeler.

Immersion blender, blender and/or food processor

These tools are especially handy for making smooth soups (see page 19).

Mortar and pestle

The mortar is the bowl and the pestle is the short, bat-shaped tool used to pound the food into a paste. Use a small (1-cup) mortar for chiles, garlic, salt and herbs and a larger (2- to 3-cup) one for pesto, guacamole and salsa.

Rasp grater (Microplane)

A long, narrow piece of curved stainless steel with razor-sharp perforations, it grates citrus zest, fresh ginger, garlic and hard cheese in seconds.

Serrated peeler

A vegetable peeler with serrated edges picks up and pulls away thin skins quickly. It is often sold as a tomato peeler. (Life is too short to peel tomatoes.)

Skillets

A large straight-sided skillet or sauté pan, 10 to 12 inches in diameter and 2½ inches deep, with a tight-fitting lid, is my all-purpose pan. I use it for everything from cooking grains to steaming greens to making risotto. Skillets that are 10 to 12 inches in diameter with shallow sloping sides are good for searing over high heat, sautéing and cooking eggs, omelets and frittatas. A small 8-inch pan is good for toasting nuts. A cast-iron skillet (10-inch) is great for high-heat cooking—searing peppers, dry-frying green beans and sautéing mushrooms or asparagus.

Soup pot or Dutch oven

A 5- to 8-quart pot has ample room for sautéing, simmering and stirring. It's great for polenta, stews and soups. A favorite is enameled cast iron.

Wok

Look for a piece of cookware called a "wok skillet." My favorite is made from anodized aluminum and has a long, soft cushioned handle. Its slightly flattened bottom ensures that it will sit securely on any cooking surface, and the material and its strong handle make it easy to lift and clean.

FAVORITE INGREDIENTS

CHEESE AND OTHER DAIRY

Cheese choices for the strict vegetarian

A wide range of cheeses use enzymes or vegetable rennet for coagulation in place of animal rennet. Search out a cheese shop with a knowledgeable staff for the best selection. In my grocery store, the cheese lists the source of the rennet on the printed labels.

Parmigiano-Reggiano

Imported from Italy, this aged, hard, granular cheese is made from skimmed or partially skimmed cow's milk and has a delicious nutty, almost buttery taste. Chopped-up rinds or chunks simmered in polenta, soup or stew are a treat.

Comté

Imported from the Jura region in east-central France, Comté is a semihard cow's-milk cheese with a rich, creamy, nutty taste. It makes a fabulous grilled cheese sandwich. To keep cheese fresh, change the wrapping each time it is used.

Feta

This cheese is imported from all over the world and can be made from cow's, goat's or sheep's milk, or a blend. I like the mild French cow's-milk feta sold in shrink-wrapped packages. Once you open feta, store it in a plastic container covered with fresh water.

Queso fresco

Available wherever Latin-American products are sold, this pressed cow's-milk cheese is dry, crumbly and salty. If it's not available, substitute a mild feta.

Crema

In Mexican cooking, crema is comparable to crème fraîche or sour cream (which may be substituted) but thin enough to drizzle on tortillas or other dishes.

CHILES

Jalapeños

These chiles are often less fiery than they are supposed to be, so I usually buy more than I need, hoping that at least half will have adequate heat. If the flesh of a jalapeño isn't hot, include some of the white membrane and seeds to add extra heat. An alternative is to use a small serrano pepper for sufficient heat.

Chipotle chiles

Delicious, smoky, and fiery hot, these chiles are sold in small cans in the Mexican section of most supermarkets, packed in a vinegary adobo sauce. Because most recipes use just a small amount, you'll want to reserve the remainder of the can for later. Remove the stems and puree the chiles, plus the sauce. Drop by teaspoonfuls onto a sheet of aluminum foil and freeze until set. Pull off the frozen chipotles and freeze in a zip-top plastic freezer bag, where they will keep for at least 6 months. See Sources (page 239).

Piquillo peppers

In Spanish, piquillo means "little beak," which describes these small pointed-tipped triangular peppers. They have a full, rich flavor and come canned or in jars in specialty markets and some supermarkets. Rinse off the brine and pat the peppers dry before using. They are excellent dressed in a vinaigrette or drizzled with olive oil and sprinkled with coarse salt. Traditionally, they are stuffed with salt cod or a mixture of fish and potatoes and served warm with a drizzle of olive oil. See Sources (page 239).

HERBS AND SPICES

Fresh herbs

I buy big bunches and store them, unwashed, standing in a plastic-bag-covered glass in the refrigerator for 1 to 2 weeks. Change the water in the glass often and wash only what you need just before using. (Water bruises the leaves and encourages rot.) For the cleanest, brightest taste, add fresh herbs at the end of the cooking time, or add half during the cooking time and save the other half to sprinkle on top. Chop the tender stems of parsley, dill and cilantro along with the leaves. Discard the woody stems.

Dried herbs

While I prefer fresh herbs, in a pinch, I use dried rosemary, oregano, mint and thyme. Simmer dried herbs in a dish to fully rehydrate them and bring out their flavor. Because drying concentrates flavor, dried herbs are strong. To substitute dried for fresh, reduce the amount by half. A trick I find useful to give dried herbs a blast of freshness is to pound them in a mortar with a sprig of Italian parsley and a pinch of coarse salt. If you don't have a mortar and pestle, make a little mound of the dried herb, coarsely chopped Italian parsley and salt and chop fine.

Smoked paprika (*Pimentón de la Vera*)

This ground red pepper has a deep, smoky aroma and a meaty taste. It comes from an area in Spain called La Vera, where the chiles are dried over wood fires before grinding. Available in specialty stores or by mail order, it comes in three strengths: *dulce,* or sweet; *agridulce,* or spicy sweet; and *picante,* or hot. I prefer the dulce and use it almost exclusively. See Sources (page 239).

Madras curry powder

All curry is a blend of spices, but I am partial to this Southern Indian mix. It contains cinnamon, anise, fenugreek, fennel and cloves, giving it a sweetness that balances the heat of the chiles and pepper. I prefer the reasonably priced Sun Brand Madras curry powder sold in a gold and white tin in many supermarkets. Feel free to substitute your favorite curry powder.

Moroccan spice blend (*ras el hanout*)

The flavors and proportions of the spices in this spice blend vary widely, but feel free to experiment with making your own from spices you have on hand (see below). Use *ras el hanout* in egg dishes, sauces and pilafs and on roasted potatoes or other vegetables. To purchase *ras el hanout*, see Sources (page 239).

✳ *Homemade Moroccan Spice Blend*
Combine ¼ to ½ teaspoon each ground cinnamon, ground cardamom, ground ginger, ground allspice, ground turmeric and freshly ground black pepper.

Za'atar

This blend of dried thyme, oregano, sumac and toasted sesame seeds makes a delicious topping, along with a rich-tasting olive oil, for yogurt, feta cheese, pilafs, vegetables and toasted breads (see Middle Eastern Bread Salad, page 64). See Sources (page 239) to purchase za'atar and sumac.

✳ *Homemade Za'atar*
Combine 2 teaspoons dried thyme, 2 teaspoons dried oregano, 2 teaspoons toasted sesame seeds, 2 teaspoons ground sumac and ½ teaspoon coarse salt.

Salt

I prefer the texture and taste of coarse salt. The staple salt in my kitchen is kosher salt. For finishing dishes, I sometimes use sea salt, which has a distinctive mineral taste. I find fine salt or the salt sold in the round boxes too metallic and salty-tasting. Because of the size of the crystals, measure by measure coarse salt contains half the sodium of fine salt.

OTHER FLAVORINGS AND SEASONINGS

Orange and lemon zest

I am partial to the fresh, bright taste that citrus zest imparts. I especially love orange with beets, tomatoes, cauliflower, broccoli and herbs like dill, mint and basil. For fine pieces, grate zest on a Microplane (see page 7). For thin strips, use a vegetable peeler to shave off pieces that are approximately ½ inch wide and 2 to 3 inches long and cut them into long, thin slivers.

Tamari and soy sauce

These two popular sauces for stir-fries are both made from soybeans, but tamari is slightly thicker and a bit smoother in taste. It is available in full-strength or reduced-sodium versions. To preserve its fresh taste, I keep tamari refrigerated once opened.

Preserved lemons

Available in jars at a steep price, this Moroccan staple can be made at home by following this simple recipe. They need several weeks to mature, so make them ahead to keep on hand.

❋ *Homemade Preserved Lemons*
Scrub 2 or 3 small lemons, trim the ends and partially cut them into 6 or 8 wedges, without separating the wedges. Spread the wedges apart and rub the cut surfaces with coarse salt, using about 1 tablespoon salt for each lemon. Press the lemons back together and pack them firmly into a clean jar. Squeeze more lemons to make about 1 cup fresh lemon juice. Add the lemon juice to fill the jar. Let stand, tightly closed, at room temperature for about 4 weeks, turning the jar every other day. To use, dice the rinds and add to stews or sprinkle over vegetables. The pulp can be whisked into salad dressings or sauces. Once the jar is opened, store it in the refrigerator.

Rice vinegar

I prefer the unseasoned Marukan brand rice vinegar because it has a light, fresh, moderately sharp taste. I especially like it tossed into rice salads. (See Japanese Rice Vinaigrette with Ginger, page 74.)

Tomato paste

I depend on the rich, concentrated flavor and salty edge that tomato paste adds to a pot of soup or stew. Because I rarely use an entire can of paste, I measure out tablespoonfuls onto a sheet of foil and freeze until firm. Once the blobs are firm, I peel them off and store them in a zip-top plastic freezer bag.

SEEDS AND NUTS

Sesame seeds

They are available in creamy white, tan and black. I prefer the tan ones, which don't have the hulls removed and are often sold as "toasted" in Asian markets. If you can only find the hull-less white seeds, you'll have to toast them in a small skillet, stirring constantly, over low heat until golden, 1 to 2 minutes. For black sesame seeds, see Sources (page 239).

Chinese sesame seed paste

This hard paste of ground toasted sesame seeds is darker in color and has a drier consistency and stronger taste than Middle Eastern sesame paste (tahini). Dig the paste out of the jar with a sturdy spoon and discard the excess oil floating on the top.

Pepitas

These hulled pumpkin seeds are often used in Mexican cooking and are sold in the nut or snack section of supermarkets in jars or plastic bags. You can choose from roasted or raw, salted or unsalted. They're great in salads and pilafs or sprinkled on soups. See Sources (page 239).

LIQUID SWEETENERS

Agave nectar

Made from the nectar of the agave, a succulent plant of Mexico, where its name translates as "honey water," this sweetener has a mild, slightly caramel taste. It is favored by some because it has a low glycemic index (about half that of sugar) and by vegans who want an alternative to honey. Agave nectar is available in plastic squeeze bottles in all health food stores and in many high-end grocery stores.

Pomegranate molasses

Sometimes called pomegranate syrup or paste, this is a thick reduction of pomegranate juice with a slightly sweet edge. It is used as a flavoring in many Middle Eastern dishes. Bottles can be found wherever Middle Eastern groceries are sold. See Sources (page 239).

BASICS

Hard-cooked eggs

Place the eggs in a single layer in a deep saucepan and add water to cover. Bring to a gentle boil, uncovered, over medium heat. Immediately remove the pan from the heat, cover and let stand for 12 to 15 minutes, depending on the doneness you prefer. When the time has elapsed, pour off the hot water and rinse the eggs with cold water. Gently tap the eggs on the side of the pan until cracked and let them sit in a pan of cold water for 5 minutes, or until cool enough to handle. Gently peel off the shells.

Gremolata

Finely chop together 1 garlic clove, bruised with the side of a knife, 1 leafy sprig fresh Italian parsley and 1 strip (about ½ by 2 inches) lemon or orange zest. Use the blend to flavor soups, stews, vegetables, pilafs, beans and grains.

Pesto

Pesto can be made with a variety of fresh herbs, nuts and hard grating cheeses. This one is classic. Other versions appear throughout the book. Toast ½ cup pine nuts in a 325°F oven until golden, 8 to 10 minutes. Combine the pine nuts in a mortar with 1 garlic clove and ½ teaspoon coarse salt and pound into a paste with the pestle. Gradually pound in 2 to 3 cups torn basil leaves to make a rough paste. Work ½ cup olive oil into the paste with the pestle. Add ¼ cup grated Parmigiano-Reggiano, or more to taste.

Variations Use a blend of herbs, mixing fresh basil, Italian parsley, mint, dill and/or arugula. Substitute toasted walnuts, almonds or pistachios for the pine nuts. Substitute Pecorino Romano for the Parmigiano-Reggiano. For a thicker sauce, use less oil; for a thinner sauce, use more oil or add water, 1 tablespoon at a time. If you don't have a mortar and pestle, make the pesto in a food processor, adding the oil in a slow, steady stream and stirring in the cheese. Makes 1 to 1½ cups.

Salsa verde

This tangy, piquant all-purpose green sauce is delicious on roasted or boiled russet or sweet potatoes and sliced tomatoes or spooned over rice or other grains and beans. In a food processor or blender, finely chop 2 cups loosely packed sprigs of fresh Italian parsley and a couple of fresh mint leaves, dill sprigs or basil leaves, ½ cup olive oil, ¼ cup fresh lemon juice, 1 garlic clove, coarsely chopped, 1 teaspoon coarse salt and ¼ teaspoon freshly ground black pepper. Taste the sauce and thin with cold water if the lemon is too sharp, or add olive oil, 1 tablespoon at a time. Stir in 1 tablespoon rinsed and drained chopped capers, if desired.

Soy or tamari nuts

Combine ½ cup whole almonds or walnut or pecan halves or pieces and 1 teaspoon extra-virgin olive oil in a heavy skillet. Cook on medium-high heat, stirring, until the nuts are lightly toasted and the skillet is hot enough to sizzle a drop of soy sauce or tamari, about 1 minute. Add 2 tablespoons soy sauce or tamari and cook, stirring, adjusting the heat between medium and medium-low to keep the nuts from burning, until the nuts are coated, about 1 minute. Turn out onto an oiled plate to cool.

Toasting nuts

The quickest way is to spread the nuts in a small, heavy skillet and cook over medium-low heat, stirring often, for 2 to 5 minutes. If you have the oven on already, toast in a 350°F oven for 10 minutes. Watch pine nuts carefully because they brown quickly and often burn. It is safest to toast them in a 325°F oven until golden brown, 8 to 10 minutes.

Glazed nuts

Almonds, walnuts, pecans or a mix can be used to make glazed nuts. Spread 1 cup nuts in a skillet and stir over medium heat until the nuts are hot and beginning to color, about 3 minutes. Drizzle 3 tablespoons agave nectar (see page 13) over the nuts and boil, stirring, until they are coated and caramelized, about 3 minutes. Transfer to a lightly oiled plate and sprinkle with coarse salt. Let stand until hardened and break into pieces. For a variation, sprinkle the nuts with sesame seeds instead of salt.

Soups That Make a Meal

Of all the meals I enjoy cooking, soup is my favorite. Soup-making technique is not etched in stone. The experience can be fluid, generous and spontaneous. You can follow a recipe or not.

Here are some quick tips to get you started.

* A large (5- to 8-quart capacity) wide pot with two opposing handles, often called a Dutch oven, works best for soup.

* The fresher the ingredients, the better the soup. Relegate limp and tired vegetables to the compost bin.

* Cook onions and other aromatic vegetables like celery, carrots and parsnips in olive oil over medium-low heat, stirring, until they are the color of straw. Golden vegetables add depth of flavor to the water, turning it into a deliciously light vegetarian broth.

* If you have a mishap and the vegetables turn black, throw them out. All the spices in the world can't mask burned vegetables. Take a deep breath and start over.

* Boxed and canned vegetable broths are inconsistent in flavor and therefore are not used in these recipes.

* Easy Basic Vegetable Broth (page 46) can be made ahead and frozen.

* If using garlic, add it after the vegetables are golden and cook briefly — 1 to 2 minutes at the most — over low heat, to soften. Dark brown or burned garlic will contribute an off taste to the soup.

* Warm spices in olive oil over low heat, 1 to 2 minutes, perhaps with the garlic, if using. Warmed, lightly toasted spices release their flavor and add a full, complex taste to the soup.

* Dried herbs are twice as strong as their fresh counterparts and should be used sparingly. Add them to the hot broth or other liquid, where they will slowly rehydrate.

* Add fresh herbs at the end of the cooking time so they retain their bright, fresh taste. Stir half of them into the soup and use the remainder to sprinkle on top as a garnish.

* Take advantage of fresh seasonal ingredients when planning your soup menu: bright-tasting herbs, green beans, fresh tomatoes, corn, summer squash and tender greens in the spring and summer and hard-shelled winter squash varieties, tender carrots, apples, leeks and dark leafy greens in the fall and winter. Freshly harvested produce adds superior taste, along with wholesome nutrients.

* Tender fresh vegetables like zucchini, peas, green beans and greens should be added at the end of the cooking time so they keep their texture and subtle flavor.

* Taste, taste, taste. A balance of fat, acid and salt is essential for a satisfying dish. The fat adds a round, full flavor. Acid acts as a counterpoint to the fat, and salt balances the first two. Olive oil is my fat of choice. If a thick vegetable soup that began with olive oil needs a fuller flavor, I drizzle a half teaspoon of my best full-bodied olive oil on top. For the acid edge, I often add a tablespoon of fresh lemon juice,

tomato paste, vinegar or chopped tomato. Salty additions include a spoonful of tamari or soy sauce, chopped olives or sun-dried tomatoes.

❋ For a hint or a big hit of heat, try a pinch of cayenne or crushed red pepper, a drop or two of hot pepper sauce, a half teaspoon of minced chipotle in adobo (it's hot!), minced jalapeño or a generous grinding of black pepper.

❋ If your soup is a little blah, it may simply need a squirt of fresh lemon or lime juice, an extra shower of finely chopped herb, a drizzle of olive oil or a swirl of yogurt.

TIPS FOR PUREED SOUPS

❋ Pureeing is a snap with a lightweight handheld immersion blender. This handy tool allows you to puree the soup directly in the pot, eliminating the need to transfer the soup back and forth and saving messy cleanup.

❋ Cool the soup slightly before pureeing in a blender or food processor. A boiling hot soup can expand and spill over dangerously. Be careful not to overfill. If the soup is warm, hold the lid down with a folded towel.

❋ For a smooth, ultracreamy soup, use a blender.

❋ An old-fashioned food mill will remove seeds and skins and produce a thicker-textured soup than a blender.

ROASTED TOMATO SOUP WITH AVOCADO Vegan

Serve this soup chilled in the summer and hot in the winter. Roasting tomatoes intensifies their fruity flavor and adds a hint of sweetness, which is especially welcome during the winter months, when tomatoes are often bland-tasting. The juices leach from the tomatoes while roasting and combine with the olive oil, giving the soup richness and a silky texture. Adjust the amount of jalapeño to your individual taste, adding more if you like your soup with a touch of fire and less if you prefer a mild bite. Keep in mind the soft, full flavor and texture of the avocado and the acid of the lime will help temper any excess heat from the chile.

Cook Time: 30 minutes
Serves: 4

- **3 pounds (10–12) ripe plum tomatoes, halved lengthwise**
- **¼ cup extra-virgin olive oil**
- **2 teaspoons ground cumin**
- **Coarse salt**
- **2 garlic cloves, sliced thin**
- **1 cup water, plus 1–1½ cups water or Easy Basic Vegetable Broth (page 46) if needed**
- **1 cup chopped sweet onion**
- **4 tablespoons fresh lime juice, plus more to taste**
- **1 tablespoon chopped seeded jalapeño pepper, plus more to taste**
- **2 avocados, halved, pitted, peeled and diced (¼ inch), about 2 cups**
- **¼ cup chopped fresh cilantro**

1 Place a heavy baking sheet in the oven and preheat to 450°F for 10 minutes.

2 Meanwhile, toss the tomatoes, oil, cumin and 1 teaspoon salt in a large bowl.

3 Carefully remove the hot pan from the oven and spread the tomatoes on the pan. With a rubber spatula, scrape the oil and seasonings from the bowl over the tomatoes. Roast the tomatoes for 15 minutes. Stir with a spatula, turning the tomatoes and moving them around on the pan so they'll roast evenly. Sprinkle with the garlic. Roast for 10 to 15 minutes more, or until the tomato juices begin to brown at the edges of the pan. Remove the pan from the oven.

4 Add 1 cup water to the hot pan and scrape up the browned bits from the bottom with the edge of the spatula to loosen. Transfer the tomatoes and all the liquid to a large bowl. Add the onion, 1 tablespoon of the lime juice and the jalapeño and puree with an

Make a Meal

If serving the soup chilled, accompany it with Green Bean, Corn, Tomato and Cucumber Salad (page 66). If serving the soup hot, pair it with Mexican Corn on the Cob (page 190) or Cumin Black Beans with Blistered Tomatoes and Corn (page 237).

immersion blender until very smooth. If you don't have an immersion blender, let the soup cool slightly, transfer it to a blender or food processor, in batches if necessary, and puree until smooth.

5 If serving the soup cold, refrigerate, covered, until chilled, 1 to 2 hours or more. If serving the soup hot, transfer it to a soup pot and heat.

6 Because the juiciness of the tomatoes will vary, thin the soup, if necessary, adding the remaining water or broth as needed to reach the desired consistency. Taste and add ½ teaspoon more salt, 1 to 2 teaspoons more jalapeño and 1 tablespoon lime juice for heightened acidity.

7 Combine the avocados, the remaining 2 tablespoons lime juice and the cilantro in a small bowl. Divide the avocado mixture among four soup bowls and ladle the soup on top.

CHILLED WATERMELON AND TOMATO SOUP Vegan

A riff on gazpacho—with watermelon sharing the stage with tomatoes—this soup is a welcome treat on a hot summer day. Try it in August, when tomatoes and watermelon are their sweetest and most flavorful.

Prep Time: About 20 minutes
Serves: 4 to 6

1½–2 pounds ripe tomatoes, cored

2–2½ pounds watermelon (preferably seedless) or cantaloupe, skin and seeds discarded

1 tablespoon chopped peeled fresh ginger

1 tablespoon chopped seeded jalapeño pepper, plus more to taste

1 tablespoon chopped fresh cilantro, plus 2 tablespoons torn leaves for garnish

¼ cup fresh lime juice, plus more to taste

Coarse salt

½ cup diced (¼ inch) red onion

½ cup diced (¼ inch) crisp, seedless cucumber

1 Cut enough tomatoes and melon into ¼-inch dice to measure 2 cups combined (1 cup of each). Place the fruit in a bowl large enough to accommodate all of the soup and refrigerate.

2 Cut the remaining tomatoes and melon into ¾-inch chunks. Puree in a blender, in batches if necessary. Add the ginger, jalapeño, chopped cilantro, lime juice and 1 teaspoon salt and puree until the mixture is smooth.

3 Add the puree to the refrigerated chunks of tomato and melon. Stir in the red onion and cucumber. Taste and add more lime juice, jalapeño and salt, if needed.

4 Refrigerate the soup until well chilled, at least 2 hours. Ladle the soup into bowls and garnish each with a shower of torn cilantro.

Make a Meal

Serve with Shredded Tuscan Kale, Tomato and Avocado Salad (page 69) and Confetti Grain Salad (page 50).

WHITE BEAN AND FENNEL SOUP   Vegan

Cannellini, fennel and sweet red onion make up one of my favorite salads, so I thought, Why not try them in a soup? The result is rich and satisfying.

Cook Time: 35 minutes
Serves: 4

- 1 **fennel bulb (about 12 ounces)**
- 2 **tablespoons extra-virgin olive oil, plus more for garnish**
- 1 **cup chopped onion**
- 1 **garlic clove, grated**
- 3½ **cups cooked or canned (two 15- to 16-ounce cans) cannellini or other white beans, rinsed and drained**
- 1 **tablespoon tomato paste**
- 2 **teaspoons coarse salt**
  Freshly ground black pepper
- ¼ **cup finely chopped red onion**
- 1 **teaspoon grated orange zest**

Make a Meal

Serve with Chopped Tomato, Celery and Kalamata Olive Salad (page 50) and Olive Bread Toasts (page 78) or Quick Melted Comté Cheese Crisps (page 90).

1 Cut a thin slice from the base of the fennel bulb. Cut off and discard most of the green stalks. Finely chop 2 tablespoons of the fernlike tops and set aside. Use a vegetable peeler to remove any bruises from the outside ribs. Halve the fennel bulb lengthwise. Place cut side down and cut into ¼-inch-thick slices. Chop enough of the slices into ¼-inch pieces to measure 1 cup. Reserve the remaining fennel for another use.

2 Heat the oil in a soup pot over medium-low heat until it is hot enough to sizzle a piece of fennel. Add the chopped fennel bulb and cook, covered, over low heat, for 10 minutes. Do not brown. Add the 1 cup chopped onion and cook, covered, over low heat for 10 minutes more, or until both the fennel and onion are soft but not browned. Stir in the garlic.

3 Add 4 cups water, the beans, tomato paste, salt and a generous grinding of pepper. Bring to a boil. Cook, uncovered, over low heat for 15 minutes, or until the flavors are blended.

4 Combine the red onion, the reserved chopped fennel tops and the orange zest in a small bowl. Ladle the soup into bowls and sprinkle the red onion mixture on top, dividing evenly. Drizzle each bowl of soup with about 1 teaspoon olive oil.

TOMATO AND WHITE BEAN SOUP WITH SPINACH PESTO

Vegan (omit cheese from pesto)

My favorite beans for this soup are those I've taken the time to cook from scratch and stash in my freezer (see page 218), but good-quality canned beans are a great alternative.

Cook Time: 30 minutes
Serves: 4

- 2 tablespoons extra-virgin olive oil
- 1 cup chopped onion
- 2 garlic cloves, grated
- 1 can (28 ounces) diced tomatoes with juice
- 1 tablespoon tomato paste
- 2 tablespoons torn fresh basil

  Coarse salt
- 1¾ cups cooked or canned (15–16 ounces) rinsed and drained cannellini or other white beans

  Freshly ground black pepper

Spinach Pesto

- 2 tablespoons pine nuts or chopped skin-on almonds or walnuts
- 1 garlic clove
- ¼ teaspoon coarse salt
- 2 cups loosely packed baby spinach leaves
- 2 tablespoons extra-virgin olive oil
- 2 tablespoons grated Parmigiano-Reggiano (optional)

1 Heat the oil in a soup pot over medium-low heat until it is hot enough to sizzle a piece of onion. Add the onion and cook, stirring, until golden, about 10 minutes. Add the garlic and cook for 1 minute.

2 Add 3 cups water, the tomatoes, tomato paste, basil and 1 teaspoon salt; bring to a boil. For a creamier texture, mash half of the beans with a fork or potato masher. Stir the beans into the soup. Cover and cook over low heat for 20 minutes. Add a generous grinding of black pepper. Taste and correct the seasoning with more salt and pepper, but keep in mind the pesto will add lots of flavor to the soup.

3 Meanwhile, make the pesto: Spread the nuts in a small skillet and toast over medium-low heat, stirring, until they turn a light golden brown, 3 to 5 minutes. By hand: Combine the nuts, garlic and salt in a large mortar and pound into a paste with the pestle. Add half of the spinach leaves and pound until reduced to a coarse paste. Repeat with the remaining spinach leaves. Gradually add the oil, stirring with the pestle. Stir in the cheese, if using. If using a blender or food processor, combine the nuts, garlic, salt and spinach and process to a coarse puree. With the motor running, add the oil in a slow, steady stream. Transfer to a small bowl and stir in the cheese, if using.

4 To serve, ladle the hot soup into bowls. Add a generous spoonful of pesto to each and serve at once.

Shortcuts

- Substitute a good-quality prepared pesto (sold next to the fresh pasta sauces in many markets) for the Spinach Pesto.
- Alternatively, stir 1 bag (5–6 ounces) baby spinach into the hot soup before serving.

Substitutions

In place of the pesto, sprinkle each bowl of soup generously with grated Parmigiano-Reggiano or orange gremolata (see page 14).

LENTIL AND VEGETABLE SOUP WITH SMOKED PAPRIKA

Vegan (omit dairy topping)

Quick-cooking and versatile lentils make a great pot of soup. A good source of protein and fiber, they are filling and luscious. The smoked paprika adds a haunting aroma and taste, reminiscent of bacon.

Cook Time: 35 minutes
Serves: 6 to 8

- 2 tablespoons extra-virgin olive oil
- 2 cups large dice (½ inch) onions
- 2 cups carrot chunks (about ½ inch)
- 1 cup large dice (½ inch) celery, plus a leafy top, chopped
- 3 garlic cloves, grated
- 1½ teaspoons smoked paprika (preferably *Pimentón de la Vera*; see page 10)
- 1½ cups brown lentils
- 1 bay leaf
- 1 tablespoon tomato paste
  Coarse salt and freshly ground black pepper
- ½ cup plain low-fat yogurt or sour cream (optional)
- 2 tablespoons finely chopped fresh cilantro

1 Heat the oil in a soup pot until it is hot enough to sizzle a piece of onion. Add the onions and cook, stirring, over medium-low heat until the onion is golden, about 10 minutes. Add the carrots, celery and celery top, garlic and paprika and cook, stirring, until the vegetables are softened and coated with the seasonings, about 5 minutes.

2 Add 6 cups water, the lentils and bay leaf and bring to a boil. Cook, uncovered, over medium-low heat until the lentils and vegetables are tender, about 20 minutes. Stir in the tomato paste, 1 teaspoon salt and a grinding of black pepper. Taste and add more salt and pepper if needed.

3 Ladle the soup into bowls. Garnish each bowl with a swirl of yogurt or sour cream (if using) and a sprinkling of cilantro.

Make a Meal

Serve with Toasted Flatbread (Naan) with Blistered Cherry Tomatoes, Arugula and Red Onion (page 93) and Roasted Cauliflower "Steaks" (page 184).

RED LENTIL SOUP WITH COCONUT MILK AND TOASTED CUMIN Vegan

Although they are a pretty pale salmon color when dried, red lentils turn yellow when cooked. They also go from a solid when they hit the pot to an almost smooth puree in a matter of minutes. Red lentils are often used in a thin, spicy Indian "soup" called dal, whose flavors inspired this soup. The addition of coconut milk helps to balance the spices.

Cook Time: 30 minutes
Serves: 4 to 6

- 2 tablespoons extra-virgin olive oil
- 1 cup chopped onion
- 1 teaspoon cumin seeds
- 1 garlic clove, grated
- 2 teaspoons Madras curry powder
- 1½ cups red lentils
- 1 can (13.5 ounces) regular or light coconut milk
   Coarse salt
- 1 teaspoon finely chopped seeded jalapeño pepper, plus more to taste
- 1 tablespoon fresh lime juice
- ¼ cup chopped fresh cilantro, for garnish

1 Heat the oil in a soup pot until it is hot enough to sizzle a piece of onion. Add the onion and cook over medium-low heat, stirring occasionally, until softened, about 5 minutes. Add the cumin and garlic and cook, stirring, for 1 minute. Add the curry powder and cook, stirring, for 30 seconds.

2 Add 4 cups water and the lentils and bring to a boil. Reduce the heat to low and cook, covered, stirring once or twice, until the lentils are very soft, about 20 minutes.

3 Stir in the coconut milk and heat through. Add 1 teaspoon salt and the jalapeño. Adjust the seasonings, adding more salt and jalapeño to taste. Stir in the lime juice.

4 Ladle the soup into bowls and sprinkle each portion generously with cilantro.

Make a Meal
Serve with Stir-Fried Tofu with Oyster Mushrooms, Bell Peppers and Spinach (page 104).

LENTIL AND SHIITAKE SOUP
WITH LEAFY GREENS Vegan

Lentils lend themselves to a wide variety of flavor combinations. Here the lentils are cooked in an excess of water, which becomes the broth on which the soup is based. Shiitake mushrooms sautéed in olive oil contribute a toasty taste. To keep the greens from overcooking, they are steamed separately and mounded in the center of each bowl before ladling over the hot soup.

Cook Time: 40 minutes
Serves: 4 to 6

- 4 tablespoons extra-virgin olive oil
- 1 cup finely chopped onion
- ½ cup chopped carrot
- ½ cup chopped celery
- 2 garlic cloves, grated
- 1 teaspoon grated peeled fresh ginger
  Coarse salt
- 2 cups brown lentils
- 5 ounces shiitake mushrooms, stems discarded, sliced (⅛ inch), about 2 cups
  Freshly ground black pepper
- 2 bunches (about 1½ pounds) Swiss chard
- 2 tablespoons tamari or soy sauce, plus more to taste
- 1 tablespoon tomato paste

1 Heat 2 tablespoons of the oil in a soup pot until it is hot enough to sizzle a piece of onion. Add the onion and cook, stirring, over medium-low heat until the onion is golden, about 10 minutes. Add the carrot, celery, garlic and ginger and stir to combine. Add 12 cups water and 2 teaspoons salt and bring to a boil.

2 Add the lentils and simmer, uncovered, over medium heat, stirring occasionally, until the lentils are tender, 15 to 25 minutes.

3 Meanwhile, heat the remaining 2 tablespoons oil in a skillet. Add the mushrooms and cook over medium heat, stirring, until golden, about 10 minutes. Sprinkle the mushrooms with salt and pepper to taste and let stand, off the heat, until needed.

4 Wash the Swiss chard and tear the leafy parts away from the thick center ribs. Reserve the ribs for another use. (You can chop and use them when making vegetable broth or an all-vegetable soup, or see the recipe for Swiss Chard Ribs Gratin, page 187.) Roughly cut the torn leaves into 2- to 3-inch pieces. Place the leaves, with the water still clinging to them, in a large pot or deep skillet

Make a Meal

Serve with Whole-Roasted Tomatoes with Warm Goat Cheese (page 207).

set over medium heat. Cover and cook until wilted and tender, about 5 minutes, depending on the maturity of the leaves. Uncover and set aside until the soup is ready to serve.

5 When the lentils are tender, stir in the mushrooms, tamari and tomato paste. Cook, uncovered, over low heat, stirring once or twice, for 5 minutes. Taste and add more tamari or salt and a grinding of black pepper, if needed.

6 To serve, place a mound of greens in each bowl and then ladle the soup over the greens.

Shortcuts

Large (16-ounce) bags of torn greens are available in the produce section of most markets. Many are a mixture of greens. Take advantage of their convenience. Although the package says "prewashed," I prefer to give the greens a quick rinse in a bowl of cold water and shake to remove excess moisture before cooking.

PUREED BLACK BEAN SOUP WITH PIQUILLO PEPPERS Vegan

The depth of flavor in this soup comes from meaty, rich-tasting black beans and the combination of piquillo peppers and smoky Spanish paprika, called *Pimentón de la Vera*. The salsa garnish is optional, but makes a pretty topping.

Cook Time: 35 minutes
Serves: 6 to 8

- 2 tablespoons extra-virgin olive oil
- 1 cup chopped onion
- 1 cup chopped green bell pepper
- 3 garlic cloves, grated
- 2 teaspoons smoked paprika (preferably *Pimentón de la Vera*; see page 10)

  Coarse salt
- 1 teaspoon ground cumin
- 1 teaspoon dried oregano
- 3 cans (15–16 ounces each) black beans, rinsed and drained, or 3¾ cups cooked dried black beans
- 1 can (14.5 ounces) diced tomatoes with juice or 1½ cups diced fresh tomatoes with juice
- 2 tablespoons tomato paste
- ½ cup chopped jarred piquillo peppers (see page 10), drained and patted dry

Salsa (optional)

- ½ cup chopped jarred piquillo peppers, drained and patted dry
- ½ cup chopped onion
- ½ cup diced avocado
- 1 tablespoon olive oil
- 1 tablespoon fresh lime juice
- 1 tablespoon minced fresh cilantro
- 2 teaspoons minced seeded jalapeño pepper

  Pinch of coarse salt

1 Heat the oil in a soup pot until it is hot enough to sizzle a piece of onion. Add the onion and green pepper and cook, stirring, over medium-low heat until golden, about 10 minutes. Add the garlic and cook for 1 minute. Stir in the paprika, 1 teaspoon salt, cumin and oregano and cook, stirring, for 30 seconds. Add 4 cups water, the black beans, tomatoes and tomato paste and bring to a boil. Cover and simmer for 10 minutes. Stir in the piquillo peppers.

2 Puree the soup with an immersion blender. If you don't have an immersion blender, let the soup cool slightly, transfer it to a blender or food processor, in batches if necessary, and puree until smooth. Return the soup to the pot and cook, covered, over low heat, for 15 minutes. Add additional salt to taste.

3 **To make the salsa (if using):** In a medium bowl, combine the piquillo peppers, onion, avocado, olive oil, lime juice, cilantro, jalapeño and salt.

4 Ladle the soup into bowls and float a rounded tablespoonful of the salsa, if using, in the center of each serving.

Shortcuts

Instead of making your own salsa, save time by using store-bought salsa. For the brightest, freshest flavors, pass over the jarred selection displayed near the chips and look in the refrigerated section of your supermarket. A variety of creative, fresh salsas are now available.

CURRIED CHICKPEA SOUP WITH SUMMER VEGETABLES Vegan

Chock-full of fresh vegetables, this hearty soup gets high marks for its many nutritional benefits. You can use fresh tomatoes, but since they need to be peeled, I prefer good-quality canned tomatoes. Although this soup requires extra time for chopping all the vegetables, the cooking time is supershort.

Cook Time: 30 minutes
Serves: 4 to 6

- 2 tablespoons extra-virgin olive oil
- ½ cup sliced (½ inch) celery
- ½ cup sliced (¼ inch) carrot
- ½ cup chopped red onion
- 2 teaspoons Madras curry powder
- 1 garlic clove, grated
- 1 can (28 ounces) diced tomatoes with juice
- 1 can (15–16 ounces) chickpeas, rinsed and drained
- 1 leafy sprig fresh basil
- 1 cup cut (½ inch) green beans (about 4 ounces)
- 1 cup diced (¼ inch) zucchini (about 4 ounces)
- 1 cup diced (¼ inch) yellow summer squash (about 4 ounces)
- 1 cup frozen green peas, thawed
- ½ teaspoon grated orange zest
  Coarse salt and freshly ground black pepper
- 4 large fresh basil leaves, for garnish

1 Heat the oil in a soup pot until it is hot enough to sizzle a piece of vegetable. Add the celery, carrot and onion and cook, stirring, over medium-low heat until the vegetables are softened, about 10 minutes. Add the curry powder and garlic and cook, stirring, for about 1 minute.

2 Add 4 cups water, the tomatoes, chickpeas and basil sprig and bring to a boil. Cover and cook over low heat for 10 minutes.

3 Add the green beans and cook for 5 minutes. Add the zucchini and summer squash and cook, stirring, for 5 minutes. Add the peas, orange zest and salt and pepper to taste and cook until the peas are heated through, about 1 minute. Retrieve and discard the basil sprig.

4 Stack the basil leaves and cut them into thin strips. Ladle the soup into bowls and garnish each bowl with basil.

Make a Meal

Serve with bruschetta with Braised Swiss Chard with Pecorino Curls (page 84) or Roasted Red Pepper and Walnut Spread (page 86) or Cheese and Mushroom Melts (page 88).

CARROT, SWEET POTATO AND GINGER SOUP WITH BABY BOK CHOY Vegan

Carrots and sweet potatoes make for sweet silkiness in this smooth, creamy, dairy-free soup. Hefty additions of fresh ginger and jalapeño contribute the right hit of heat and create a sophisticated flavor profile. To keep the juicy crunch of the bok choy, add it just before serving.

Cook Time: 35 minutes
Serves: 4

- 2 **tablespoons extra-virgin olive oil**
- 1 **pound carrots, sliced (½ inch), about 3 cups**
- 1 **pound sweet potatoes, scrubbed, skins left on and cubed (½ inch), about 3 cups**
- 1 **bunch scallions (white and green parts), sliced (about 1 cup)**
- ½ **cup chopped celery**
- 1 **garlic clove, grated**
- 1 **tablespoon chopped peeled fresh ginger**
  Coarse salt
- 4 **tablespoons chopped fresh cilantro**
- 1 **tablespoon fresh lime juice**
- 1 **tablespoon finely chopped seeded jalapeño pepper, or to taste**
- 6 **ounces baby bok choy, stem ends trimmed and sliced (½ inch), about 2 cups lightly packed**

Make a Meal
Serve with Curried Quinoa and Apple Salad with Dried Cranberries (page 73).

1 Heat the oil in a soup pot until it is hot enough to sizzle a piece of vegetable. Add the carrots, sweet potatoes, scallions, celery, garlic, ginger and 2 teaspoons salt. Cook, covered, stirring occasionally, over medium-low heat until lightly browned and softened, about 10 minutes. Add 6 cups water and 2 tablespoons of the cilantro and bring to a boil. Cover and cook over medium heat until the vegetables are tender, 20 to 25 minutes.

2 Ladle out about 2 cups of the solid vegetables and set aside. Use an immersion blender to puree the soup in the pot. If you don't have an immersion blender, let the soup cool slightly, transfer it to a blender or food processor, in batches if necessary, and puree until smooth. Return the soup to the pot.

3 Add the reserved vegetables, lime juice and jalapeño. Taste and add more salt, if needed. Bring the soup to a boil. Stir in the bok choy and cook for 30 seconds. Ladle the soup into bowls and garnish with the remaining 2 tablespoons chopped cilantro.

Shortcuts
If you can find real baby carrots, use them. Leave the thin skins on and cut the carrots into 1½-inch pieces. Instead of peeling the sweet potatoes, scrub them with a stiff brush. Their skins soften when cooked.

LEEK AND POTATO SOUP WITH ROASTED CAULIFLOWER Vegan

You'd swear this thick, creamy soup is loaded with dairy, but it isn't. Through the magic of pureeing, leeks, potatoes and roasted cauliflower take on the consistency of a cream soup. Two surprise ingredients—a touch of curry powder and some grated orange zest—add a subtle sweetness that helps to smooth out the vegetative quality of the soup.

Cook Time: 30 minutes
Serves: 4

- 6 **cups cauliflower florets (from 1 large head, cored and thick stems removed)**
- 5 **tablespoons extra-virgin olive oil**
  Coarse salt and freshly ground black pepper
- 2 **medium leeks, roots and dark green tops trimmed, halved lengthwise, washed thoroughly and thinly sliced (about 3 cups)**
- 1 **tablespoon Madras curry powder**
- 1½ **pounds russet potatoes, peeled and diced (½ inch), about 3 cups**
- 1 **tablespoon tomato paste**
- 2 **teaspoons packed coarsely chopped fresh oregano**
- 1 **teaspoon grated orange zest**
- 1 **garlic clove, grated**

1 Place a heavy baking sheet in the oven and preheat to 450°F for 10 minutes.

2 Meanwhile, toss the cauliflower in a bowl with 3 tablespoons of the oil, 1 teaspoon salt and a generous grinding of black pepper.

3 Carefully remove the hot pan from the oven and spread the cauliflower florets on the pan. Roast the cauliflower for 10 minutes. Stir with a spatula, turning the florets and moving them around on the pan so they'll roast evenly. Roast until browned and tender, about 10 minutes more.

4 Meanwhile, combine the remaining 2 tablespoons oil and the leeks in a soup pot. Cook, covered, over medium-low heat until the leeks are wilted, about 10 minutes. Add the curry powder and cook, stirring, for 1 minute. Add 6 cups water, the potatoes and tomato paste. Cover and cook until the potatoes are tender, about 20 minutes.

5 Combine the oregano, orange zest and garlic in a small bowl. Stir into the roasted cauliflower.

6 When the potatoes are tender, add half of the seasoned roasted cauliflower to the soup and puree with an immersion blender. If you don't have an immersion blender, let the soup cool slightly, transfer it to a blender or food processor, in batches if necessary, and puree until smooth. Return the soup to the pot. Taste and add more salt and a generous grinding of black pepper if needed.

7 To serve, ladle the soup into bowls. Divide the remaining roasted cauliflower florets among the soup bowls and serve at once.

Shortcuts

Use bags of precut cauliflower florets in place of the cauliflower head. For best results, soak the florets in a bowl of ice water for 10 minutes to refresh them before roasting.

WINTER BORSCHT   Vegan (omit dairy topping)

One trip to Russia and many bowls of delicious borscht later, I was inspired to create my own version of this iconic beet soup, modeled after an especially aromatic version made with caramelized apples. Although the list of ingredients is long, you can pare it down if you'd like. Use your discretion and what's in your larder, but don't forgo the orange zest. It adds a fresh, bright taste to the mélange of vegetables.

Cook Time: 45 minutes
Serves: 8 with leftovers

- 1½ pounds beets (about 5 medium-large), preferably with leafy green tops attached
- 2 tablespoons extra-virgin olive oil
- 1 medium leek, roots and dark green tops trimmed, halved lengthwise, washed thoroughly and chopped (about 1 cup)
- 1 cup diced parsnip or carrot
- 1 cup diced fennel or celery
- 2 garlic cloves, grated
- 1 cup canned diced tomatoes with juice (about half a 14.5-ounce can)
  Coarse salt
- 8 round white, Yukon Gold or other small potatoes, unpeeled
- 2 cups finely chopped red or green cabbage
- 1 cup diced peeled tart apple, such as Granny Smith
- 2 tablespoons chopped fresh dill, plus more for garnish
- 2 teaspoons grated orange zest
  Freshly ground black pepper
- 2–3 tablespoons red wine vinegar, or more to taste
- 1 cup sour cream, plain yogurt or crème fraîche, or to taste (optional)

1 If your beets have tops, remove them, cutting the stems close to the beets. Set the tops aside. Scrub the beets or peel them if the skins are thick. Cut 3 of the beets into ¼-inch dice and set aside. Coarsely shred the remaining beets on a box grater or the wide shredding attachment of a food processor. Set the beets aside.

2 Wash the beet tops in two or three changes of water to make sure they are grit-free. Pull the large leafy parts off the thick center stems and discard the stems, or reserve for broth. Coarsely chop the beet greens until you have 2 cups and set aside. Reserve the leftovers for braised greens (see Braising, page 156 and Swiss Chard with Fragrant Garlic and Salt, page 186).

3 Heat the oil in a soup pot until it is hot enough to sizzle a piece of vegetable. Add the leek, parsnip or carrot and fennel or celery and cook, stirring, over medium heat until the vegetables are soft and golden, about 10 minutes. Add the garlic and cook for 1 minute. Add the reserved diced and shredded beets, 6 cups water, the tomatoes and 2 teaspoons salt and bring to a boil. Cook, covered, for 20 minutes.

4 Meanwhile, place the potatoes in a separate saucepan. Cover the potatoes with water, add a pinch of salt and boil until fork-tender, 10 to 20 minutes, depending on their size. Drain the water. Let stand, covered, until ready to serve.

Make a Meal

Serve with thick toasted slices of crusty whole-grain bread, perhaps smeared with Multi-Mushroom Pâté (page 87). If your beets have no greens, consider serving Swiss Chard with Fragrant Garlic and Salt (page 186) or Stir-Fried Asian Greens with Crisp Golden Garlic (page 195).

5 Add the cabbage, apple, dill, orange zest and a generous grinding of black pepper to the soup pot. Cook, covered, stirring once or twice, over medium heat for 10 minutes, or until the vegetables are wilted. Add the reserved beet greens, if using, 5 minutes before serving.

6 When the soup is hot, stir in the vinegar. Taste and adjust the salt, pepper and vinegar. Place a hot potato in each bowl and halve or quarter it. Ladle the soup over the potatoes and garnish each bowl with a spoonful of sour cream, yogurt or crème fraîche (if using) and a generous sprinkling of chopped dill.

Shortcuts

To save time, use the conveniently precooked and peeled beets available in some markets and skip steps 1 and 2. Dice half of the beets and shred the rest. Add them to the soup in step 3 halfway through the cooking time, then proceed with the recipe, omitting the addition of the beet greens.

PUMPKIN AND TOMATO SOUP WITH CHEESE

The unlikely combination of pumpkin and tomatoes makes a delightfully easy soup. This version uses canned pumpkin, but if you happen to have some fresh winter squash or blocks of frozen squash in the freezer, you can use that instead (see Substitutions). The soup's flavors are rounded out with the addition of cumin and a generous topping of shredded cheese. Omit the cheese for a vegan variation.

Cook Time: 35 minutes
Serves: 6 to 8

- 2 tablespoons extra-virgin olive oil
- 1 cup chopped onion
- ½ cup chopped celery
- 1 garlic clove, grated
- 2½ teaspoons ground cumin
- 1 can (28 ounces) whole plum tomatoes with juice or 2½ pounds ripe, juicy tomatoes, cored and coarsely chopped
- 2 cans (15 ounces each) pureed pumpkin
- 1 tablespoon tomato paste
- Coarse salt
- 2 tablespoons fresh lime or lemon juice
- Freshly ground black pepper
- ½ cup coarsely shredded Comté, Pecorino Romano or sharp cheddar cheese, or plain yogurt or crème fraîche

1 Heat the oil in a soup pot until it is hot enough to sizzle a piece of onion. Add the onion and celery and cook, stirring occasionally, over medium-low heat until the onion is golden, about 10 minutes. Add the garlic and cumin and cook, stirring, for 1 minute.

2 Add the tomatoes, pumpkin, 2½ cups water, tomato paste and 1 teaspoon salt. Bring to a boil and cook, covered, over medium-low heat for 10 minutes. Uncover and cool slightly. Puree the soup with an immersion blender. If you don't have an immersion blender, transfer the soup to a blender or food processor, in batches if necessary, and puree until smooth. Return the soup to the pot. Add additional water to thin the soup if necessary.

3 Cover and simmer for 15 minutes. Stir in the lime juice. Add more salt, if needed, and black pepper to taste. Ladle the soup into bowls and divide the cheese among the bowls, mounding it in the center of each serving, or add a dollop of yogurt or crème fraîche. Serve at once.

Vegan Variation

Make a batch of Crispy Kale (page 197) and sprinkle a handful on top of each bowl of soup instead of the cheese topping.

Substitutions

To make this soup truly fresh (though not fast), substitute roasted butternut or kabocha squash for the pumpkin. You will need 2½ to 3 cups mashed cooked squash. To save preparation time, roast the squash a day or two ahead and refrigerate until ready to use. Or you can use 2 boxes (14 ounces each) frozen pureed squash, thawed, or 2 bags (10 to 12 ounces each) fresh squash chunks, cooked in the soup until tender.

FARRO AND KALE SOUP WITH ORANGE GREMOLATA Vegan

This flavorful soup is elegant enough to serve in shallow bowls as a starter and hearty enough to ladle into deep bowls to offer as a main course. As a nonvegan bonus, simmer chunks of Parmigiano-Reggiano in the soup. As they cook, the hard rinds soften and turn chewy, becoming soft morsels to savor. If you have a batch of homemade vegetable broth on hand, use it here, but otherwise use water.

Cook Time: 35 minutes
Serves: 6 to 8

- 3 tablespoons extra-virgin olive oil, plus more for garnish
- 1 cup chopped onion
- 1 cup thick-sliced (¼ inch) carrots
- ½ cup diced (¼ inch) celery
- 1 tablespoon chopped celery leaves
- 2 garlic cloves, grated
- 8 cups water or Easy Basic Vegetable Broth (page 46) or a combination
- 1 cup farro (see page 216)
- ½ cup diced fresh or drained canned tomato
  Coarse salt
- 1 bay leaf
- 1 bunch Tuscan (lacinato) kale (about 12 ounces), leaves stripped from ribs and chopped, ribs discarded
  Freshly ground black pepper

Orange Gremolata
- ½ cup lightly packed fresh Italian parsley leaves
- 2 strips (½ by 2 inches each) orange zest
- 1 garlic clove, bruised with the side of a knife

1 Heat 2 tablespoons of the oil in a soup pot until it is hot enough to sizzle a piece of onion. Add the onion and cook, stirring, over medium-low heat until it is golden, about 10 minutes. Add the carrots, celery, celery leaves and half of the garlic and cook, stirring, for 2 minutes. Add the water and/or vegetable broth. Stir in the farro, tomato, 1 teaspoon salt and the bay leaf and bring to a boil. Cook, uncovered, stirring occasionally, until the farro is tender, about 25 minutes.

2 Meanwhile, heat the remaining 1 tablespoon oil and the remaining garlic over medium-low heat in a large skillet until sizzling (do not brown). Immediately add the kale. Drizzle the kale with 2 tablespoons water and toss to coat. Cover and cook over medium-low heat until the leaves are tender, 8 to 12 minutes, depending on their maturity and tenderness. Add the cooked kale and any liquid in the bottom of the skillet to the soup. Season with salt and pepper to taste. Thin the soup with broth or water if it is too thick.

3 To make the orange gremolata: Gather the parsley, orange zest and garlic together and chop until the pieces are very fine.

4 To serve, ladle the soup into bowls. Drizzle olive oil on top. Sprinkle with the gremolata and serve at once.

Substitutions

- Add 1¾ cups cooked or canned cannellini or other white beans, rinsed and drained, along with the kale.
- In place of the farro, you can use quick-cooking barley.

MISO SOUP WITH SPINACH, CURRIED TOFU AND SHIITAKE Vegan

Nothing like the austere but nonetheless comforting miso that you'll find in a Japanese restaurant or your neighborhood vegetarian gathering place, this is a thoroughly westernized version, hearty with rice, spinach, tofu and shiitake mushrooms and flavored with curry. Miso—fermented soybean paste—is sold in 16-ounce plastic containers in the refrigerated section of many supermarkets, next to the tofu.

Cook Time: 25 minutes
Serves: 4

- ½ block (about 7 ounces) medium-firm tofu, drained and cut into 2 horizontal slices
- ½ cup white or yellow miso
- 2 tablespoons extra-virgin olive oil
- ½ cup stemmed shiitake mushrooms, cut into thin slices
- 1 teaspoon Madras curry powder
- 2 cups thin-sliced (¼ inch) spinach leaves
- ½ cup cooked brown rice, Forbidden Rice (see page 217) or Bhutanese red rice (see page 218)
- 1 tablespoon tamari or soy sauce
- 1 tablespoon diagonally sliced scallions (green parts only), for garnish

1 Place the tofu slices on a folded dish towel and cover with a second folded towel. Press down gently but firmly with the palm of your hand to extract some of the moisture. Cut the tofu into ½-inch cubes and set aside.

2 In a large pot, bring 6 cups water to a slow boil over medium heat. Add the miso and gently stir until dissolved. Keep warm over low heat.

3 Heat a large skillet over medium heat until it is hot enough to sizzle and evaporate a drop of water. Add 1 tablespoon of the oil and heat until it is hot enough to sizzle a slice of mushroom. Add the mushrooms and ½ teaspoon of the curry powder and cook, stirring, adjusting the heat to maintain a steady sizzle, until the mushrooms are tender, about 5 minutes. Add the mushrooms to the soup.

4 Add the remaining tablespoon of oil to the skillet and heat over medium heat until it is hot enough to sizzle a piece of tofu. Add the tofu to the hot oil. Sprinkle with the remaining ½ teaspoon curry powder and cook, turning with a spatula, until browned on at least two sides, about 2 minutes per side. As the tofu browns, add it to the soup.

5 Add the spinach, rice and tamari to the soup and heat through. Ladle the soup into bowls and sprinkle with the scallions.

CURRIED COCONUT-SQUASH SOUP WITH PEANUTS Vegan

Rich and creamy canned coconut milk and convenient blocks of frozen pureed winter squash make a luscious soup spiked with curry powder, fresh ginger and cayenne. Chopped peanuts add a welcome crunch to every steaming spoonful.

Cook Time: 10 minutes
Serves: 4

- 1 **tablespoon Madras curry powder**
- 2 **boxes (10 ounces each) frozen pureed winter squash, thawed**
- 2 **cans (13.5 ounces each) regular or light coconut milk**
- 2 **teaspoons grated peeled fresh ginger**
- 1 **teaspoon tamari or soy sauce**
  Coarse salt
- ⅛ **teaspoon cayenne**
- ¼ **cup fresh lime juice, plus more to taste**
- 2 **tablespoons thin-sliced scallions (white and green parts)**
- 1 **tablespoon minced seeded jalapeño pepper**
- ½ **cup dry-roasted unsalted peanuts**
- 2 **tablespoons chopped fresh cilantro**

1 Sprinkle the curry powder in a soup pot and heat, stirring, over low heat for 1 minute. Add the squash, coconut milk, ginger, tamari, ½ teaspoon salt and cayenne. Bring to a simmer, stirring, over medium heat. Cover and cook over low heat for 10 minutes.

2 Add the lime juice, scallions and jalapeño. Taste and correct the seasonings with more lime juice and salt, if needed.

3 Crush the peanuts with a mortar and pestle or finely chop. Ladle the hot soup into bowls. Garnish each bowl with a sprinkling of peanuts and cilantro.

Make a Meal

Serve with crostini with Beet and Tahini Puree (page 83) and a side dish of Green and Yellow Wax Beans with Almond Pesto (page 165) and Toasted Flatbread (Naan) with Goat Cheese, Sautéed Greens and Crispy Shallots (page 92; omit the fried shallots, if you like).

VEGETABLE, BLACK-EYED PEA AND ORZO SOUP

Vegan (omit the cheese topping)

Think of this as a version of minestrone, with frozen black-eyed peas, orzo, Kalamata olives, dried oregano and lemon zest giving it a Greek twist. To extend the theme, top each steaming bowl of soup with crumbled feta. If you don't have the precooked vegetables from the broth on hand, follow the "from scratch" recipe.

Cook Time: 30 minutes
Serves: 4 to 6

- 6 cups Easy Basic Vegetable Broth (page 46)
- 2 cups frozen black-eyed peas
- ¼ cup orzo
- 2 cups cooked vegetables from Easy Basic Vegetable Broth
- ¼ cup chopped pitted Kalamata olives
- 1 teaspoon dried oregano
- 1 teaspoon grated lemon zest
- Coarse salt and freshly ground black pepper
- ½–¾ cup crumbled feta cheese (optional)

Make a Meal

Serve with Twice-Cooked Broccoli Rabe with Red Pepper and Garlic Oil (page 179).

1 Bring the broth to a boil in a soup pot. Add the black-eyed peas and the orzo and cook over low heat, stirring occasionally, until the orzo and peas are both soft to the bite, about 20 minutes.

2 Add the cooked vegetables, olives, oregano and lemon zest and cook over medium-low heat for 10 minutes. Season with salt and pepper to taste.

3 To serve, ladle the warm soup into bowls and sprinkle each with about 2 tablespoons crumbled feta, if using.

Variation

"From-Scratch" Vegetable, Black-Eyed Pea and Orzo Soup: Cook the vegetables in oil as instructed in step 1 of Easy Basic Vegetable Broth (page 46). Add 6 cups (instead of 9 cups) water and simmer for about 20 minutes. Scoop the vegetables out of the broth with a slotted spoon and set aside. Add the orzo and black-eyed peas to the broth as instructed in step 1 of the soup recipe and proceed.

EASY BASIC VEGETABLE BROTH Vegan

Quick, easy and great to have on hand in the freezer, this vegetable broth is far better than the boxed broths on supermarket shelves. It's based on staple aromatic vegetables—onions, carrots, celery, and garlic—but if I have shiitake mushrooms or Swiss chard stems in the freezer, a few green beans, a chunk of parsnip, a piece of zucchini or other unassertive-tasting vegetables, I add them to the pot. Avoid strongly flavored vegetables like cabbage, broccoli, cauliflower or turnips. Often I save bits and pieces of vegetables in a zip-top plastic freezer bag and add those too. Sometimes I rescue the vegetables and give them another life in a second soup (see Vegetable, Black-Eyed Pea and Orzo Soup, page 45).

Cook Time: 45 minutes
Makes 8 cups

- 2 **tablespoons extra-virgin olive oil**
- 2 **cups chopped onions**
- 2 **celery stalks, cut into ¼-inch slices**
- 2 **medium carrots, cut into ¼-inch slices**
- 2 **leafy sprigs fresh Italian parsley**
- 3 **garlic cloves, grated**
- ½ **cup chopped fresh or canned tomatoes with juices or 1 tablespoon tomato paste (optional)**
- ¼–½ **cup shiitake mushroom stems or sliced cremini mushrooms (optional)**
- 1 **bay leaf**
- 1 **tablespoon coarse salt**
- ¼ **teaspoon coarsely ground black pepper**

1 Heat the oil in a soup pot until it is hot enough to sizzle a piece of onion. Add the onions and cook, stirring, over medium-low heat until the onions are golden, about 10 minutes. Add the celery, carrots, parsley and garlic and cook, stirring, for 2 minutes.

2 Add 9 cups water, the tomatoes (if using), shiitake stems or mushrooms (if using), bay leaf, salt and pepper. Bring to a boil. Reduce the heat to medium-low so that the broth maintains a slow boil and cook, uncovered, for about 30 minutes.

3 Cool the broth. Place a strainer over a big bowl and carefully pour the broth through the strainer. Reserve the vegetables (see headnote). Divide the broth among freezer containers, label and freeze for 2 to 3 months or until needed.

Main and Side-Dish Salads

Vegetarian salads offer, in one bold, often brilliant stroke, all the elements that any good meal requires: crisp texture, bright color, juiciness and contrasting sweet and acid notes. Add to that the zing of a tangy dressing, a hint of salt and the comforting crunch of nuts or seeds, and you have all sorts of possibilities.

Keep in mind that the base of your salad — lettuce, spinach and other leafy greens — is primarily comprised of water. That moisture begins to evaporate once the greens are picked and continues as they are transported from the field, to the warehouse, to the market and, finally, to your vegetable bin. But you can reverse the dehydration at least partially by giving the greens a good soaking in cold water. The result is the starting point for a fresh, crisp, delicious salad.

SALAD TIPS

* Soak the greens in cold water in a salad spinner with the basket in place. When they are crisp, lift out the basket, drain the excess water, return the basket to the bowl and spin the greens dry. Use immediately or refrigerate in the salad spinner. Alternatively, you can soak the greens in a large bowl of cold water with a handful of ice cubes for at least 10 minutes. To dry, shake them in a colander, then wrap them in a clean towel or whirl in a salad spinner.

* Bags of baby spinach and other greens are time-saving, but they should be washed and crisped in ice water before using.

* Head lettuce and other greens from farmers' markets can be gritty. Swish in a large bowl of warm water to relax the leaves and free the sand from any crevices. Crisp and refresh in a second bath of ice water.

* Always lift greens out of the rinse water, so you leave behind any grit and the dirty water in the bowl.

* Jazz up your salads with torn leaves of fresh herbs like dill, mint and basil.

* Boost the protein and bulk up your salad with a handful of toasted nuts or seeds, crumbled cheese or chopped hard-cooked eggs (see page 14).

* Grain salads absorb the flavors in dressing quickly. Make a double batch of dressing but add only half at a time, increasing the amount as you taste and evaluate the flavors. The secret is to taste and correct the seasonings right up to serving.

QUICK HITS FOR SALADS

Crispy Chickpeas

These multi-use crisp chickpeas are great for snacking or sprinkling on top of green salads, grain salads or pilafs. They are best eaten freshly made, since they lose their crunch as they stand. Place a large baking sheet in the oven and preheat to 450°F for 10 minutes. Rinse and drain 1 can (15–16 ounces) chickpeas, spread the chickpeas on a folded towel and blot dry. Whisk 1 egg white in a bowl until frothy. Add the chickpeas to the egg white and toss to coat. Turn out the chickpeas onto the towel and blot to remove any excess egg. Place the chickpeas in a bag with ¼ cup all-purpose flour and ¼ teaspoon cayenne and shake to coat. Carefully remove the heated pan from the oven and add 3 tablespoons olive oil. Spread the chickpeas on the hot pan and roast, stirring occasionally, until crisp and golden brown, 15 to 20 minutes. To recrisp, spread them on a baking sheet and place in a 400°F oven for 10 to 15 minutes.

MIXED GREENS WITH DRIED OR FRESH FRUIT AND CHEESE

Toss 4 to 6 cups lightly packed torn greens with Basic Vinaigrette (page 74). Toss in one of the following combinations of dried or fresh fruit and nuts or cheese:

Dates, Pistachio and Feta

½ cup snipped pitted dates, 2 tablespoons toasted pistachios and ½ cup cold crumbled feta cheese (preferably mild French).

Dried Apricot, Glazed Walnuts and Stilton

½ cup thin strips dried apricots, ¼ cup glazed walnuts (see page 15) and ½ cup cold crumbled Stilton cheese.

Fresh Apple, Hazelnuts and Parmigiano-Reggiano

1 large or 2 small crisp Fuji or other apples, cut into 16 paper-thin slices, ¼ cup chopped toasted and peeled hazelnuts and curls of Parmigiano-Reggiano. Substitute hazelnut oil for the olive oil and use lemon juice in the vinaigrette.

Fresh Pear, Walnuts and Comté

1 large ripe Bartlett pear, cut into 16 paper-thin slices, ½ cup toasted walnut pieces and curls of Comté cheese. Substitute walnut oil for the olive oil and use lemon juice in the vinaigrette.

Fresh Peach, Toasted Almonds and Manchego

1 large peach, peeled, or nectarine, unpeeled, cut into 16 thin (¼-inch) slices, or 8 small ripe apricots, halved or quartered, ¼ cup toasted sliced skin-on almonds and curls of Manchego cheese. If available, substitute Marcona almonds imported from Spain for the sliced almonds.

TOMATO SALADS

During tomato season, enjoy meaty plum (Roma) tomatoes in mixed salads and juicy round tomatoes in sliced or composed salads. Brightly flavored, acidic tomatoes stand up to richer, bolder-flavored olive oils. This is the time to invest in a big, fruity olive oil, often called "finishing" oil.

Tomato and Mint Salad

Toss 2 to 3 cups firm, ripe tomato wedges with ¼ cup finely chopped fresh mint, 2 tablespoons extra-virgin olive oil, 1 grated garlic clove and ½ teaspoon coarse salt. Taste, and if the salad needs a kick, splash on 1 tablespoon fresh lime juice or mild fruit wine vinegar. If preferred, substitute chopped fresh tarragon or dill or torn fresh basil leaves for the mint.

Tomato and Cannellini Salad

Toss 2 to 3 cups diced (½ inch) ripe tomatoes with 1 can (15–16 ounces) cannellini, rinsed and drained, ½ cup chopped fennel or celery,

½ cup chopped sweet onion, ¼ cup torn fresh basil leaves, 2 tablespoons extra-virgin olive oil, 2 tablespoons red wine vinegar and ½ teaspoon coarse salt.

Tomato, Corn and Cilantro Salad

Toss 2 to 3 cups firm, ripe tomato wedges with 1 cup fresh raw corn kernels, ¼ cup coarsely chopped fresh cilantro, 2 tablespoons extra-virgin olive oil, 2 tablespoons fresh lime juice, 1 grated garlic clove, 1 teaspoon finely chopped seeded jalapeño pepper and ½ teaspoon coarse salt.

Chopped Tomato, Celery and Kalamata Olive Salad

Toss 2 to 3 cups cubed firm, ripe tomatoes, ½ cup sliced (½ inch) celery, ¼ cup chopped pitted Kalamata or cracked Sicilian green olives, 2 tablespoons extra-virgin olive oil, 2 tablespoons chopped celery leaves, 1 grated garlic clove, ½ teaspoon coarse salt, a pinch of dried oregano and a generous grinding of black pepper. Taste, and if the salad needs a kick, splash on 1 tablespoon fresh lime juice or mild fruit wine vinegar.

OTHER SALADS

Warm New Potato Salad with White Wine and Scallions

Cook 1½ pounds quartered or halved small new red potatoes until tender. Drain, and while the potatoes are still hot, toss in a bowl with ½ cup dry white wine, ¼ cup extra-virgin olive oil, ½ cup thin-sliced scallions (white and green parts), 1 teaspoon coarse salt and a generous grinding of black pepper. The potatoes will absorb the wine and olive oil as they stand. Serve warm or at room temperature.

Chickpea Salad with Celery, Lemon and Herbs

Rinse and drain 1 can (15–16 ounces) chickpeas, spread on a folded towel and blot dry. Toss the chickpeas with ½ cup each chopped (about the size of a chickpea) celery and red onion, ¼ cup chopped celery leaves, 2 tablespoons extra-virgin olive oil, 2 tablespoons fresh lemon juice and 1 tablespoon each finely chopped fresh Italian parsley, oregano, dill, mint, or basil or any combination of fresh herbs to equal ¼ cup. Season with ½ teaspoon coarse salt and a generous grinding of black pepper. Add 2 cups shredded romaine leaves, mixed salad greens or torn crinkly spinach leaves and toss to combine.

Black Bean and Mango Salad

Rinse and drain 1 can (15–16 ounces) black beans and toss with 1 mango, diced, ¼ cup sliced scallions (white and green parts) or chopped red onion, 2 tablespoons chopped fresh cilantro, 2 tablespoons extra-virgin olive oil, 2 tablespoons lime juice and 1 teaspoon finely chopped seeded jalapeño pepper. Season with ¼ teaspoon coarse salt and a generous grinding of black pepper.

CONFETTI GRAIN SALADS

Leftover cooked grains make great quick salads. To 2 to 3 cups cooked rice, quinoa, bulgur, couscous, farro (see page 216) or other grain, add 1 to 2 cups chopped vegetables. Select a maximum of 3 or 4 from the following, mixing and matching according to the season and compatibility: raw corn kernels, thawed frozen or cooked fresh peas, cooked and cooled frozen shelled edamame (green soybeans), chopped carrot, red, yellow or green bell pepper, red onion, scallions (white and green parts), celery, fennel, cucumbers and any number of other vegetables. Add ¼ to ½ cup chopped toasted nuts, seeds or raisins or snipped dried fruit.

Brown Rice, Scallion and Peanut Salad

Combine 2 to 3 cups cooked brown rice, ½ cup thin-sliced scallions (white and green parts), ½ cup chopped carrot and ½ cup chopped dry-roasted unsalted peanuts. Toss with Japanese Rice Vinaigrette with Ginger (page 74). Top with chopped fresh cilantro or dill.

Arborio Rice, Green Pea and Toasted Pine Nut Salad

Combine 2 to 3 cups freshly cooked warm Arborio rice, 1 cup thawed frozen green peas and ¼ cup toasted pine nuts. Toss with Basic Vinaigrette (page 74) made with red wine vinegar.

RED RICE SALAD WITH EDAMAME, TAMARI WALNUTS AND GINGER Vegan

The earthy flavors of Bhutanese red rice complement the sweet nutty taste of the green soybeans (edamame) and the soy-coated walnuts. Look for shelled edamame; the unshelled are too time-consuming to peel. If they are unavailable, see Substitutions below.

Cook Time: 30 minutes
Serves: 4

- 1½ cups frozen shelled edamame (green soybeans)
- 1 teaspoon coarse salt
- 1 cup Bhutanese red rice (see page 218)

Tamari Walnuts

- ½ cup walnut pieces
- ½ teaspoon mild-flavored extra-virgin olive oil or other vegetable oil
- 1½ tablespoons tamari or soy sauce

Rice Vinaigrette

- 3 tablespoons mild-flavored extra-virgin olive oil or other vegetable oil
- 3 tablespoons unseasoned Japanese rice vinegar
- 1 teaspoon grated peeled fresh ginger
- 1 garlic clove, grated
- ½ teaspoon coarse salt

- ½ cup thin-sliced scallions (white and green parts)
- 1 tablespoon finely chopped seeded jalapeño pepper, or to taste
- ¼ cup chopped fresh cilantro leaves or dill

1 Bring a medium saucepan three-fourths full of water to a boil. Add the edamame and salt and simmer until the edamane are tender, about 3 minutes. Remove the edamame from the boiling water with a perforated spoon or skimmer and place in a strainer. Rinse with cold water and set aside to cool. Add the rice to the boiling water and cook until the grains are tender, about 25 minutes. Drain in a strainer. Rinse with cold water and set aside to cool.

2 To make the tamari walnuts: Combine the walnuts and oil in a heavy skillet over medium-high heat and cook, stirring, until the skillet is hot enough to sizzle a drop of tamari, about 1 minute. Add the tamari and boil, stirring and adjusting the heat between medium and medium-low, until the walnuts are glazed with the thickened tamari, about 1 minute. Turn the walnuts out onto a plate to cool.

3 To make the vinaigrette: Whisk the oil, rice vinegar, ginger, garlic and salt in a large bowl until blended.

4 Add the rice, edamame, scallions and jalapeño to the dressing and toss to coat. Sprinkle with the walnuts and cilantro or dill. Serve at room temperature.

Substitutions

- You can use 2 cups broccoli florets in place of the edamame.
- If red rice is not available, substitute medium- or long-grain brown rice. You can also use a combination of red, Forbidden Rice (see page 217) and brown rice.

BLACK RICE, MANGO AND SUGAR SNAP PEA SALAD Vegan

Black rice studded with sunny orange squares of ripe mango and bright green sugar snaps makes a stunning presentation. The best rice to use for this salad is the Chinese black rice marketed as Forbidden Rice (see page 217). Unlike the more typical Japonica black rice, which has a round grain that cooks up soft and sticky, Forbidden Rice has a long grain with a less starchy consistency, making it perfect for savory dishes. If Forbidden Rice is not available, make this salad with brown or white basmati rice.

Cook Time: 25 minutes
Serves: 4

- 8 ounces stringless sugar snap peas (about 2 cups)
- 1 teaspoon coarse salt
- 1 cup Forbidden Rice (see headnote)

Sesame and Tamari Dressing

- 3 tablespoons unseasoned Japanese rice vinegar
- 2 tablespoons mild-flavored extra-virgin olive oil or other vegetable oil
- 1 tablespoon tamari or soy sauce
- 2 teaspoons toasted sesame oil
- 1 teaspoon grated peeled fresh ginger
- 1 garlic clove, grated
- ¼ teaspoon coarse salt

- 1 ripe mango, peeled, pitted and diced (¼ inch), about 1½ cups
- ½ cup chopped red onion
- 4 tablespoons finely chopped fresh cilantro
- 2 teaspoons sesame seeds

1 Bring a medium saucepan three-fourths full of water to a boil. Add the sugar snaps and salt and simmer until tender, about 1 minute. Remove the sugar snaps from the boiling water with a perforated spoon or skimmer and place in a strainer. Rinse with cold water and set aside to cool. Add the rice to the boiling water and cook until the grains are tender, about 25 minutes. Drain in a strainer. Rinse with cold water and set aside to cool.

2 To make the sesame and tamari dressing: Whisk the vinegar, oil, tamari, sesame oil, ginger, garlic and salt in a large bowl.

3 Add the cooled rice, sugar snaps, mango, red onion and 2 tablespoons of the cilantro to the dressing and gently toss to combine. Spoon the rice salad onto a platter and sprinkle with the remaining 2 tablespoons cilantro and the sesame seeds.

Shortcuts

Look for stringless sugar snap peas, which take less time to trim.

> ## Make a Meal
>
> Start with one of the Asian-flavored soups: Carrot, Sweet Potato and Ginger Soup with Baby Bok Choy (page 33) or Miso Soup with Spinach, Curried Tofu and Shiitake (page 42). This salad is also excellent with Cabbage, Pineapple and Peanut Salad (page 72) or Green Bean, Corn, Tomato and Cucumber Salad (page 66).

TOMATOES AND POTATOES WITH AVOCADO-DILL DRESSING

This is a satisfying and pretty salad created by a friend. It was Lynda Barber's brilliant idea to spread half of the avocado dressing on the plate as a bed for the potatoes, tomatoes and salad greens and then dollop the remaining dressing on top. The important flavor here is dill — lots of it. Thin-sliced red onion and quartered hard-cooked eggs are optional but delicious additions.

Cook Time: 30 minutes
Serves: 4 as a main dish or 8 as a side dish

- 1½ pounds small to medium Yukon Gold potatoes, halved if large

Avocado-Dill Dressing

- 1 ripe avocado, halved, pitted and peeled
- ½ cup mayonnaise
- ½ cup plain Greek-style yogurt (0% or 2%)
- ½ cup coarsely chopped crisp, seedless cucumber
- ½ cup lightly packed coarsely chopped fresh dill, including delicate stems
- ¼ cup chopped scallions (white and green parts)
- 1 tablespoon fresh lemon or lime juice
- ½ teaspoon coarse salt
  Pinch of cayenne

- 12 thin diagonal slices crisp, seedless cucumber
- 3–4 cups lightly packed mixed salad greens, small leaves of watercress, arugula or baby spinach
- 8 thick slices (½ inch) tomato (2 large)
- ½ cup paper-thin lengthwise slices red onion (optional)
- 2 hard-cooked eggs (see page 14), peeled and quartered (optional)
- ½ cup lightly packed coarsely chopped fresh dill
  Coarse salt and freshly ground black pepper

1 Place the potatoes in a medium saucepan and cover with water. Bring to a boil and cook, covered, over medium heat until the potatoes are tender when pierced with a skewer, 15 to 20 minutes, depending on their size. Rinse with cold water and drain. Set the potatoes aside and cool to lukewarm. When cool enough to handle, remove the skins and cut the potatoes into thick (¼- to ½-inch) slices.

2 To make the dressing: Combine the avocado, mayonnaise, yogurt, cucumber, dill, scallions, lemon juice, salt and cayenne in a food processor. Process until smooth.

3 Spread half of the avocado dressing on a large serving platter. Layer the sliced potatoes on top of the dress-

ing and top with the cucumber slices. Distribute the salad greens over the potatoes and cucumbers and top with overlapping tomato slices and onion slices, if using. Place the eggs, if using, around the edge of the platter.

4 Spoon a dollop of the remaining avocado dressing on top of each tomato slice. Reserve the remaining dressing to serve on the side. Sprinkle the salad with the dill and add salt and pepper to taste.

TOASTED BULGUR, TOMATO AND FETA SALAD

Middle Eastern in origin, bulgur is best known as the grain used in tabbouleh salad. Here I put my own twist on tabbouleh by toasting the bulgur and adding pine nuts browned in olive oil and three different fresh herbs along with tomato and feta cheese. Allow at least 20 minutes to soak the bulgur.

Cook Time: 30 minutes
Serves: 4

- 1 cup medium- or coarse-grain bulgur
- 2 tablespoons mild-flavored extra-virgin olive oil or other vegetable oil
- ½ teaspoon coarse salt

Dressing

- ⅓ cup mild-flavored extra-virgin olive oil or other vegetable oil
- ¼ cup fresh lemon juice
- 1 garlic clove, grated
- ½ teaspoon coarse salt

- ¼ cup pine nuts
- 1 cup loosely packed fresh mint leaves
- ½ cup loosely packed chopped fresh dill, including tender stems
- ½ cup loosely packed chopped fresh Italian parsley, including tender stems
- 2 firm, ripe tomatoes, cored and cut into ½-inch cubes (about 2 cups)
- 1 cup cubed (½ inch) crisp, seedless cucumber
- 1 cup cubed (½ inch) red onion
- 4 ounces crumbled feta cheese (about 1 cup)
- ½ cup pitted Kalamata olives (optional)

1 Preheat the oven to 350°F. Spread the bulgur on a baking sheet and bake until lightly toasted, stirring once, about 10 minutes. Transfer the bulgur to a bowl. Add 1½ cups boiling water, 1 tablespoon of the oil and the salt and stir to blend. Let stand, covered tightly, until all the water is absorbed, about 20 minutes.

2 **To make the dressing:** In a small bowl, whisk the oil, lemon juice, garlic and salt until blended. Set aside.

3 Combine the pine nuts and the remaining 1 tablespoon oil in a small skillet and cook over low heat, stirring, until they are browned, about 5 minutes.

4 Finely chop the mint, dill and parsley in a food processor. Combine the bulgur, dressing, herbs, tomatoes, cucumber and onion and toss to blend. Spoon onto a large platter and garnish with the feta cheese, pine nuts and olives, if using. Serve at room temperature.

Make a Meal

Serve with Warm Green Bean and Tomato Salad with Mint (page 67) or a half recipe of Middle Eastern Bread Salad (page 64), cutting the amount of the herbs in half so as not to overwhelm the palate.

Shortcuts

If time doesn't allow, skip the bulgur-toasting step. See directions for cooking bulgur, page 215.

Substitutions

In place of the pine nuts, use chopped walnuts. I also like to add 1 tablespoon sesame seeds.

SOBA NOODLE SALAD WITH SNOW PEAS   Vegan

Soba, the Japanese buckwheat noodles most often served in both hot and chilled broths, appear here in a salad. They are widely available, usually sold in boxes or plastic bags in the Asian section of the supermarket. I've kept the vegetable additions basic, but feel free to put in slivered radishes for more color or to substitute slivered green beans for the snow peas.

Cook Time: 5 minutes
Serves: 4

- 6 ounces snow peas, cut into ¼-inch diagonals (about 1½ cups)
- 1 teaspoon coarse salt
- 12 ounces soba noodles
- 2 teaspoons toasted sesame oil

Dressing

- ⅓ cup unseasoned Japanese rice vinegar
- ¼ cup mild-flavored extra-virgin olive oil or other vegetable oil
- 3 tablespoons tamari or soy sauce
- 1 teaspoon grated peeled fresh ginger
- 1 garlic clove, grated
- ½ teaspoon coarse salt

- 4 scallions (white and green parts), cut into thin (⅛-inch) diagonals (about ½ cup)
- 1 medium carrot, finely shredded (about ½ cup)
- ½ cup thin matchsticks (⅛ by 1 inch) crisp, seedless cucumber
- 1 tablespoon sesame seeds

1 Bring a medium saucepan three-fourths full of water to a boil. Add the snow peas and salt and simmer until crisp-tender, about 1 minute. Remove the snow peas from the boiling water with a perforated spoon or skimmer and place in a bowl of ice water. Add the noodles to the boiling water and cook until tender, 3 to 4 minutes. Drain the noodles in a strainer. Rinse with cold water. Transfer the noodles to a bowl and toss with the sesame oil. Refrigerate until ready to mix with other ingredients.

2 **To make the dressing:** In a small bowl, whisk the rice vinegar, oil, tamari, ginger, garlic and salt until blended.

3 Drain the snow peas and pat dry. Add the snow peas, scallions, carrot, cucumber and half of the sesame seeds to the soba noodles. Add the dressing and toss with your hands to thoroughly blend. Top with the remaining sesame seeds. Serve cold.

Make a Meal

The noodles are delicious with one of the shredded Tuscan kale salads (pages 69 and 70) or with Miso Soup with Spinach, Curried Tofu and Shiitake (page 42).

Substitutions

- Substitute diagonally sliced asparagus, 1-inch lengths of green beans or whole sugar snap peas (cooked until crisp-tender using the same technique as in this recipe) for the snow peas.
- Sesame seeds (an excellent source of protein) are the garnish of choice, but feel free to substitute peanuts, almonds or other nuts.

TOASTED QUINOA, CORN AND AVOCADO SALAD   Vegan

The nutty taste and irresistible crunch of toasted quinoa make it a natural for a refreshing, yet hearty, main-dish salad. Here I dress it with a favorite dressing of toasted ground cumin and lots of lime juice.

Cook Time: 30 minutes
Serves: 4 as a main dish or 8 as a side dish

- 1½ cups quinoa
- 1 tablespoon mild-flavored olive oil or other vegetable oil

Jalapeño Dressing

- 2 teaspoons ground cumin
- 5 tablespoons mild-flavored olive oil or other vegetable oil
- ½ cup fresh lime juice, plus more to taste
- 1 tablespoon finely chopped seeded jalapeño pepper, plus more to taste
- 1 garlic clove, grated
- 1 teaspoon coarse salt

- 1 cup fresh corn kernels (from 2 ears)
- 1 cup diced (½ inch) firm, ripe plum tomatoes
- ½ cup thin-sliced (¼ inch) scallions (white and green parts)
- 1 ripe avocado, halved, pitted, peeled and diced (½ inch)
- ½ cup finely chopped fresh cilantro

1 Rinse the quinoa in a fine-mesh strainer under cold running water for at least 45 seconds. Shake the strainer to remove as much water as possible.

2 Heat the oil in a large skillet. Add the rinsed quinoa and cook, stirring, over medium heat until it is a light golden brown, about 10 minutes. Add 2 cups water and bring to a boil. Cook, covered, over medium-low heat until the water is absorbed and the quinoa is translucent and appears to be uncoiling, 18 to 20 minutes. Let stand, covered, until cool, about 10 minutes.

3 **To make the dressing:** Sprinkle the cumin in a small skillet and toast over medium-low heat, stirring, until fragrant and a shade darker in color, about 3 minutes. Remove from the heat. When the skillet is cool to the touch, add the oil, lime juice, jalapeño, garlic and salt. Transfer to a large bowl and whisk to blend.

4 Add the cooled quinoa, corn, tomatoes and scallions to the dressing and toss to blend. Spoon the salad onto a large platter and sprinkle the avocado and cilantro on top.

Make a Meal

Serve with Tomato and Mint Salad (page 49) or with a platter of thick-sliced tomatoes drizzled with extra-virgin olive oil and sprinkled with coarse salt.

Shortcuts

You can toast a large batch of quinoa ahead of time. Store at room temperature in a tightly closed container. It will keep for 3 or more months. Use in main dishes, side dishes or other salads.

MIDDLE EASTERN BREAD SALAD   Vegan

This is my version of fattoush, a popular Middle Eastern salad made with lettuce, herbs and torn pita bread. I prefer sheets of soft lavash, an Armenian bread sold in plastic bags and often used to make wrapped sandwiches. (Lavash is also sold as cracker bread, but that version needs to be spritzed with water and softened before using.) Here I brush the soft bread with olive oil and then sprinkle it with za'atar, a popular Middle Eastern spice blend.

Cook Time: 20 minutes
Serves: 4 as a main course or 8 as a side
    dish (recipe can be halved)

- 1 large sheet or 2 half sheets (approximately 24 by 12 inches total) whole wheat lavash
- About 2 tablespoons extra-virgin olive oil
- 1–2 tablespoons za'atar (see page 11)
- Coarse salt
- 2 cups lightly packed fresh Italian parsley, including tender stems
- 1 cup lightly packed fresh mint leaves
- ½ cup lightly packed chopped fresh dill, including tender stems (use less if you're not a dill fan)
- 1 medium head romaine lettuce, cut into ½-inch crosswise slices (4 cups lightly packed)
- ½ cup thin-sliced (⅛ inch) scallions (white and green parts)
- ½ cup thin-sliced (⅛ inch) crisp, seedless cucumber
- 1 cup cubed (½ inch) firm, ripe tomato

Dressing

- 6 tablespoons extra-virgin olive oil
- ¼ cup fresh lemon juice
- 1 garlic clove, grated

1 Preheat the oven to 350°F. Brush both sides of the lavash lightly with the olive oil. Place the lavash on a large baking sheet, slightly overlapping or, if necessary, cutting to fit. Sprinkle the top evenly with za'atar and a light dusting of salt. Bake until toasted and crisp, 15 to 20 minutes. Cool. Break or cut into rough 1-inch pieces. You should have about 4 cups.

2 Place the parsley, mint and dill in a food processor and pulse 2 or 3 times, or until coarsely chopped. Transfer to a large bowl. Add the lettuce, scallions, cucumber and tomato.

3 **To make the dressing:** In a small bowl, whisk the oil, lemon juice and garlic until blended. Add to the salad and toss to coat. Add the toasted lavash and toss to combine. Serve immediately.

Make a Meal

Top the salad with Crispy Chickpeas (page 48) or serve with Chickpea Salad with Celery, Lemon and Herbs (page 50).

Substitutions

- I find lavash in my supermarket's deli department, but if it is unavailable, use pita. You will need 2 pita (whole wheat preferred), halved along the folds. Brush with oil and sprinkle with za'atar and coarse salt and bake following the directions for the lavash until crisp and browned, 15 to 18 minutes.
- You can omit the za'atar and use a more generous sprinkling of salt.

GREEN BEAN, CORN, TOMATO AND CUCUMBER SALAD   Vegan

This simple salad calls out to me in early summer when fresh corn, tender green beans and ripe tomatoes make their appearance at my produce market. The corn available today is so sweet that I cut it from the cobs and use it raw in salads. You can give it a quick steaming if you prefer, but I like its raw crunch.

Cook Time: 5 minutes
Serves: 4

- 6 ounces green beans, cut into 1-inch lengths (about 1½ cups)
- 1½ teaspoons coarse salt
- 1 cup fresh corn kernels (from 2 ears)
- 2 medium tomatoes, cut into thin wedges
- ½ cup sliced (⅛ inch) crisp, seedless cucumber
- ¼ cup loosely packed torn fresh basil leaves
- 2 tablespoons extra-virgin olive oil
- 2 tablespoons fresh lime or lemon juice

Make a Meal

This is good with Red Rice Salad with Edamame, Tamari Walnuts and Ginger (page 52) or Toasted Bulgur, Tomato and Feta Salad (page 58). If desired, adjust the ingredients so there won't be any repetitions.

1 Bring a medium saucepan three-fourths full of water to a boil. Add the beans and 1 teaspoon of the salt and cook until crisp-tender, about 5 minutes. Drain and rinse with cold water. Place in a bowl with a handful of ice cubes to chill.

2 Combine the corn, tomatoes, cucumber, basil, oil, lime juice and the remaining ½ teaspoon salt in a salad bowl. Drain the green beans, remove the ice, and blot the beans dry. Add the beans to the salad bowl and toss to blend. Serve at room temperature.

Substitutions
- There are many variations on this theme. For instance, limit the vegetables to beans and corn, omitting the tomatoes and cucumbers. Increase the beans from 8 ounces to 12 ounces if you omit any of the other vegetables.
- Substitute a fruit-flavored vinegar for the citrus juice in the dressing.

WARM GREEN BEAN AND TOMATO SALAD WITH MINT Vegan

As a kid, I spent hours in my grandmother's kitchen watching her every move. During the height of summer, when Nana's garden was in high gear, the additions to her green bean and mint salad varied. If green beans were plentiful, the salad would be all beans. If they were scanty, she would stretch them with wedges of tomato or sliced cucumber.

Cook Time: 5 minutes
Serves: 4 to 8

- 12 ounces green beans, slender beans left whole, more mature beans cut into 2-inch lengths
  Coarse salt
- 1 garlic clove
- ½ cup lightly packed finely chopped fresh mint
- 1 pound ripe tomatoes, cut into ½-inch wedges
- ¼ cup full-flavored extra-virgin olive oil
  Freshly ground black pepper

Make a Meal

This is the perfect accompaniment to almost any main-dish salad or as part of a salad buffet. Serve with Middle Eastern Bread Salad (page 64) or Summer Tomato and Olive Bread Salad (page 71). For a buffet of salads, pair with Spinach, Avocado and Chopped-Egg Salad (page 68) and Warm New Potato Salad with White Wine and Scallions (page 50).

1 Bring a large pot three-fourths full of water to a boil. Add the beans and 1 teaspoon salt and cook, stirring once, until the beans are crisp-tender, about 5 minutes. Meanwhile, lightly bruise the garlic clove with the side of a knife and rub it on the inside of a large salad bowl. Leave the garlic in the bowl. Drain the beans and immediately add the hot beans and mint to the salad bowl. (The mint will darken, but it is essential to add it while the beans are hot so its flavor permeates the beans.)

2 Add the tomatoes, oil, a sprinkling of salt and a grinding of black pepper. Gently fold the ingredients together until blended. Serve warm or at room temperature.

Variations

- Prepare as directed, using 1 pound green beans and half a medium red onion cut into thin lengthwise slices. Add 1 tablespoon red wine vinegar, if desired.
- Add 1 avocado, cut into thin wedges, to the cooked beans, onion and mint. Add 1 tablespoon fresh lime or lemon juice, if desired
- Add 2 warm hard-cooked eggs (see page 14), cut into thin wedges, to the green bean and mint mixture. Thin-sliced red onion and a dash of red wine vinegar are optional.

SPINACH, AVOCADO AND CHOPPED-EGG SALAD

Of all the bags of prewashed greens in the produce section, the one I grab when I need a salad in a hurry is the baby spinach. Refresh bagged greens with a quick dip in cold water and spin them dry in your salad spinner. The creamy, tangy dressing for this salad comes together quickly in a food processor.

Prep Time: About 15 minutes
Serves: 4

Dressing

- ¼ **cup light mayonnaise**
- ¼ **cup plain low-fat yogurt**
- 2 **tablespoons coarsely chopped fresh dill**
- 2 **tablespoons coarsely chopped scallions (white and green parts)**
- 1 **tablespoon cider vinegar**
- ½ **teaspoon coarse salt**

- 1 **bag (5–6 ounces) baby spinach, rinsed and dried (about 5 cups lightly packed)**
- 2–4 **hard-cooked eggs (see page 14), quartered and cut crosswise (½ inch)**
- 1 **avocado, halved, pitted, peeled and cubed (¼ inch)**
- ¼ **cup thin-sliced radishes**
  Freshly ground black pepper
- ¼ **cup toasted salted sunflower seeds**

1 **To make the dressing:** Combine the mayonnaise, yogurt, dill, scallions, vinegar and salt in a food processor and pulse until the dill is finely chopped and the mixture is blended.

2 In a large serving bowl, combine the spinach, eggs, avocado, radishes, a generous grinding of black pepper and the dressing and toss to combine. Sprinkle the sunflower seeds on top. Serve immediately.

Substitutions

- Large-leaf spinach is also delicious in this salad. Its crinkly leaves are thicker and have a richer taste, adding textural interest. Bunches of spinach require a bit more work, since you'll have to trim off the long stems, tear the leaves into pieces and carefully wash them. (See Salad Tips, page 48.)
- Substitute salted roasted pepitas (hulled pumpkin seeds; see page 13) for the sunflower seeds.

Make a Meal

Serve with Warm Green Bean and Tomato Salad with Mint (page 67) and Confetti Rice Salad (page 50).

SHREDDED TUSCAN KALE, TOMATO AND AVOCADO SALAD Vegan

This recipe is based on a delicious and revolutionary idea: raw kale salad. Because it's on many restaurant menus, I suspect it is from an innovative raw foods chef. Having tested this salad with every variety of kale I can find, I've decided the mild-tasting, tender, pebbly-leafed Tuscan (lacinato) kale, often sold as "dinosaur kale," is the best. Although the kale is raw, it is softened by rubbing it in your hands with the lime juice, olive oil and salt dressing.

Prep Time: About 10 minutes
Serves: 4

- 1 small bunch (about 10 ounces) Tuscan (lacinato) kale, washed and dried
- 2 tablespoons fresh lime juice
- 1 tablespoon extra-virgin olive oil
- ½ teaspoon coarse salt

Salsa

- 1 avocado, halved, pitted, peeled and diced (¼ inch)
- 1 ripe tomato, diced (¼ inch), with seeds and juice (about 1 cup)
- ½ cup diced (¼ inch) red onion
- 1 teaspoon finely chopped seeded jalapeño pepper, plus more to taste
- 1 small garlic clove, grated
- 1 tablespoon lime juice
- 1 tablespoon extra-virgin olive oil
- ½ teaspoon coarse salt

- ¼ cup unsalted roasted pepitas (hulled pumpkin seeds; see page 13)

1 To prepare the kale, cut along both sides of the stem of each leaf with a sharp knife or pull the ruffled leaves away from the stems with your hands. Discard the stems. Gather a bunch of the long kale leaves together on the cutting board and slice into thin (⅛-inch) crosswise slices. You should have 4 to 6 cups lightly packed.

2 Combine the kale, lime juice, oil and salt in a large bowl. Rub the ingredients together with your hands (as though giving the kale a massage) until the leaves wilt, 1 to 2 minutes. Set aside.

3 **To make the salsa:** Combine the avocado, tomato, red onion, jalapeño, garlic, lime juice, oil and salt and stir to blend.

4 Add the salsa to the kale and toss to combine. Sprinkle the salad with the pepitas. Serve at room temperature.

Substitutions

Substitute roasted sunflower seeds for the pepitas.

Make a Meal

Serve with Black Rice, Mango and Sugar Snap Pea Salad (page 54) or Summer Tomato and Olive Bread Salad (page 71).

SHREDDED TUSCAN KALE SALAD WITH TAMARI AND SESAME Vegan

Everyone who tastes this salad (even my kale-phobic husband) devours it. The best kind to use is the mild, tender Tuscan (lacinato) variety, often sold as dinosaur kale.

Prep Time: 10 minutes
Serves: 4

- 1 small bunch (about 10 ounces) Tuscan (lacinato) kale, washed and dried
- 3 tablespoons unseasoned Japanese rice vinegar
- 2 tablespoons tamari or soy sauce
- 2 tablespoons mild-flavored olive oil
- 1 teaspoon toasted sesame oil
- 1 teaspoon grated peeled fresh ginger
- 1 garlic clove, grated
- ½ cup finely chopped carrot
- ¼ cup finely chopped red onion
- 1 tablespoon sesame seeds

1 To prepare the kale, cut along both sides of the stem of each leaf with a sharp knife or pull the ruffled leaves away from the stems with your hands. Discard the stems. Gather a bunch of the long kale leaves together on the cutting board and slice into thin (⅛-inch) crosswise slices. You should have 4 to 6 cups lightly packed.

2 Combine the kale, rice vinegar, tamari, olive oil, sesame oil, ginger and garlic in a large bowl. Rub the ingredients together with your hands (as though giving the kale a massage) until the leaves wilt, 1 to 2 minutes.

3 Add the carrot, onion and sesame seeds and toss with a fork until blended. Serve at room temperature.

Make a Meal

I like this with Green Bean, Corn, Tomato and Cucumber Salad (page 66) and a rice salad, such as the simple Brown Rice, Scallion and Peanut Salad (page 51).

SUMMER TOMATO AND OLIVE BREAD SALAD Vegan

You'll need ripe, luscious tomatoes for this salad, so save this recipe for the height of the season. Seek out a coarse-grained, chewy loaf of artisanal bread studded with black Kalamata olives. If olive bread is unavailable, use any whole-grain rustic loaf and toss in a handful of pitted Kalamata olives.

Cook Time: 20 minutes
Serves: 4 to 6

4–6 thick (1-inch) slices olive bread, crusts left on (see headnote)

Extra-virgin olive oil

1 garlic clove, bruised with the side of a knife

¼–½ cup ice water

5–6 large tomatoes (1½–2 pounds)

1 cup diced (¼ inch) red onion

1 cup lightly packed torn fresh basil leaves

Coarse salt and freshly ground black pepper

1–2 tablespoons aged red wine vinegar

Make a Meal

Serve with Warm Green Bean and Red Onion Salad with Mint (see Variations, page 67) and corn on the cob Mexican-style (page 190) or plain with olive oil and a sprinkling of coarse salt.

1 Preheat the oven to 350°F. Arrange the bread slices on a large baking sheet. Brush both sides of the bread lightly with oil and bake until crisp and golden, about 20 minutes, turning over halfway through the baking time. When the bread is cool enough to handle, cut it into rough 1-inch squares. You should have 4 to 6 cups. Set aside.

2 Rub the bruised garlic all over the surface of a large salad bowl. Leave the garlic in the bowl. Add the bread cubes. Sprinkle the bread with ¼ cup ice water, a tablespoon at a time, tossing after each addition. Reserve the remaining ¼ cup water to add later, if needed. (If the tomatoes are especially juicy, you may not need to add more water.)

3 With the tip of a paring knife, cut the stem ends from the tomatoes. Cut the tomatoes into ½-inch slices. Stack the slices and cut into ½-inch cubes. Add the tomatoes to the salad bowl, along with the onion, basil, a generous sprinkling of salt and a grinding of black pepper. Drizzle 3 tablespoons oil over the mixture. Toss to blend. Sprinkle with 1 tablespoon vinegar. Taste and season with more salt, pepper, oil and/or vinegar, if needed. If the salad seems dry, add the remaining ¼ cup ice water, 1 tablespoon at a time, and toss to combine. Serve at room temperature.

CABBAGE, PINEAPPLE AND PEANUT SALAD   Vegan

Full of crunch, heat and bright fresh flavors, this salad is a favorite. I even like leftovers the next day when the cabbage has lost some of its crunch.

Prep Time: About 15 minutes
Serves: 4 to 6

- 12 ounces green or savoy cabbage, cored and sliced thin (about 4 cups)
- ½ pineapple, halved lengthwise, cored, skin cut away and fruit coarsely chopped (about 2 cups)
- ½ cup coarsely chopped dry-roasted un-salted peanuts
- 1 jalapeño pepper, halved lengthwise, seeded and cut into ⅛-inch crosswise slices

Dressing

- 3 tablespoons mild-flavored olive oil or other vegetable oil
- 3 tablespoons unseasoned Japanese rice vinegar
- 1 teaspoon grated peeled fresh ginger
- 1 garlic clove, grated
- 1 teaspoon coarse salt

- ¼ cup chopped fresh cilantro (optional)

1 Combine the cabbage, pineapple, peanuts and jalapeño in a large bowl.

2 **To make the dressing:** In a small bowl, whisk the oil, vinegar, ginger, garlic and salt until blended. Add the dressing to the cabbage and toss to blend. Add the cilantro, if using. Serve at room temperature.

Shortcuts

Use a food processor fitted with the slicing blade to make quick work of the cabbage. Chop the pineapple with the chopping blade of the food processor.

Substitutions

- Omit the peanuts and substitute 1 to 2 tablespoons sesame seeds.
- Replace the head cabbage with bagged sliced cabbage crisped in ice water for 10 minutes.
- In a pinch, use chunks of unsweetened canned pine-apple instead of the fresh.

Make a Meal

Serve with Red Rice Salad with Edamame, Tamari Walnuts and Ginger (page 52).

CURRIED QUINOA AND APPLE SALAD WITH DRIED CRANBERRIES Vegan

This salad is heady with the aroma of toasted curry and crunchy with quinoa, raw apple and walnuts.

Cook Time: 30 minutes
Serves: 4

- 1 **cup quinoa**
- 3 **tablespoons extra-virgin olive oil, or more to taste**
- 2½ **teaspoons Madras curry powder**
  Coarse salt
- 2 **tablespoons fresh lemon juice, or more to taste**
- 1 **cup chopped peeled crisp apple, such as Fuji, Granny Smith or Pink Lady**
- ½ **cup chopped walnuts**
- ½ **cup dried cranberries**
- 2 **tablespoons thin-sliced scallions (green parts only)**

Make a Meal
Serve with Red Lentil Soup with Coconut Milk and Toasted Cumin (page 27).

1 Rinse the quinoa in a fine-mesh strainer under cold running water for at least 45 seconds. Shake in the strainer to remove as much water as possible.

2 Heat 1 tablespoon of the oil in a large skillet. Add the quinoa and cook, stirring, over medium-low heat until the quinoa is light golden brown, about 10 minutes. Add the curry powder and cook, stirring, for 1 minute. Add 2 cups water and 1 teaspoon salt and bring to a boil. Cook, covered, over medium-low heat until the water is absorbed and the quinoa is translucent and appears to be uncoiling, 18 to 20 minutes. Let stand, covered, until cool.

3 Whisk the remaining 2 tablespoons oil and the lemon juice in a large bowl until blended. Add the cooled quinoa, apple, walnuts, cranberries and scallions and toss to blend. Taste and correct the seasonings, adding a bit more lemon juice, oil and/or salt, if needed. Serve at room temperature.

Shortcut
A large batch of quinoa can be toasted ahead of time (see page 217).

BASIC VINAIGRETTE Vegan

Whisk 3 tablespoons extra-virgin olive oil, 1 tablespoon red wine vinegar, sherry vinegar, lemon juice or lime juice, 1 small garlic clove, grated, ½ teaspoon coarse salt and a generous grinding of black pepper in a small bowl. You can add 1 to 2 teaspoons Dijon mustard, 1 tablespoon minced red onion or shallot or 1 to 2 tablespoons finely chopped fresh tarragon, mint, basil, dill or other fresh herbs.

JAPANESE RICE VINAIGRETTE WITH GINGER Vegan

Whisk 3 tablespoons mild-flavored extra-virgin olive oil or other vegetable oil, 2 tablespoons unseasoned Japanese rice vinegar (my preferred brand is Marukan), 1 teaspoon grated peeled fresh ginger, 1 to 2 teaspoons tamari or soy sauce, 1 teaspoon toasted sesame oil and coarse salt to taste.

Topped and Stuffed Breads
That Make a Meal

A steaming bowl of soup, a buffet of vegetables or a light main dish call out for an accompaniment. I often yearn for a crisp or chewy side dish, something to add texture and extra satiety. For me, that means bread.

A grand selection of toppings for crostini, bruschetta and open-faced sandwiches as well as creative fillings for grilled sandwiches and tortillas offer a broad range of choices.

In the wide world of open-faced sandwiches, including bruschetta and crostini, there is a huge selection of "flat-form" possibilities for toppings, while grilled sandwiches, tortillas and other "wrappers" call out for creative fillings.

Bubbly mozzarella cheese layered with tomato slices on crisped Italian bread, for example, or braised Swiss chard and curls of Pecorino Romano cheese on bruschetta make a terrific lunch with a steaming bowl of soup. Others, like Grilled Comté Sandwich with Apple and Mango Chutney (page 91) or Summer Veggie Burritos with Goat Cheese (page 98), are hearty enough to stand alone or can be paired with a simple salad or cup of soup.

Flour and corn tortillas are staples in my refrigerator. The typical Mexican quesadilla is simply a cheese-filled tortilla folded into a half circle and heated in a skillet until the cheese is meltingly hot and the tortilla is golden and crunchy. But over the years, I've taken liberties with the concept of quesadil-

las, adding all sorts of ingredients that taste great together.

Mix and match fillings and toppings, experiment with different types of cheese and try a variety of mustards, spreads and relishes. Use the enticing recipes in this chapter as a springboard and let your culinary imagination take flight.

SANDWICH TIPS

❋ Seek out the best artisanal bread you can find, preferably a multigrain loaf that can be hand-cut into thick slices.

❋ Bread with a coarse crumb absorbs hot oil best and browns to a perfectly crunchy golden crust.

❋ To refresh day-old pita, tortillas or naan (flatbread), wrap in foil and warm in a moderate oven for about 10 minutes. Or crisp in a toaster or toaster oven.

❋ For grilled cheese sandwiches, keep a stash of good melting cheese on hand. A few favorites are mozzarella, Monterey Jack, Comté, cheddar and Manchego.

❋ Make quick work of cheese "curls" by pressing down hard with a vegetable peeler or cheese plane and pulling it along the smooth surface of the cheese. Hard or semihard cheeses are best for making curls.

❋ Use up small amounts of leftover chopped cooked greens, broccoli or cauliflower, smashed peas or beans or grilled sliced vegetables for sandwich fillings or toppings for crostini and bruschetta.

❋ Fresh goat's-milk cheese warmed to room temperature spreads smoothly on bread. For a crumbled topping for bruschetta or crostini, use cold cheese.

❋ A thin layer of pickle slices or chopped olives balances the richness of melted cheese and adds a great flavor hit to sandwiches.

❋ For a tender, golden brown crust on grilled sandwiches, use a silicone brush to apply olive oil to the griddle or skillet.

❋ For grilled sandwiches, olive oil is better than butter because it will brown without burning.

QUICK HITS FOR BREADS

Broiled Open-Faced Cheese Sandwiches with Tapenade or Sun-Dried Tomato Spread

Broil slices of bread until light golden brown on both sides. Spread each with a thin layer of black olive spread (called tapenade in France and olivada in Italy) or sun-dried tomato spread. Top with a ¼-inch-thick slice of mozzarella and broil until the cheese is bubbly, 3 to 5 minutes.

Lemony Goat Cheese Spread

Mash 3 to 4 ounces softened fresh goat cheese, 2 tablespoons extra-virgin olive oil, 1 teaspoon each grated lemon zest and snipped rosemary, half a clove of garlic, grated, and a grinding of black pepper until blended. Spread on crostini or bruschetta, drizzle each with about ¼ teaspoon extra-virgin olive oil and sprinkle with a little chopped fresh rosemary or other herb.

Warm Hard-Cooked Egg Spread with Parmigiano-Reggiano

Hard-cook 4 large eggs (see page 14) and peel while still warm. Mash the eggs in a bowl with 2 tablespoons extra-virgin olive oil, 2 tablespoons minced red onion, 1 tablespoon finely chopped fresh basil or Italian parsley, ½ teaspoon coarse salt and a grinding of black pepper. Broil ½- to ¾-inch-thick slices of Italian bread, preferably whole-grain, on both sides until golden. Spread the toast with the egg mixture and cover with shaved curls of Parmigiano-Reggiano. Broil until the cheese is softened and the egg mixture is warm, about 3 minutes.

Fried-Egg Quesadillas with Tomato and Cheese

Heat 1 teaspoon olive oil in a small skillet over medium-low heat. Add an 8-inch corn or flour tortilla and warm it, turning once, about 1 minute. Remove the tortilla from the pan and keep warm. Break 1 large egg into the pan and fry, breaking the yolk with the tip of a spatula, until the white and yolk are partially set, about 1 minute. Slide the spatula under the egg and transfer to the warm tortilla. Top the egg with ¼ cup chopped tomato and a few fresh cilantro leaves. Sprinkle with ¼ cup shredded Monterey Jack cheese. Fold the tortilla in half and, with the spatula, transfer the folded tortilla to the hot skillet. Cook until golden and the cheese is melted, turning once, about 1 minute. Cut into wedges.

Manchego-Fig Quesadillas

Heat 1 teaspoon olive oil in a small skillet over medium-low heat. Add an 8-inch corn or flour tortilla and warm it, turning once, about 1 minute. Off the heat, cover the bottom half of the tortilla with 1 large fresh fig, cut into ¼-inch-thick slices. Sprinkle with 1 to 2 teaspoons chopped seeded jalapeño pepper, 1 tablespoon chopped fresh cilantro and about ¼ cup shredded Manchego cheese. Fold the top half of the tortilla over the filling. Return the quesadilla to the warm skillet and reheat until the cheese is melted, about 1 minute. Cut into wedges.

BRUSCHETTA VS. CROSTINI

Bruschetta (bruce-*ket*-ta) and crostini (kroh-*stee*-nee), two Italian favorites, are often confused.

Bruschetta is basically a thick slice of bread, grilled or broiled, rubbed with garlic and drizzled with extra-virgin olive oil. Because it is thick and sturdy, I like to use it as the platform for hearty toppings such as cooked greens, chopped tomatoes and avocado or white beans seasoned with red onion, rosemary and garlic.

Crostini, or toasts, are made with thinner pieces. Typically, the bread is toasted, oiled and then spread with a thin topping. I've adjusted the concept for speed and efficiency by toasting thin-sliced, lightly oiled pieces on baking sheets until crisp and golden. More like crackers than toast, these platforms won't support chunky or chopped toppings, so keep your spreads on the thin side. Crostini can be made ahead and kept on hand in zip-top plastic bags or airtight containers for a week or longer.

The kind of bread is important. Make sure you select a solid, rustic Italian loaf or a French baguette from a good bakery. The bread should have an even crumb and not be riddled with airholes.

Olive Bread Toasts

Seek out a good loaf of artisanal olive bread. This bread makes the most delightful grilled sandwiches, bruschetta, crostini and plain crispy toasts. For toasts, slice it thin and prepare as you would crostini. Serve with a smear of Lemony Goat Cheese Spread (page 77).

Crostini

Preheat the oven to 400°F. Line up ¼- to ½-inch-thick rounds or diagonal slices of crusty French or Italian bread on a baking sheet. Lightly brush the tops of the slices with olive oil. Bake for 10 to 15 minutes, or until the bread is light golden brown. If the toasts become too dry, the bread won't be able to soak up the flavors in the topping.

Bruschetta

Position the top oven rack 5 inches from the heat source. Preheat the broiler. Cut hearty Italian bread, preferably a whole-grain loaf, into ½- to ¾-inch-thick slices. Line up the slices on a baking sheet and brush with olive oil (optional). Broil until golden, about 5 minutes. Turn the bread with tongs and broil on the other side until golden, about 3 minutes. Another option is to fire up the grill and toast thick slices of bread on the grill until lightly browned.

Quick-Toasted Bruschetta

For two servings, or 4 pieces bruschetta, I cut the bread into ½- to ¾-inch-thick slices and toast it in my toaster until golden brown on both sides, 2 to 3 minutes, then brush with olive oil.

Pita Chips

Preheat the oven to 350°F. Separate a package of pita bread along the folded edges to make flat circles. Spread the rough side of each lightly with olive oil. If desired, sprinkle with coarse salt, za'atar (see page 11), smoked paprika (preferably *Pimentón de la Vera*; see page 10) or Madras curry powder, or leave plain. Stack 2 or 3 of the circles and cut into 6 pie-shaped wedges. Spread the wedges in a single layer on a baking sheet and bake until golden, 12 to 15 minutes. Repeat until all the chips are baked. Stored in a zip-top plastic bag, the pita chips will keep for up to 2 weeks.

ROSEMARY-FENNEL WHITE BEAN SPREAD Vegan

Canned cannellini or white kidney beans make a quick topping for crostini or bruschetta when gussied up with minced red onion, fennel seed and snipped rosemary.

Serves: 4 to 6

- 1 garlic clove
- 1 teaspoon fennel seed
- Coarse salt
- 1¾ cups cooked or canned (15–16 ounces) cannellini or white kidney beans, rinsed and drained
- ¼ cup extra-virgin olive oil, plus more for topping
- ¼ cup minced red onion
- 1 tablespoon red wine vinegar
- Freshly ground black pepper
- 8–12 crostini or bruschetta (page 78), for serving
- 2 tablespoons snipped fresh rosemary

Make a Meal

Serve with Artichoke and Potato Stew with Black Olives and Tomatoes (page 134) or Skillet-Baked Eggs with Blistered Cherry Tomatoes (page 149).

1 Combine the garlic, fennel seed and ½ teaspoon salt in a mortar and crush into a paste with the pestle. If you don't have a mortar and pestle, grate the garlic and finely chop the fennel seed with a knife. Combine with the salt in a small bowl and mash with the back of a spoon until blended.

2 In a food processor, combine the mashed garlic mixture, beans and oil and process into a coarse puree. Transfer the puree to a bowl and stir in the red onion, vinegar and a generous grinding of black pepper. Taste and add more salt if needed.

3 Spread the crostini or bruschetta with the bean mixture. Top each portion with a light sprinkling of rosemary and a ¼-teaspoon drizzle of olive oil. Serve.

BROCCOLI, DILL AND LEMON SPREAD Vegan

This silken spread of cooked broccoli and fresh dill pureed with garlic and olive oil and enlivened with a generous squirt of lemon juice also makes a fresh dip for crudités or pita chips (page 78).

Cook Time: 6 minutes
Serves: 4 to 6

- 4 **cups broccoli florets (about 10 ounces)**
  Coarse salt
- 5 **tablespoons extra-virgin olive oil**
- 1 **garlic clove, grated**
- ⅛ **teaspoon crushed red pepper**
- ¼ **cup plus 1 tablespoon chopped fresh dill**
- 1 **tablespoon fresh lemon juice, plus more to taste**
- 8–12 **crostini (page 78), for serving**

Make a Meal

Serve with Tomato and White Bean Soup with Spinach Pesto (page 24) or Pumpkin and Tomato Soup with Cheese (page 38).

1 Bring a large saucepan half full of water to a boil. Add the broccoli and 1 teaspoon salt and cook, uncovered, until the broccoli is tender but still bright green, 3 to 5 minutes. Drain well.

2 Meanwhile, combine 2 tablespoons of the oil and the garlic in a small skillet and cook over medium-low heat, stirring, until the garlic begins to sizzle, about 1 minute. Do not brown. Remove from the heat. Add the crushed red pepper.

3 Combine the broccoli, ¼ cup of the dill, the oil-garlic mixture and the lemon juice in a food processor and puree. With the motor running, gradually add the remaining 3 tablespoons oil. Add ½ teaspoon salt, or to taste.

4 Spread on the crostini and sprinkle with the remaining 1 tablespoon dill. Serve immediately.

CHICKPEA SPREAD WITH POMEGRANATE MOLASSES   Vegan

Thick and syrupy with a rich sweet-and-sour taste, pomegranate molasses is used in Middle Eastern cooking. Use this quick, delicious puree as a spread on crostini or as a dip for warm pita bread or crisps. If pomegranates are in season, sprinkle the spread with the pretty jewel-like seeds.

Serves: 4 to 6

- 1 can (15–16 ounces) chickpeas, rinsed and drained
- 2 tablespoons pomegranate molasses (see page 13), plus more for drizzling (if not using pomegranate seeds)
- 2 tablespoons fresh lemon juice
- 1 garlic clove, grated
- ½ teaspoon coarse salt
- 3 tablespoons extra-virgin olive oil
- 8–12 crostini (page 78) or 1 recipe pita chips (page 78), for serving
- 2 tablespoons finely chopped fresh mint
- ¼ cup fresh pomegranate seeds, for garnish (optional)

1 Combine the chickpeas, pomegranate molasses, lemon juice, garlic and salt in a food processor and puree. With the motor running, gradually add the oil, processing until the mixture is smooth and creamy.

2 Spread about 2 tablespoons of the puree on each crostini. Sprinkle with mint and drizzle with pomegranate molasses and/or scatter over a few pomegranate seeds, if using. If serving as a dip, spread the puree on a serving plate, sprinkle it with the mint and drizzle with pomegranate molasses and/or garnish with the fresh pomegranate seeds.

Make a Meal

Serve with a vegetable buffet of Carrots with Moroccan Spices and Lemon (page 182), Steamed Spinach with Ginger and Garlic Oil (page 196) and Curried Quinoa and Apple Salad with Dried Cranberries (page 73).

BEET AND TAHINI PUREE

I was introduced to this intriguing spread of finely chopped cooked beets and tahini by the Lebanese-born cookbook author Anissa Helou. In this version, I add yogurt, lemon juice and fresh dill to the mix. Serve it on bread as I do here, as a spread in a sandwich with slices of avocado or as a salad spooned onto a crisp lettuce leaf.

Cook Time: 15 minutes
Serves: 4 to 6

- 2 cups cubed (½ inch) beets (about 6 medium beets), peeled if large
- 2 tablespoons tahini
- 2 tablespoons plain nonfat or low-fat yogurt
- 2 tablespoons fresh lemon juice
- 2 tablespoons chopped fresh dill
- ½ teaspoon coarse salt
  Freshly ground black pepper
- 8–12 crostini (page 78), for serving
- 2 hard-cooked eggs (see page 14), chopped, or diced avocado (optional)

Make a Meal

Serve with hard-cooked eggs, halved and sprinkled with za'atar (see page 11) and coarse salt (omit the hard-cooked egg garnish on the puree). Accompany with wedges of ripe avocado topped with lime juice and sprinkled with sesame seeds.

1 Bring the cubed beets and 2 tablespoons water to a boil in a small heavy saucepan. Cover and cook over medium-low heat until the beets are tender, 12 to 15 minutes. Do not allow the water to evaporate or the beets will burn. If there is any water left in the pan when the beets are done, cook, uncovered, over medium heat until the water cooks off. Transfer the beets to a food processor and cool slightly.

2 Add the tahini, yogurt, lemon juice, 1 tablespoon of the dill, the salt and a grinding of black pepper and process until finely chopped, stopping to scrape down the sides of the bowl as needed. Transfer the mixture to a bowl.

3 Spread the puree on the crostini. Top each crostini with about 1 tablespoon chopped egg or diced avocado, if using, and sprinkle with the remaining 1 tablespoon dill.

Shortcuts

To save time, use the packaged cooked beets available in some markets. Add to the food processor in step 2 and continue with the recipe.

BRAISED SWISS CHARD WITH PECORINO CURLS

Greens are a favorite topping, no matter what the season. You won't need the full wedge of cheese for this recipe, but you will need a good-sized chunk from which to shave curls of Pecorino to crown the tops of the bruschetta.

Cook Time: 10 minutes
Serves: 4

- 2 **bunches (about 1½ pounds) Swiss chard**
- 2 **tablespoons extra-virgin olive oil, plus more as needed**
- 2 **garlic cloves, finely sliced**
  Coarse salt and freshly ground black pepper
- 8 **bruschetta (page 78), for serving**
  Wedge of Pecorino Romano cheese, at room temperature

Make a Meal

Serve as an accompaniment to a hearty soup. Try Tomato and White Bean Soup with Spinach Pesto (page 24) or White Bean and Fennel Soup (page 23).

1 Wash the Swiss chard and tear the leafy parts away from the thick center ribs. Reserve the ribs for another use (see Swiss Chard Ribs Gratin, page 187) or add to vegetable soup or broth. Tear the leaves into 2-inch pieces.

2 Combine the oil and garlic in a large heavy pot and cook over low heat until the garlic sizzles, about 1 minute.

3 Add the wet Swiss chard leaves to the pot and cook, covered, over medium heat, until wilted, 3 to 5 minutes. Add a sprinkling of salt and a generous grinding of black pepper. Transfer to a strainer to drain off any excess moisture.

4 Drizzle about ½ teaspoon oil on the surface of each bruschetta. Top with a layer of the hot Swiss chard.

5 Hold the wedge of cheese firmly in one hand. With a cheese plane or a heavy-duty vegetable peeler pressed hard into the flat surface of the cheese, slice off curls of cheese and place on top of the Swiss chard. Serve immediately.

TOMATO, AVOCADO AND TARRAGON SPREAD Vegan

This recipe is best when tomatoes are big and juicy. If you're forced to use less-than-stellar tomatoes, the "bath" of salt, lime juice, oil and tarragon will jazz them up a bit. I am not as liberal in my use of tarragon as I am with other herbs, but I do like its aniselike taste. If you prefer, substitute cilantro, dill, mint or basil for the tarragon.

Serves: 4 to 6

- 2 **tablespoons extra-virgin olive oil**
- 2 **tablespoons fresh lime juice**
- 2 **tablespoons chopped fresh tarragon** (see headnote)
- 1 **garlic clove, grated**
- 1 **teaspoon coarse salt**
- 3 **large ripe tomatoes, sliced ¼ inch thick**
- 2 **avocados, halved and pitted**
- 1 **teaspoon finely chopped seeded jalapeño pepper**
- 12 **bruschetta (page 78), for serving**

1 Whisk the oil, 1 tablespoon of the lime juice, 1 tablespoon of the tarragon, the garlic and ½ teaspoon of the salt in a small bowl until blended. Place the tomatoes on a platter and spoon the dressing over them.

2 With a tablespoon, scoop the avocado flesh into a small bowl and mash it with a fork. Add the remaining 1 tablespoon lime juice, the remaining ½ teaspoon salt and the jalapeño and stir to blend.

3 Pour the juices from the tomato platter into a small bowl and drizzle each bruschetta with about 1 teaspoon of the juice. Spread the bruschetta with a layer of the mashed avocado. Place a slice of tomato on top of each. Top the tomato with a pinch of the remaining 1 tablespoon tarragon. Serve immediately.

Make a Meal

Serve with Black Rice, Mango and Sugar Snap Pea Salad (page 54) and Chilled Watermelon and Tomato Soup (page 22).

ROASTED RED PEPPER AND WALNUT SPREAD Vegan

This spread, called muhammara, is eaten widely throughout the Middle East. The ingredients differ from kitchen to kitchen, but generally it is based on roasted red peppers, walnuts and pomegranate molasses. The recipe was introduced to me by a friend, Turkish food and travel expert Kathleen O'Neill. Eaten primarily as a dip with pita chips or vegetable crudités, it is also delicious on crostini or bruschetta, topped with finely chopped walnuts.

Prep Time: About 15 minutes
Serves: 8

1½ cups walnut pieces

1 slice whole wheat bread crumbled (about ½ cup)

1 jar (12 ounces) roasted red peppers, rinsed, drained and coarsely chopped (about 1½ cups)

¼ cup extra-virgin olive oil, plus more to taste

2 tablespoons pomegranate molasses (see page 13), plus more to taste

1 tablespoon fresh lemon or lime juice, plus more to taste

¾ teaspoon ground cumin

¼ teaspoon cayenne, or to taste

Coarse salt

Pinch of sugar (optional)

Pita chips (page 78), for serving

1 Combine the walnuts and bread in a food processor and process until finely chopped. Add the roasted peppers and oil and process until smooth. Add the pomegranate molasses, lemon juice, cumin, cayenne and 1 teaspoon salt. Process until blended.

2 Add more oil, 1 tablespoon at a time, until the mixture is thick but easy to scoop or spread. Taste and add more pomegranate molasses and salt if needed. (If the pomegranate molasses is sweet, the spread may need a dash more lemon or lime juice; if it is tart, it might need a pinch of sugar.)

3 Refrigerate the spread, covered, until ready to serve. The flavors will mellow as it stands. Serve with pita chips.

Make a Meal

Serve spread on crostini or bruschetta (page 78) as an accompaniment to Tomato Couscous with Cinnamon and Raisins (page 226), Toasted Bulgur Pilaf with Cumin, Dried Fruit and Crispy Shallots (page 222), Broccoli and Red Onion Stir-Fry with Tamari Walnuts (page 175) or Twice-Cooked Broccoli Rabe with Red Pepper and Garlic Oil (page 179).

MULTI-MUSHROOM PÂTÉ Vegan

This smooth, spreadable mixture of mushrooms spiked with sautéed garlic, sun-dried tomatoes and a trio of fragrant herbs can be made ahead. It keeps well for up to 1 week.

Cook Time: 15 minutes
Serves: 6 to 8

- 4 tablespoons extra-virgin olive oil
- 12 ounces mushrooms (any combination of white button, cremini and/or oyster mushrooms), coarsely chopped (about 4 cups)
- 4 ounces shiitake mushrooms, stems discarded, coarsely chopped (about 1½ cups)
- 2 garlic cloves, grated
- 2 tablespoons chopped fresh Italian parsley
- 2 teaspoons fresh thyme leaves
- 1 teaspoon chopped fresh rosemary
- 1 teaspoon coarse salt
  Freshly ground black pepper
- ¼ cup oil-packed sun-dried tomatoes, drained, blotted dry and finely chopped
- 12–16 crostini or bruschetta (page 78), for serving

1 Heat 2 tablespoons of the oil in a large skillet over medium heat until hot enough to sizzle a piece of mushroom. Add all of the mushrooms and cook, stirring, over medium-high heat until softened and lightly browned, about 10 minutes. Add the garlic, 1 tablespoon of the parsley, 1 teaspoon of the thyme, ½ teaspoon of the rosemary, the salt and a generous grinding of pepper and cook over low heat, stirring, for 2 minutes. Cool slightly.

2 Transfer the mushroom mixture and the remaining 2 tablespoons oil to the food processor and pulse until the mushrooms are finely chopped and the mixture is blended. Transfer the mixture to a bowl and fold in the sun-dried tomatoes.

3 Spread the mushroom mixture on the crostini or bruschetta and garnish each with a light sprinkling of the remaining parsley, thyme and rosemary. Serve immediately.

Make a Meal

Serve as an accompaniment to Winter Borscht (page 36) or Leek and Potato Soup with Roasted Cauliflower (page 34).

CHEESE AND MUSHROOM MELTS

Keep mushrooms on hand for this gooey, rich and satisfying open-faced melt. Use a crusty round or other wide loaf that will make substantial-sized slices about 3 inches wide and 6 inches long. If a wide loaf isn't available, cut a long loaf into large diagonal slices.

Cook Time: 15 minutes
Serves: 4

- 3 tablespoons extra-virgin olive oil, plus more to brush bread
- 8 ounces large white or cremini mushrooms, thickly sliced (¼ to ⅓ inch)
- 2 tablespoons chopped fresh Italian parsley, including tender stems
- 1 teaspoon chopped fresh thyme leaves
- 1 teaspoon chopped fresh rosemary
- 1 garlic clove, grated
- ½ teaspoon coarse salt
  Freshly ground black pepper
- 4 large, thick (½-inch) slices whole wheat bread (see headnote)
- 4 ounces mozzarella, Comté, Manchego, Italian fontina, Gruyère, Parmigiano-Reggiano or other good melting cheese

Make a Meal

Serve with a green salad with fresh or dried fruit, Warm Green Bean and Tomato Salad with Mint (page 67) or Lentil and Vegetable Soup with Smoked Paprika (page 26).

1 Heat the oil in a large skillet over medium heat until it is hot enough to sizzle a slice of mushroom. Add the mushrooms and cook, stirring, adjusting the heat as needed to maintain a steady sizzle, until the mushrooms are golden and tender, about 5 minutes. Add the parsley, thyme, rosemary, garlic, salt and a generous grinding of pepper and cook, stirring, over low heat, for 2 minutes.

2 Adjust the oven rack so that the top of the bread will be about 3 inches from the broiler. Preheat the broiler. Arrange the bread on a baking sheet, brush lightly on both sides with oil and broil on one side until lightly browned, about 2 minutes. Turn the bread over and broil for 2 minutes more. Remove the pan from the oven; leave the broiler on. Spoon the mushrooms on top of the bread in a flat layer, dividing evenly.

3 Use a cheese plane or a vegetable peeler to cut enough cheese into curls or thin slices to cover the mushrooms on each slice of bread. Return the pan to the broiler and broil until the cheese melts, about 2 minutes. Serve hot.

TOASTED ITALIAN BREAD WITH MOZZARELLA, TOMATO AND OLIVES

Childhood memories of a favorite after-school snack of broiled mozzarella cheese on thick slices of Italian bread inspired this delicious open-faced sandwich. It's hearty enough for lunch, with a side of greens or a bowl of soup.

Cook Time: 10 minutes
Serves: 2 or 4

    Extra-virgin olive oil

4 **thick slices Italian bread**

1 **cup coarsely shredded mozzarella cheese**

4 **tomato slices**

2 **tablespoons coarsely chopped pitted Kalamata olives**

Make a Meal

Serve with Farro and Kale Soup with Orange Gremolata (page 40) or Curried Chickpea Soup with Summer Vegetables (page 32).

1 Heat a thin film of oil in a skillet large enough to fit all the bread (or make the sandwiches in batches, if necessary). Add the bread and cook over medium-low heat until golden, about 3 minutes. Turn the bread with a spatula and mound ¼ cup mozzarella on each slice. Top each with a tomato slice and sprinkle with the olives.

2 Cover the skillet and cook until the cheese is melted and the bread is golden on the bottom, 3 to 5 minutes. Serve immediately.

QUICK MELTED COMTÉ CHEESE CRISPS

Whenever I'm faced with a half-eaten loaf of good bread, I stuff it into a zip-top plastic bag and freeze it for another day. Then I thaw it partially and, with a serrated knife, cut it into ½-inch (or thinner) slices, brush the slices with olive oil and toast, adding a thin slice of cheese during the last few minutes. These crisps, once made, will keep in an airtight bag or container for a week or more.

Cook Time: 20 minutes
Serves: 4 or more

8 or more thin (¼- to ½-inch) slices oval or round rustic bread

1–2 tablespoons extra-virgin olive oil

16–24 thin slices or shavings Comté cheese (about 3 ounces)

1 Preheat the oven to 400°F. Place the sliced bread in a single layer on a baking sheet. Brush the bread lightly with the oil.

2 Bake until the bread is lightly browned on the bottom, 10 to 15 minutes. Remove the pan from the oven and turn the slices browned side up. Place 2 or 3 thin slices of cheese on each piece of bread, covering the surface in a single layer. Return the pan to the oven and bake until the cheese is melted and bubbly, 3 to 5 minutes. Serve immediately.

Substitutions

Substitute Parmigiano-Reggiano, Asiago, Pecorino Romano, Gruyère or other firm, easy-to-shave cheese for the Comté.

GRILLED COMTÉ SANDWICH WITH APPLE AND MANGO CHUTNEY

In my cheese drawer, snuggled next to a wedge of Parmigiano-Reggiano, is a slab of Comté, the luscious, buttery cow's-milk cheese of France. It melts like a dream, making it my first choice for the quintessential grilled cheese sandwich. Its rich, nutty taste pairs perfectly with the crisp acidity of the apple and the tangy heat of the mango chutney.

Cook Time: 10 minutes
Serves: 2

- 1 slab (¾ by 3 by 3 inches) Comté (about 4 ounces), rind trimmed
- 4 slices multigrain bread
- 1–2 crisp juicy apples (Fuji, Granny Smith, Gala or other), cored and sliced
- 6–8 leaves crinkly spinach
- ¼ cup mango or ginger chutney
- 1 tablespoon extra-virgin olive oil

Make a Meal

This is a rich sandwich. Serve with a mixed green salad tossed with a drizzle of walnut oil, a squirt of fresh lemon juice and a sprinkling of toasted walnut pieces.

1 Cut the cheese into enough ⅛-inch-thick rectangles to make a single layer on 2 slices of the bread, completely covering the surface. Top with a slightly overlapping layer of the apple slices. Add the spinach leaves.

2 Spread the chutney on the remaining 2 bread slices. Sandwich the bread together and press down lightly.

3 Heat a skillet large enough to hold both sandwiches. When the skillet is hot enough to sizzle a drop of water, brush it with a thin film of oil.

4 Use a wide spatula to transfer the sandwiches to the skillet, positioning them cheese side down. Place a lid slightly smaller than the skillet on the surface of the sandwiches (this is a good place to use a panini press if you have one) to weight the sandwiches. Cook over medium-low heat until the bottoms are a dark golden brown, 4 to 5 minutes.

5 Remove the cover and turn the sandwiches over. Return the lid to the surface of the sandwiches. Cook the other side until the bread is golden brown and the cheese is melted, 3 to 4 minutes.

6 Transfer the sandwiches to a cutting board, cut each sandwich in half with a serrated knife and serve.

TOASTED FLATBREAD (NAAN) WITH GOAT CHEESE, SAUTÉED GREENS AND CRISPY SHALLOTS

Naan, a slightly puffy, leavened flatbread from India, is now widely available in the bread section of the supermarket. It makes the perfect platform for many toppings. If naan is unavailable, substitute packaged prebaked pizza crusts.

Cook Time: 15 minutes
Serves: 4

- ¼ cup extra-virgin olive oil
- ½ cup thinly sliced shallots, separated into rings
  Crushed red pepper (optional)
- 1 bunch (about 12 ounces) greens, such as Swiss chard, kale or curly-leafed spinach
- 4 naan or other ½-inch-thick flatbread (see headnote)
- ¼ cup sun-dried tomato tapenade or other dried-tomato spread (optional)
- ½ cup crumbled cold fresh goat cheese (about 2 ounces)

1 Preheat the oven to 450°F.

2 Combine the oil and shallots in a small skillet and cook, stirring, over medium heat until the shallots turn dark golden brown, 4 to 5 minutes. Remove from the heat. Stir in a pinch of crushed red pepper, if desired. Set aside.

3 Meanwhile, prepare the greens: Pull the leaves of the Swiss chard or kale from the sturdy stems. Coarsely chop the chard, kale or spinach leaves. Rinse the greens in cold water and drain.

4 Add the wet leaves to a large skillet and cook, covered, over medium heat until wilted, 2 to 3 minutes. Uncover and toss until the greens are tender, 2 to 3 minutes, depending on the greens (kale will take more time and spinach less). Drain off any excess liquid. Pour the shallots and oil over the greens and toss over medium-high heat until the greens are coated with oil, about 1 minute. Remove from the heat.

5 Place the naan directly on the oven rack and bake until heated through, about 5 minutes. Remove the bread from the oven to a platter. Spread the bread with the

Make a Meal

Serve with Pumpkin and Tomato Soup with Cheese (page 38) or Carrot, Sweet Potato and Ginger Soup with Baby Bok Choy (page 33).

tomato tapenade, if using, and sprinkle the goat cheese evenly on top. Distribute the greens mixture on top. Spoon any excess oil in the skillet over the greens. Serve immediately.

Variations

- Goat Cheese, Sautéed Greens and Hard-Cooked Eggs: Skip the shallots and slice 4 hard-cooked eggs (see page 14) into thin rounds and place on top of the sautéed greens.
- Blistered Cherry Tomatoes, Arugula and Red Onion: Prepare the blistered cherry tomatoes according to the recipe on page 149. With a slotted spoon, transfer about ½ cup of the tomatoes and some of the juices to each naan. Top each hot naan with a handful of torn arugula leaves and a few thin lengthwise slices of red onion. Sprinkle each bread lightly with 1 tablespoon grated Parmigiano-Reggiano.

CURRIED EGG AND FETA BREAKFAST QUESADILLAS

Scrambled eggs folded into a tortilla sounds like breakfast, but it is also great for lunch or dinner.

Cook Time: 10 minutes
Serves: 4

Extra-virgin olive oil

¼ cup chopped onion

1 teaspoon Madras curry powder

6 large eggs, beaten until frothy

4 (8- to 10-inch) flour tortillas

½ cup crumbled feta cheese (about 2 ounces)

¼ cup tomato salsa, freshly made (pages 69 and 100) or store-bought (optional)

2 tablespoons finely chopped fresh dill or cilantro

Make a Meal

Serve with Oven-Roasted Mini Bell Peppers with Rosemary (page 170) and Summer Stew of Zucchini, Tomatoes, Corn and Basil (page 211).

1 Preheat the oven to 400°F. Brush a large baking sheet lightly with oil.

2 Heat 1 tablespoon oil in a medium skillet over medium heat until hot enough to sizzle a piece of onion. Add the onion and cook, stirring, until tender, about 3 minutes. Stir in the curry powder. Add the eggs and cook, stirring with the flat edge of a rubber spatula, adjusting the heat as needed, until the eggs begin to set, about 2 minutes. Turn the eggs out of the skillet onto a plate.

3 Place the tortillas on the baking sheet and sprinkle half of each tortilla with 2 tablespoons feta. Spoon the scrambled-egg mixture on top of the cheese, distributing it evenly. Top each with a spoonful of salsa, if using, and a generous sprinkling of dill or cilantro. Fold the tortillas over to make half circles and press down lightly.

4 Bake until the tortillas are warm and the cheese is beginning to melt, about 3 minutes. Turn with a wide spatula and bake for 2 to 3 minutes more. Transfer the quesadillas to a cutting board, cut into wedges and serve.

Substitutions

Try Manchego or another melting cheese in place of the feta.

ROASTED VEGETABLE AND MOZZARELLA QUESADILLAS

Make these luscious quesadillas when you have leftover roasted vegetables. I like them so much that I often roast a batch especially for this recipe. A mixture of eggplant, zucchini and red bell pepper is especially good.

Cook Time: 10 minutes
Serves: 4

Extra-virgin olive oil

4 (8- to 10-inch) flour tortillas

1⅓ cups shredded mozzarella cheese

1⅓ cups chopped roasted vegetables (see page 156)

4 tablespoons coarsely chopped pitted Kalamata olives

1 Preheat the oven to 400°F. Brush a large baking sheet lightly with oil.

2 Place the tortillas on the pan and sprinkle half of each tortilla with ⅓ cup cheese. Top the cheese with a layer of the chopped roasted vegetables and sprinkle each with 1 tablespoon olives. Fold the tortillas over to make half circles and press down lightly.

3 Bake until the tortillas are warm and beginning to color and the cheese is melted, about 5 minutes. Turn with a wide spatula and bake for 5 minutes more. Transfer the quesadillas to a cutting board, cut into wedges and serve.

Make a Meal

Serve with Shredded Tuscan Kale, Tomato and Avocado Salad (page 69) and Warm Green Bean and Tomato Salad with Mint (page 67).

CORN TORTILLAS WITH MUSHROOMS, SPINACH AND MANCHEGO CHEESE

This dish of stacked corn tortillas was inspired by chilaquiles, a classic Mexican casserole made from leftover corn tortillas layered with tomato salsa and shredded cheese. When made in a casserole dish, it is reminiscent of lasagna. You may want to make a double batch of the quick salsa in the recipe to keep on hand for soups, salads, quesadillas or dips. Refrigerate for 1 week or freeze for up to 3 months.

Cook Time: 30 minutes
Serves: 4

- 8 (6- to 8-inch) corn tortillas
  Extra-virgin olive oil

Salsa

- 2 tablespoons extra-virgin olive oil
- ½ cup chopped onion
- 2 teaspoons chili powder
- 1 teaspoon ground cumin
- 1 can (28 ounces) diced tomatoes with juice
- 2 teaspoons minced seeded jalapeño or serrano pepper, or more to taste
- 1 tablespoon finely chopped fresh cilantro, including tender stems

- 10–12 ounces sliced cremini mushrooms (about 4 cups)
  Coarse salt and freshly ground black pepper
- 1 bag (5–6 ounces) baby spinach, rinsed and drained (about 5 cups, lightly packed)
- 1 cup shredded Manchego or Monterey Jack cheese

- 1 cup (approximately) crema (Mexican sour cream; see page 9) or light or regular sour cream
- 2 scallions (white and green parts), cut into thin diagonal slices
- 2 tablespoons chopped fresh cilantro, for garnish

1 Preheat the oven to 350°F. Brush one side of each of the tortillas with oil and arrange, slightly overlapping, on a baking sheet. Bake the tortillas until warmed and slightly crisp, about 5 minutes.

2 To make the salsa: Heat the oil in a large skillet until it is hot enough to sizzle a piece of onion. Add the onion and cook, stirring, over medium-low heat until tender, about 5 minutes. Add the chili powder and cumin and cook, stirring, for 1 minute. Add the tomatoes and bring to a boil. Cook, uncovered, until thickened, about 15 minutes. Stir in the jalapeño and cilantro.

3 While the salsa is cooking, heat 2 tablespoons oil in a large skillet until it is hot enough to sizzle a slice of mushroom. Add the mushrooms and cook, stirring, over medium heat until they are golden and tender, about

5 minutes. Sprinkle the mushrooms with salt and pepper to taste. Add the spinach all at once and cook, covered, over medium-low heat until it is wilted, about 2 minutes. Uncover. If there is moisture in the pan, cook on high heat until the liquid evaporates, about 30 seconds.

4 Remove 4 of the tortillas from the pan and set aside. Ladle about ¼ cup of the salsa in the center of each of the tortillas on the pan and spread it to the edges with the underside of the ladle. Using half of the mushroom and spinach mixture, place a portion on top of each tortilla. Sprinkle each with 2 tablespoons of the cheese. Top with the remaining 4 tortillas. Spread the remaining salsa over each tortilla and top with the remaining mushroom and spinach mixture, dividing evenly. Sprinkle each stack with 2 tablespoons of the remaining shredded cheese.

5 Return the pan to the oven and bake until the tortilla stacks are heated through and the cheese is melted, about 5 minutes.

6 Slide each tortilla stack onto a dinner plate. Top with a spoonful of crema to taste and a sprinkling of scallions and cilantro. Serve at once.

Shortcuts

For a quicker version, use a good-quality store-bought salsa in place of the homemade salsa.

SUMMER VEGGIE BURRITOS WITH GOAT CHEESE

Crunchy and fresh, these burritos bear little resemblance to the hefty commercial ones that I call torpedoes because of their heaviness. This version, filled with colorful summer vegetables, is lighter and healthier. When our favorite teenager gave me a thumbs-up with her mouth full, I knew I'd gotten it right. Take a few minutes to make the fresh tomato and chipotle chile salsa, or use your favorite store-bought version.

Cook Time: 10 minutes
Serves: 4 to 8

   8 (10-inch) flour tortillas
   1 tablespoon extra-virgin olive oil
   ½ cup chopped red onion
   1 cup chopped zucchini
2½ cups cooked quinoa (see page 216)
   1 cup fresh corn kernels (from 2 ears) or thawed frozen corn
   ½ cup chopped jarred piquillo peppers (see page 10) or roasted red peppers, drained and patted dry
   2 tablespoons chopped fresh cilantro
   ½ teaspoon coarse salt
   2 cups lightly packed slivered romaine or other crisp lettuce
   4 ounces cold fresh goat cheese, crumbled (about 1 cup)
   2 cups Spicy Chipotle Chile Salsa (page 100) or store-bought salsa

1 Preheat the oven to 350°F. Stack the tortillas, wrap them tightly in aluminum foil and warm the stack in the oven for about 10 minutes. Warming the tortillas makes them more pliable for rolling. Cut 8 additional pieces of foil, each 12 inches square, for wrapping the burritos.

2 Heat the oil in a large skillet until it is hot enough to sizzle a piece of onion. Add the onion and cook, stirring, over medium-low heat until tender, about 5 minutes. Add the zucchini and cook, stirring, until heated through, about 2 minutes. Off the heat, add the quinoa, corn, peppers, cilantro and salt and stir to combine.

3 Place a warm tortilla in the center of each square of foil. Place about ½ cup of the quinoa mixture in the center of each tortilla. Top with ¼ cup lettuce, 3 or 4 bits of crumbled goat cheese and a rounded tablespoon of the salsa, including some of the juice.

4 Working on one tortilla at a time, fold the two sides of the tortilla in until the edges are almost touching in the

Make a Meal

Serve with Curried Coconut-Squash Soup with Peanuts (page 44) or Black Bean and Mango Salad (page 50).

center. Then roll the tortilla from the bottom of the circle, enclosing the filling to make a roll about 5 inches long and 2½ inches thick. Wrap each burrito tightly in foil and serve at once or refrigerate until ready to serve. These will keep for 1 day, although they are best eaten soon after filling.

5 Serve with the remaining salsa, spooning it over the filling while eating, if desired.

SPICY CHIPOTLE CHILE SALSA Vegan

Fresh and zesty, this easy salsa is spiced with the smoky, haunting flavor of chipotle. Use as a topping for burritos or quesadillas or spoon it into a bowl of soup. If tasty plum tomatoes are unavailable, use good-quality canned diced tomatoes, well drained.

Prep Time: About 10 minutes
Makes about 2 cups

- 2 **cups diced ripe tomatoes, preferably plum tomatoes**
- 2 **tablespoons finely chopped red onion**
- 2 **tablespoons chopped fresh cilantro**
- 2 **teaspoons minced seeded jalapeño pepper**
- 2 **teaspoons minced chipotle chile in adobo sauce**
- 2 **tablespoons fresh lime juice**
- ½ **teaspoon coarse salt**

In a medium bowl, combine the tomatoes, onion, cilantro, jalapeño, chipotle, lime juice and salt. Stir to blend. Cover and refrigerate until ready to use. It will keep, refrigerated, for up to 5 days.

Main Dishes

A vegetarian main dish need not be daunting. Think of the traditional meat, potato and vegetable main dish, then exclude the meat, reconceptualize the potato as any starch, increase the quantity and move it to the center of the plate. The array of starches available is almost endless: bulgur, polenta, quinoa, rice, beans and pasta, to name a few. Add one or two vegetable side dishes, and dinner is ready. Almost.

For excitement, richness, crunch and bold flavors, add spices, a shower of chopped fresh herbs, sautéed garlic, squirts of fresh lemon or lime juice, strips or gratings of orange or lemon zest, a topping of cheese and/or a sprinkling of toasted nuts or seeds.

Toasted Quinoa with Spinach, Blistered Tomatoes and Walnuts (page 114) is a perfect illustration of how to elevate a vegetarian main dish from ho-hum to memorable. First, toast the quinoa in olive oil to impart a rich, nutty taste. Blister grape or cherry tomatoes in hot olive oil and watch the juices turn sweet and syrupy. Barely wilt the spinach so it remains fresh and flavorful. Add crunch and richness with walnuts and cheese and fresh brightness with torn basil leaves.

To add a spark to your vegetarian kitchen, keep these ingredients and tips in mind:

* The most-used spices in my spice drawer are ground cumin, cinnamon, chili powder, smoked paprika (preferably *Pimentón de la Vera*; see page 10), Madras curry powder and an exotic Moroccan spice blend called *ras el hanout* (see page 11).

* Keep ginger fresh in the freezer, grating it still frozen on a rasp grater (Microplane) as needed. If you use it frequently, store ginger in the vegetable drawer of your refrigerator, wrapped in a paper towel, not plastic.

* Grate garlic, orange and lemon zest, ginger and cheese on a rasp grater.

* If possible, shop where fresh herbs are sold in bunches instead of small plastic boxes. Herbs remain perky in a wide-mouthed container half filled with water and covered with an inverted plastic bag. Add fresh water to the container every few days. Wash the herbs just before using.

* A combination of chopped dill, mint and basil adds a fresh taste to almost any dish. For an extra jolt of flavor, place a ½-inch-wide strip of lemon or orange zest under the herbs and chop them together.

* For a fresh, bright taste, squirt fresh lemon or lime juice on a dish just before serving.

STIR-FRIED TOFU WITH OYSTER MUSHROOMS, BELL PEPPERS AND SPINACH

Tofu is the perfect background for zippy marinades and flavorful ingredients. Here I use oyster mushrooms, but shiitake, big white button or another exotic variety also works. Serve plain or over rice, quinoa or other grain.

Cook Time: 15 minutes
Serves: 4

- 1 block (16 ounces) firm tofu, drained

Marinade

- ¼ cup orange juice
- 2 tablespoons tamari or soy sauce
- 2 tablespoons unseasoned Japanese rice vinegar
- 1 tablespoon honey, maple syrup or agave nectar (see page 13)
- 1 teaspoon toasted sesame oil
- 1½ tablespoons cornstarch
- ½ teaspoon coarse salt
  Pinch of crushed red pepper

- 3 tablespoons peanut oil
- 8 ounces multicolored mini bell peppers (about 8), left whole, or 1 large red bell pepper, cut into 1- by ½-inch pieces
- 8 ounces oyster mushrooms, including stems, cut into ½-inch pieces (about 3 cups)
- 1 tablespoon finely chopped peeled fresh ginger

- 2 teaspoons grated orange zest
- 1 garlic clove, grated
- 1 bag (5–6 ounces) baby spinach, rinsed and drained (about 5 cups lightly packed)

1 Slice the block of tofu into ¾-inch-thick slices. Arrange the slices on a folded dish towel, cover with a second folded towel and press down gently but firmly with the palm of your hand for 30 seconds to remove the excess moisture. Cut the slices into ¾-inch cubes.

2 To make the marinade: Combine the orange juice, tamari, rice vinegar, honey, sesame oil, cornstarch, salt and crushed red pepper in a large bowl. Whisk to blend. Add the tofu and toss to coat.

3 Heat a wok or large skillet over high heat until it is hot enough to sizzle and evaporate a drop of water. Add 2 tablespoons of the peanut oil. Remove the tofu from the marinade with a slotted spoon (reserve the remaining marinade) and add it to the pan, adjusting the heat as needed to keep the oil sizzling hot. Cook the tofu, turning with a spatula or tongs, until it is evenly browned,

Serve with Carrot, Sweet Potato and Ginger Soup with Baby Bok Choy (page 33) or Red Lentil Soup with Coconut Milk and Toasted Cumin (page 27) and Soba Noodle Salad with Snow Peas (page 60).

about 8 minutes. Scoop the tofu from the pan with a slotted spoon and set aside.

4 Add the remaining 1 tablespoon peanut oil and the peppers to the pan and stir-fry until the peppers begin to blister, 3 to 5 minutes. Add the mushrooms, ginger, orange zest and garlic and stir-fry for 2 minutes. Add the tofu and the reserved marinade and stir-fry to coat, about 1 minute. Add the spinach and stir-fry for about 1 minute. Remove from the heat. The spinach will continue to wilt from the heat of the other ingredients as it stands. Serve.

TOFU "STEAKS" WITH SPICY ALMOND BUTTER SAUCE AND BABY BOK CHOY Vegan

A variety of nut butters have been popping up on supermarket and specialty store shelves. Being partial to almond butter, I use it here in an otherwise fairly classic rendition of Asian peanut sauce. (Peanut butter can be used instead of the almond butter, if you prefer.) Use a skillet or wok to first sear the tamari-glazed tofu, then cook the small heads of baby bok choy in the same pan.

Cook Time: 15 minutes
Serves: 4

- 4–6 heads baby bok choy, halved lengthwise
- 1 block (16 ounces) medium or firm tofu, drained
- ½ cup smooth almond butter
- 3 tablespoons Chinese rice wine or dry sherry
- 2 tablespoons Chinese sesame seed paste (see page 12)
- 2 tablespoons unseasoned Japanese rice vinegar
- 4 tablespoons tamari or soy sauce
- 1 tablespoon toasted sesame oil
- 1 tablespoon chopped peeled fresh ginger
- 2 garlic cloves, grated
- ½ teaspoon spicy Chinese chile paste
- 2 tablespoons extra-virgin olive oil
  Pinch of crushed red pepper
- 2 tablespoons toasted sliced skin-on almonds
- 2 tablespoons thin diagonally sliced scallions (green parts only)

1 Place the bok choy in a bowl and cover with water. Add a couple of ice cubes and let stand until ready to use.

2 Slice the block of tofu into four ¾-inch-thick slices. Arrange the slices on a folded dish towel, cover with a second folded towel, and press down gently but firmly with the palm of your hand for 30 seconds to remove the excess moisture.

3 In a blender, combine the almond butter, ¼ cup water, wine, sesame paste, rice vinegar, 2 tablespoons of the tamari, the sesame oil, ginger, garlic and chile paste. Blend, scraping the sides of the jar at least once, until smooth. Transfer to a small saucepan and heat, stirring, until simmering, about 5 minutes. Let stand off the heat until ready to serve.

4 Place the tofu slices on a plate and drizzle evenly with the remaining 2 tablespoons tamari. Heat a large skillet over medium heat until it is hot enough to sizzle and evaporate a drop of water. Add 1 tablespoon of the olive oil. When the oil is hot enough to sizzle a piece of tofu, add the tofu, reserving the tamari on the plate, and sear, adjusting the heat as needed to keep the oil

sizzling hot, until the tofu is browned on the bottom, about 3 minutes. Turn the tofu with a spatula and drizzle with the tamari left on the plate. Cook the tofu until browned on the bottom, about 2 minutes more. Transfer the browned tofu to a platter and cover with foil to keep warm.

5 Add the remaining 1 tablespoon olive oil to the skillet. Drain the bok choy and add it to the hot skillet, cut sides down, with the water still clinging to the leaves. Cook over medium-high heat until golden brown, about 2 minutes. Turn and brown the other side until the bok choy is crisp-tender, about 2 minutes. Sprinkle with the crushed red pepper.

6 Meanwhile, reheat the almond butter sauce, stirring, over medium-low heat. If the sauce seems too thick, thin it with 1 tablespoon boiling water. Arrange the bok choy on the platter with the tofu and spoon the warm sauce on top. Garnish with the almonds and scallions and serve.

STIR-FRIED CURRIED TOFU WITH COCONUT GREEN RICE AND CASHEWS Vegan

Tender tofu, brightly colored vegetables and hot rice are coated with a bright green sauce of cilantro leaves pureed with creamy coconut milk, flavored with pungent fresh ginger and jalapeño and topped with a crunchy halo of chopped roasted cashews.

Cook Time: 25 minutes
Serves: 4

1 block (16 ounces) medium or firm tofu, drained

1½ cups basmati or jasmine rice

Coarse salt

1 cup regular or light coconut milk

1 cup packed fresh cilantro, including tender stems

2 teaspoons chopped seeded jalapeño or serrano pepper, or more to taste

4 teaspoons chopped peeled fresh ginger

2 garlic cloves, grated

1 tablespoon fresh lime juice

2 tablespoons extra-virgin olive oil

1 large red bell pepper, diced (½ inch), about 1 cup

½ cup diagonally sliced (½ inch) scallions (white and green parts)

1 tablespoon Madras curry powder

1 bag (5–6 ounces) baby spinach, rinsed and drained (about 5 cups lightly packed)

6 tablespoons chopped fresh cilantro

¼ cup coarsely chopped roasted cashews, preferably unsalted

1 Slice the block of tofu into six ½-inch-thick slices. Arrange the slices on a folded dish towel, cover with a second folded towel and press down gently but firmly with the palm of your hand for 30 seconds to remove the excess moisture. Cut the slices into ½-inch cubes. Set aside.

2 Cook the rice in boiling salted water following the directions on the rice package. I prefer to use a 10-inch or large skillet for even cooking. Cover to keep warm.

3 Meanwhile, combine the coconut milk, cilantro, jalapeño, 1 teaspoon of the ginger, half of the garlic, the lime juice and ½ teaspoon salt in a blender and puree until smooth. Leave the sauce in the blender until ready to use.

4 Heat a wok or large skillet over high heat until it is hot enough to sizzle and evaporate a drop of water. Add the oil. When the oil is hot enough to sizzle a piece of tofu, add the tofu. Cook, adjusting the heat as needed to keep the oil sizzling hot and turning the tofu with a spatula or tongs, until golden, about 6 minutes.

Serve with a crisp salad of chopped napa cabbage tossed with chopped fresh pineapple and Japanese Rice Vinaigrette with Ginger (page 74), sprinkled with black sesame seeds.

5 Add the red bell pepper, scallions, curry powder, the remaining 3 teaspoons ginger and the remaining garlic. Cook, stirring gently with a spatula, for 2 minutes. Add the spinach, 2 tablespoons of the cilantro and half of the sauce to the pan and cook, stirring, until blended and the spinach starts to wilt, 1 to 2 minutes.

6 Uncover the hot cooked rice and drizzle the remaining sauce on top. Toss once or twice with a fork. Divide the rice among four bowls and spoon the vegetable and tofu mixture on top, dividing evenly. Sprinkle each bowl with about 1 tablespoon each cashews and cilantro.

Shortcuts

Instead of cooking rice, use the convenient pouches of microwaveable rice found in the frozen-foods section in many supermarkets.

Substitutions

Instead of garnishing the dish with cashews, use unsweetened flaked coconut (available in bulk in most health food stores), toasted and sprinkled on top with the cilantro.

PAN-SEARED TOFU WITH EGGPLANT AND CURRIED TOMATO-MINT SAUCE Vegan

Eggplant and curried tomato sauce are the stars of this dish, which bursts with flavor. The eggplant soaks up the bright-tasting curry sauce. I sometimes eat this spooned over a plate of cooked quinoa or bulgur, with or without the tofu. If you prefer, substitute cilantro for the mint.

Cook Time: 30 minutes
Serves: 4

- 1 block (16 ounces) medium or firm tofu, drained
- 1 can (28 ounces) diced or whole peeled tomatoes with juice
- 2 teaspoons Madras curry powder
- 1 garlic clove, grated
- 1 teaspoon grated peeled fresh ginger
- 1 cinnamon stick
- ½ teaspoon coarse salt
- Pinch of crushed red pepper
- 4 tablespoons finely chopped fresh mint
- 12 slices (½ inch thick) peeled eggplant (about 1½ pounds or 2 medium eggplants)
- 4 tablespoons extra-virgin olive oil

1 Place a large baking sheet in the oven and preheat to 450°F for 10 minutes.

2 Slice the block of tofu into four ¾-inch-thick slices. Arrange the slices on a folded dish towel, cover with a second folded towel and press down gently but firmly with the palm of your hand for 30 seconds to remove the excess moisture.

3 Puree the tomatoes using a food mill or a food processor. Add the puree to a large skillet and bring to a boil. Add ½ cup water, the curry powder, garlic, ginger, cinnamon stick, salt and crushed red pepper. Cook, uncovered, stirring occasionally, until the sauce is thickened, about 15 minutes. Add 2 tablespoons of the mint.

4 While the sauce is cooking, lightly brush the eggplant slices on both sides with 2 tablespoons of the oil. Carefully remove the hot pan from the oven and arrange the oiled eggplant slices in a single layer. Return the pan to the oven and roast for 10 minutes. Turn the eggplant and roast the other side until lightly browned and tender, about 10 minutes.

5 Heat a large skillet over medium heat until it is hot enough to sizzle and evaporate a drop of water. Add the remaining 2 tablespoons oil. When the oil is hot enough to sizzle a piece of tofu, add the tofu slices. Sear the tofu until lightly browned, about 3 minutes per side.

6 Add the roasted eggplant and the tofu to the pan with the tomato sauce. Cook, covered, over low heat until heated through, about 10 minutes. Sprinkle with the remaining 2 tablespoons mint and serve.

BULGUR PILAF WITH ROASTED VEGETABLES Vegan

Crunchy and nutty, bulgur is the fastest-cooking grain in the cupboard. Topped with almost any stir-fried, pan-seared or roasted vegetable, it makes a meal. In this recipe, I use bell peppers, zucchini, carrots and red onion for their year-round availability, taste, color and texture.

Cook Time: 25 minutes
Serves: 4 to 6

- 3 red bell peppers, diced (½ inch)
- 3 zucchini (about 6 ounces each), diagonally sliced (¼ inch)
- 2 large carrots, diagonally sliced (¼ inch)
- 1 large red onion, cut into wedges (¼ inch)
- 4 tablespoons extra-virgin olive oil
- 1½ teaspoons coarse salt
  Freshly ground black pepper
- 1 cup chopped onion
- 1½ cups coarse-grain bulgur
- ¼ cup raisins
- ¼ cup coarsely chopped pitted Kalamata olives
- 1 tablespoon chopped fresh mint
- 1 tablespoon chopped fresh dill
- 1 tablespoon chopped fresh Italian parsley
- 1 teaspoon grated orange zest
- 2 tablespoons toasted pine nuts or ¼ cup toasted chopped walnuts or skin-on almonds

1 Place a heavy baking sheet in the oven and preheat to 450°F for 10 minutes.

2 Meanwhile, combine the peppers, zucchini, carrots and red onion in a bowl. Drizzle the vegetables with 3 tablespoons of the oil and sprinkle with ½ teaspoon of the salt and a generous grinding of black pepper.

3 Carefully remove the hot pan from the oven and spread the vegetables on the pan. Roast the vegetables for 15 minutes. Stir with a spatula, turning the vegetables and moving them around on the pan so they'll brown evenly. Roast until browned and tender, about 10 minutes more.

4 Meanwhile, heat the remaining 1 tablespoon oil in a large skillet. Add the chopped onion and cook, stirring, over medium heat until golden, about 10 minutes. Stir in the bulgur and raisins. Add 2 cups water and the remaining 1 teaspoon salt and bring to a boil. Stir once to blend. Cover and cook over low heat until the water is absorbed, about 10 minutes.

5 Add the olives, mint, dill, parsley and orange zest to the hot roasted vegetables. Add half of the vegetables to the bulgur and fluff with a fork. Spoon the bulgur into a serving dish and mound the remaining vegetables on top. Sprinkle with the nuts and serve.

Substitutions

Feel free to mix and match the vegetables: try asparagus in spring, tender green beans in summer and cauliflower florets in fall.

TOASTED QUINOA WITH SPINACH, BLISTERED TOMATOES AND WALNUTS

Quinoa has an irresistibly nutty taste and a texture that is crunchy yet delicate, and it cooks in less than 20 minutes. For a pretty touch, use tricolor grape or cherry tomatoes.

Cook Time: 35 minutes
Serves: 4

- 1½ cups quinoa
- 2 tablespoons extra-virgin olive oil
- 1 garlic clove, grated
- 1 teaspoon coarse salt
- 1 cup grape or petite cherry tomatoes, stems removed
- 1 bag (5–6 ounces) baby spinach, rinsed and drained (about 5 cups lightly packed)
- ½ cup walnut pieces
- ½ cup grated Parmigiano-Reggiano
- Torn fresh basil leaves (optional)

Make a Meal

Serve with Chickpea Salad with Celery, Lemon and Herbs (page 50).

1 Rinse the quinoa in a fine-mesh strainer under cold running water for at least 45 seconds. Shake in a strainer to remove as much water as possible.

2 Heat 1 tablespoon of the oil in a large skillet. Add the rinsed quinoa and cook, stirring, over medium heat until it is a light golden brown, about 10 minutes.

3 Add the garlic and cook, stirring, for 30 seconds. Add 3 cups water and the salt and bring to a boil. Cook, covered, over medium-low heat until the water is absorbed and the quinoa is translucent and appears to be uncoiling, 18 to 20 minutes.

4 Meanwhile, heat the remaining 1 tablespoon oil in a small skillet over medium-high heat until it is hot enough to sizzle a tomato. Add the tomatoes and cook, shaking the pan, until the tomatoes are blistered and softened, about 5 minutes. Set aside.

5 Add the spinach to the quinoa and cook, stirring occasionally, over medium heat until wilted, about 3 minutes. Add the tomatoes, sprinkle with the walnuts and cheese, and fluff to combine. Garnish with the basil, if using, and serve.

FARROTTO WITH TOMATOES AND PECORINO

Farrotto is an Italian adaptation of risotto that substitutes farro for the more typical rice. Traditionally, it is left quite soupy and can be eaten either with a spoon or with a fork. Pearled farro, imported from Italy, is labeled *perlato*, which means that most of the bran has been removed and the grain will cook in about 20 minutes.

Cook Time: 35 minutes
Serves: 4

- 1 **bouquet garni (1 bay leaf, 1 sage leaf, 1 rosemary sprig, 1 parsley sprig and 1 garlic clove, tied together with kitchen string)**
- 1½ **cups farro (see page 216)**
  Coarse salt
- 1½–2 **cups Easy Basic Vegetable Broth (page 46) or water**
- 3 **tablespoons extra-virgin olive oil**
- ½ **cup finely chopped onion**
- 1 **garlic clove, grated**
  Pinch of crushed red pepper
- 1 **can (14.5 ounces) diced tomatoes with juice**
- 8 **fresh basil leaves, torn**
- ⅓ **cup grated Pecorino Romano cheese, plus shavings for garnish**
  Freshly ground black pepper

Make a Meal
Serve topped with Swiss Chard with Fragrant Garlic and Salt (page 186).

1 Bring a large saucepan half full of water to a boil. Add the bouquet garni, farro and 1 teaspoon salt and cook, stirring, until the farro is almost tender but not fully cooked, about 15 minutes. Drain the farro. Remove and discard the bouquet garni.

2 Bring the broth to a boil in a small saucepan. Keep warm over low heat.

3 Heat the oil in a large, wide saucepan over medium heat until it is hot enough to sizzle a piece of onion. Add the onion and cook, stirring, until softened, about 3 minutes. Stir in the garlic and crushed red pepper and cook for 1 minute. Add the tomatoes, half the basil, the farro and about ½ cup of the hot broth.

4 Cook over medium heat, uncovered, stirring occasionally. Add the remaining broth in ½-cup increments as the farro absorbs the previous addition. Keep adding the broth until the farro is tender but still has a bit of bite, about 15 minutes. You may not need all of the broth. The mixture should have the consistency of risotto, neither soupy nor pilaf-like.

5 Stir in the grated cheese and the remaining basil. Season to taste with salt and pepper. Ladle the farrotto into soup bowls and top with shaved Pecorino.

CUMIN-SCENTED ISRAELI COUSCOUS WITH CARAMELIZED CABBAGE Vegan

Forget braising or boiling: the way to cook cabbage is to slowly caramelize it in olive oil. With the tomato salad on top of the cooked couscous and cabbage, this is almost a meal. The round grains of Israeli couscous are much larger than the fine granular kind.

Cook Time: 30 minutes
Serves: 4

- 4 tablespoons extra-virgin olive oil
- 2 teaspoons cumin seeds
- 1½ cups Israeli couscous
- 1¾ cups Easy Basic Vegetable Broth (page 46) or water
- ½ teaspoon coarse salt
- 1½ pounds cabbage, chopped (about 8 cups)
- 1 cup chopped onion
- ¼ cup dried currants or raisins
- 1 garlic clove, grated

Tomato Salad

- 1 cup diced plum tomatoes
- 1 tablespoon finely chopped fresh Italian parsley
- 1 tablespoon finely chopped fresh mint
- 1 tablespoon fresh lemon juice
- ½ teaspoon grated lemon zest or 1 tablespoon finely chopped preserved lemon rind (see page 12)
- Pinch of coarse salt

- ½ cup chopped toasted walnuts

1 Heat 2 tablespoons of the oil and the cumin seeds in a medium skillet over medium heat until hot and fragrant, about 2 minutes. Add the couscous and cook, stirring, over medium-low heat until golden, about 10 minutes. Add the broth and salt and bring to a boil. Cook, covered, over medium-low heat until the water is absorbed and the couscous is tender, about 15 minutes. Keep warm over low heat.

2 Meanwhile, heat the remaining 2 tablespoons oil in a large skillet over medium heat until hot enough to sizzle a piece of cabbage. Add the cabbage and onion and cook, stirring frequently, until the cabbage begins to turn golden brown, about 12 minutes. Add the currants and cook, stirring, until the cabbage is slightly darker, about 5 minutes. Stir in the garlic and keep warm over low heat.

3 To make the tomato salad: Combine the tomatoes, parsley, mint, lemon juice, lemon zest and salt in a small bowl. Stir to blend.

Make a Meal

Serve with a side dish of Carrots with Moroccan Spices and Lemon (page 182).

4 Add the couscous and walnuts to the cabbage and stir to combine. Transfer the mixture to a serving bowl, top with the tomato salad and serve.

RED QUINOA WITH SCRAMBLED EGGS, ASPARAGUS AND TAMARI ALMONDS

The deep, earthy taste of red quinoa is reminiscent of smoky bacon. When I first tasted it, I immediately wanted to pair it with asparagus, eggs and nuts.

Cook Time: 30 minutes
Serves: 4

- 1½ cups red quinoa (see page 216)
- 2 tablespoons extra-virgin olive oil
- 4 ounces asparagus, diagonally sliced (¼ inch), about 1 cup
- ½ cup thin-sliced scallions (white and green parts)
- ½ cup chopped red bell pepper (optional)
- 1 garlic clove, grated
- 1 teaspoon grated orange zest
- 1 tablespoon tamari or soy sauce, plus more for serving
- 4 large eggs
- ¼ teaspoon coarse salt
- ⅛ teaspoon crushed red pepper
- 2 tablespoons torn or slivered fresh basil or cilantro leaves
- ¼ cup chopped Tamari Almonds (page 14)

1 Rinse the quinoa in a fine-mesh strainer under cold running water for at least 45 seconds. Shake in the strainer to remove as much water as possible.

2 Heat 1 tablespoon of the oil in a large skillet. Add the rinsed quinoa and cook, stirring, over medium heat until the grain dries out and turns a shade darker, 5 to 8 minutes. Add 3 cups water and bring to a boil. Cook, covered, over medium-low heat until the water is absorbed and the quinoa is fluffy and appears to be uncurling, 18 to 20 minutes. Remove from the heat and set aside.

3 Add the remaining 1 tablespoon oil to a wok or large skillet and heat until hot enough to sizzle a piece of vegetable. Add the asparagus, scallions and bell pepper, if using, and stir-fry over medium-high heat until the asparagus is crisp-tender, about 4 minutes. Add the garlic and orange zest and cook, stirring, for 1 minute.

4 Add the cooked quinoa and the tamari to the vegetables and cook, stirring, until heated through, about 2 minutes. Whisk the eggs, salt and crushed red pepper until blended. Push the quinoa to the sides of the pan, making a space in the center. Pour in the eggs and cook,

without stirring, over medium-high heat until set, about
30 seconds. Reduce the heat to medium and cook,
gently stirring with a rubber spatula to distribute fluffy
clumps of cooked egg throughout the quinoa mixture,
about 30 seconds.

5 Top with the basil and almonds and serve with more
tamari on the side.

Substitutions

If red quinoa is not available, substitute regular quinoa.

SHORTCUT CORN RISOTTO WITH SUMMER "SUCCOTASH"

Come summer, I celebrate fresh corn, sweet juicy tomatoes and tender green beans with a vegetable medley I call summer "succotash." It's pretty and tasty, and a big bowl of it can make a meal. I also love it served over a creamy risotto that needs little or no stirring. Look for a mild goat's-milk feta from France for this recipe, as other feta may be a bit too sharp for the delicate summer vegetables. If unavailable, substitute a crumbly fresh goat cheese.

Cook Time: 25 minutes
Serves: 4

- 3 tablespoons extra-virgin olive oil
- 1 cup chopped red onion
- 1½ cups Arborio or other medium-grain white rice
- ½ cup dry white wine
- Coarse salt
- 3 cups fresh corn kernels (from 6 ears) or canned or frozen corn
- 5 ounces creamy, mild goat's-milk feta cheese or fresh goat cheese, crumbled (about 1 cup)
- 1 cup diagonally sliced (¼ inch) green beans (about 5 ounces)
- 1 garlic clove, grated
- 2 cups diced (½ inch) tomatoes (about 12 ounces)
- ¼ cup loosely packed torn fresh basil leaves
- Freshly ground black pepper

1 Heat 1 tablespoon of the oil in a large skillet until it is hot enough to sizzle a piece of onion. Add ½ cup of the onion and cook, stirring, over medium-low heat until tender, about 5 minutes. Add the rice and stir until coated with the oil. Add 2½ cups water, the wine and 1 teaspoon salt. Bring to a boil, stirring once. Cook, covered, over low heat, stirring once or twice, until the rice is creamy and tender, 12 to 15 minutes. Stir in 1 cup of the corn and cook, stirring, for 2 minutes. Fold in ½ cup of the cheese.

2 Meanwhile, heat the remaining 2 tablespoons oil in a large skillet until it is hot enough to sizzle a piece of onion. Add the remaining ½ cup onion and cook, stirring, until tender, about 5 minutes. Add the remaining 2 cups corn, the green beans and garlic and cook, stirring, until the beans are crisp-tender, about 5 minutes. Add the tomatoes, basil, a pinch of salt and a generous grinding of black pepper.

Serve with a mixed green salad with slices of ripe melon and perhaps a fresh fig, if available. Serve Quick Melted Comté Cheese Crisps (page 90) on the side.

3 To serve, spoon the risotto into four shallow bowls. Top with the succotash and sprinkle with the remaining ½ cup cheese.

VEGETABLE PAELLA   Vegan

The most important step in making paella is the slow cooking of the onion, tomato, garlic and seasonings in oil. This is called the *sofrito* and is essential for flavor. The dish is sometimes seasoned with saffron, but in this version, I use a delicious smoked paprika called *Pimentón de la Vera*. The preferred rice for paella is medium-grain sticky rice with a firm core. Imported Spanish varieties include Bomba, Calasparra and Valencia, but you can substitute more widely available Arborio or any other medium-grain white rice. Cook the rice uncovered and do not stir the paella while it is cooking. The grains will absorb the complex taste of the seasonings and will be separate, but soft and moist, when done. To get a browned crust on the bottom—considered a delicacy—turn the heat to high during the last few minutes of cooking. Include some of this crunchy layer (called the *socarrat*) with each serving.

Cook Time: 50 minutes
Serves: 4 to 6

- 5 tablespoons extra-virgin olive oil
- 8 ounces multicolored mini bell peppers (about 8), left whole, or 1 large red bell pepper, cut into 2- by ½-inch pieces
- 6 ounces shiitake mushrooms, stems discarded, caps halved or quartered if large (about 2½ cups)
- 2 teaspoons chopped fresh thyme
- 2 teaspoons coarse salt
  Freshly ground black pepper
- 1½ cups cauliflower florets (from ½ small head, cored and thick stems removed)
- 8 ounces green beans, cut into ½-inch lengths (about 1½ cups)
- 2 cups chopped onions
- 1 garlic clove, grated

- 1 can (14.5 ounces) diced tomatoes with juice
- 1½ teaspoons smoked paprika (preferably *Pimentón de la Vera*; see page 10)
- 1¼ cups medium-grain white rice (see headnote)
  Lemon wedges, for garnish
  Sprigs of fresh thyme or Italian parsley, for garnish (optional)

1 In a small saucepan, bring 6 cups water to a boil; cover and keep hot over low heat.

2 Heat 2 tablespoons of the oil in a large skillet or paella pan over medium heat. Add the peppers and mushrooms and cook, stirring, until the peppers are blistered and browned and the mushrooms are golden, 6 to 8 minutes. Sprinkle with 1 teaspoon of the chopped thyme, ¼ teaspoon of the salt and a grinding of black pepper. Remove the peppers and mushrooms from the pan with a slotted spoon and set aside.

Precede the paella with a soup course. Tomato and White Bean Soup with Spinach Pesto (page 24) or White Bean and Fennel Soup (page 23) are good choices.

3 Add 1 tablespoon of the oil and the cauliflower and green beans to the pan and cook, stirring, over medium-high heat until the cauliflower begins to brown and is crisp-tender, about 5 minutes. Add the remaining 1 teaspoon chopped thyme, ¼ teaspoon of the salt and a grinding of black pepper. Transfer the vegetables to a bowl, keeping them separate from the peppers and mushrooms.

4 Add the remaining 2 tablespoons oil to the hot pan. Add the onions and cook, stirring, over medium-low heat until softened and golden, 5 to 8 minutes. Add the garlic and cook for 1 minute. Add the tomatoes and boil over high heat, stirring, until all the tomato juice evaporates. Reduce the heat to medium and stir in the paprika. Add the rice and stir until coated with the tomato mixture, about 1 minute. Add 4 cups of the hot water and the remaining 1½ teaspoons salt and bring to a boil. Cook, uncovered, at a gentle simmer over medium-low heat, without stirring, until most of the liquid is evaporated and the rice is almost tender, about 15 minutes.

5 Spoon the mushrooms and peppers onto the center of the rice. Spoon the cauliflower and green beans around the edges. Pour 1 cup of the hot water on top and cook, uncovered, on medium-low until all the water is absorbed and the rice is tender, 5 to 8 minutes. Do not stir. (If the rice is still slightly firm, add about ½ cup more hot water and cook for another 5 minutes.)

6 Turn the heat to high for 1 to 2 minutes until the rice forms a browned crust on the bottom of the pan. Push the tip of a spoon into the rice to take a peek. Let the paella stand, uncovered, for 5 minutes before serving. Garnish with lemon wedges and thyme or parsley sprigs, if using.

LENTIL AND SHIITAKE RAGOUT WITH GREEN BEANS Vegan

This quick-cooking stew of tender lentils, earthy shiitake mushrooms and bright green beans is a hearty, soul-warming dish great hot from the pan or chilled and served as a salad, with raw spinach leaves tossed in along with a splash of rice vinegar.

Cook Time: 25 minutes
Serves: 4

- 1½ cups brown lentils
- 1 garlic clove, bruised with the side of a knife, plus 1 tablespoon finely chopped garlic
- 1 thick (½-inch) onion slice
- 1 leafy celery top
- 3 tablespoons extra-virgin olive oil
- 8 ounces shiitake mushrooms, stems removed, sliced (¼ inch), about 3½ cups
- ½ cup chopped red bell pepper
- 2 teaspoons grated peeled fresh ginger
- 8 ounces green beans, cut into 1-inch lengths (about 2 cups)
- 1 cup carrot chunks (½ inch), about 2 medium carrots
- 2 tablespoons tamari or soy sauce, plus more to taste
- 1 tablespoon tomato paste
  Freshly ground black pepper
- 2 tablespoons thin-sliced scallions (green parts only)
- 2 tablespoons chopped fresh cilantro (optional)

1 Combine 6 cups water, the lentils, garlic clove, onion slice and celery top in a large saucepan and bring to a boil. Cook, uncovered, at a gentle simmer over medium-low heat until the lentils are almost tender but not quite cooked, about 15 minutes. Set a fine-mesh strainer over a bowl and strain the lentils, reserving the cooking water. Discard the onion and celery top. You should have about 4 cups cooked lentils.

2 Meanwhile, heat the oil in a large skillet over medium heat until it is hot enough to sizzle a slice of mushroom. Add the mushrooms and cook, stirring, until they are golden and soft, about 5 minutes. Add the bell pepper, chopped garlic and ginger and cook, stirring, for 2 minutes.

3 Add the lentils, 2 cups of the reserved lentil cooking water, the green beans, carrots, tamari and tomato paste. Cover and cook over medium heat until the lentils and vegetables are tender, about 10 minutes. Add a generous grinding of black pepper and more tamari if needed. Sprinkle the ragout with the scallions and cilantro, if using, ladle into shallow bowls and serve.

Make a Meal

Serve with Broccoli with Olives, Orange Zest and Parsley (page 176).

CURRIED LENTILS WITH WALNUTS, SPINACH AND CHERRY TOMATOES

Vegan (omit the yogurt)

Earthy lentils and sweet, crunchy walnuts are among the most compatible of foods. This dish is the perfect canvas for a variety of additions. The simplest is to stir tender spinach leaves into the hot lentils until the greens wilt. Other options are to add steamed broccoli florets, stir-fried asparagus or sautéed red bell peppers or mushrooms.

Cook Time: 35 minutes
Serves: 4

- 1 **cup brown lentils**
- ¼ **cup extra-virgin olive oil**
- 1 **cup chopped onion**
- 2 **teaspoons Madras curry powder**
- 1 **garlic clove, grated**
- 2 **bags (5–6 ounces each) baby spinach (8–10 cups packed), rinsed and drained**
- 1 **cup small cherry or grape tomatoes, stems removed**
- 2 **tablespoons finely chopped fresh mint**
- ½ **cup chopped walnuts**
- ½ **cup plain low-fat yogurt (optional)**

1 Bring a medium saucepan half full of water to a boil. Add the lentils and cook, uncovered, until tender but not mushy, 18 to 20 minutes. Drain and set aside.

2 Heat the oil in a large skillet until hot enough to sizzle a piece of onion. Add the onion and cook, stirring, until tender, about 5 minutes. Add the curry powder and garlic and cook, stirring, for 1 minute. Add the cooked lentils, spinach, tomatoes and mint and cook, stirring, until heated through, about 5 minutes.

3 Meanwhile, heat the walnuts in a small skillet over medium heat, stirring, until toasted, about 5 minutes. Sprinkle the walnuts over the lentils and serve with the yogurt, if using, to spoon over the top.

Make a Meal

For nonvegans, a steaming bowl of curried lentils calls out for a topping of a soft fried or poached egg. I also like this dish with Roasted Cauliflower, Red Bell Pepper and Red Onion with Rosemary and Garlic (page 185).

CURRIED POTATO, SHIITAKE AND BROCCOLI STIR-FRY Vegan (omit the yogurt)

My love for crisp fried potatoes inspired this delicious stir-fry. All the ingredients come together in a salty, earthy, spicy mélange that is topped off with a tangy drizzle of plain yogurt, if desired, and a sprinkling of toasted almonds.

Cook Time: 25 minutes
Serves: 4

- 4 cups broccoli florets (from 1 bunch)
- 1½ teaspoons coarse salt
- ½ cup skin-on almonds, coarsely chopped
- 3 tablespoons extra-virgin olive oil
- 1½ pounds Yukon Gold, red-skinned or round white potatoes, unpeeled, diced (¼ to ½ inch), about 3 cups
- 5 ounces shiitake mushrooms, stems discarded, caps cut into ½-inch pieces (about 2 cups)
- 1 cup coarsely chopped (½ inch) onion
- ½ cup moist sun-dried tomatoes or oil-packed sun-dried tomatoes, drained, blotted dry and cut into ½-inch pieces
- 2 teaspoons Madras curry powder
  Pinch of crushed red pepper
- 1 garlic clove, grated
- 1 cup plain low-fat yogurt (optional)

1 Bring a large saucepan half full of water to a boil. Add the broccoli and ½ teaspoon of the salt and boil, uncovered, over medium heat until tender, about 3 minutes. Drain, rinse with cold water and set aside.

2 Place the almonds in a large skillet and cook over medium-high heat, stirring frequently, until toasted, about 2 minutes. Pour the almonds into a small bowl and set aside.

3 Reheat the skillet over medium heat until it is hot enough to sizzle and evaporate a drop of water. Add the oil. When it is hot enough to sizzle a piece of potato, add the potatoes. Cook, stirring, over medium-high heat until browned, about 8 minutes.

4 Add the mushrooms, onion, sun-dried tomatoes, curry powder, the remaining 1 teaspoon salt and crushed red pepper. Stir-fry, adjusting the heat to maintain a steady sizzle, until the potatoes and mushrooms are tender, 8 to 10 minutes.

5 Add the cooked broccoli and the garlic and stir-fry until heated through, about 2 minutes. Transfer the stir-fry to a serving bowl. Sprinkle with the almonds. Serve the yogurt on the side, if using.

Make a Meal

Serve with Apple-Glazed Acorn Squash (page 209).

Substitutions

Substitute 4 cups lightly packed baby spinach leaves for the broccoli florets. Add the spinach to the hot potato and mushroom mixture in step 5 and cook until wilted, 1 to 2 minutes.

TWICE-BAKED POTATOES WITH ROASTED POBLANO CHILES AND QUESO FRESCO

This is the iconic twice-baked potato given a Tex-Mex twist, with Mexican cheese and mildly spicy roasted poblano chiles. The recipe is easily doubled.

Cook Time: 35 minutes
Serves: 2 to 4

- 2 large russet potatoes, halved lengthwise
- 1 tablespoon extra-virgin olive oil
- 2 poblano chiles
- ¼ cup light or regular sour cream or crema (Mexican sour cream; see page 9)
- ½ cup crumbled queso fresco, mild feta cheese or soft fresh goat cheese (about 2 ounces)
- 2 tablespoons oil-packed sun-dried tomatoes, drained, blotted dry and chopped
- 2 tablespoons chopped fresh cilantro
  Coarse salt
- ½ cup shredded Monterey Jack, Manchego or other melting cheese (about 2 ounces)

1 Place a large baking sheet in the oven and preheat to 450°F for 10 minutes. Lightly brush the cut sides of the potatoes with the oil. Carefully remove the hot pan from the oven and arrange the oiled potatoes, cut sides down, in a single layer. Roast for 15 minutes. Use a wide spatula to turn the potatoes and roast until tender when pierced with the tip of a knife, 5 to 10 minutes more. Leave the oven on.

2 Meanwhile, evenly char the poblanos on all sides using a stove top pepper roaster or grill pan set over medium-high heat, a chef's torch or simply by holding the peppers with tongs (held with a mitted hand) over an open flame. Wrap the charred poblanos in foil to cool. When they are cool enough to handle, rub off the charred skins, split the peppers in half and discard the stems and seeds. Finely chop the chiles.

3 Holding the hot cooked potatoes with a dish towel or oven mitt, scoop out the flesh with a spoon, leaving a thin layer of flesh on the skins. Set skins aside. In a large bowl, combine the potato flesh, chopped chiles, sour cream, queso fresco, sun-dried tomatoes and cilantro and mash with a fork until blended. Taste and add salt, if needed.

Make a Meal

For hearty appetites, serve 2 potato halves as a main course with a side of Blistered Cherry Tomatoes with Balsamic (page 206). Or serve one half as an accompaniment to a bowl of soup such as Pumpkin and Tomato Soup with Cheese (page 38).

4 Arrange the hollowed-out potato halves on the baking sheet and mound the potato mixture into each one. Sprinkle the cheese generously on top.

5 Bake until the cheese is melted and the potatoes are reheated, about 10 minutes, and serve. These can be made several hours ahead and reheated before serving. If you refrigerated them, they will take about 20 minutes in a 400°F oven to reheat.

ROASTED SWEET POTATOES TOPPED WITH QUICK BLACK BEAN CHILI Vegan (omit the yogurt)

Quick and easy to prepare, sweet potatoes topped with black bean chili make a great-tasting meal. The chipotles add a blast of heat and an alluring smoky taste to the beans. Use dried black beans, cooked ahead, if you have them on hand, but canned beans are a fine substitute. The sweet potatoes can be cooked ahead and reheated.

Cook Time: 30 minutes
Serves: 4

- 2 **large or 4 medium sweet potatoes, scrubbed, skins left on and halved lengthwise**
- 2 **tablespoons extra-virgin olive oil**
- ½ **cup chopped onion**
- 2 **garlic cloves, grated**
- 2 **teaspoons chili powder**
- 1 **teaspoon ground cumin**
- 2 **cans (15–16 ounces each) black beans, rinsed and drained**
- 1 **can (14.5 ounces) diced tomatoes with juice**
- 1 **teaspoon chipotle chile in adobo sauce, or more to taste**
- ½ **teaspoon coarse salt, or more to taste**
  Plain low-fat yogurt (optional)
- 2 **tablespoons finely chopped fresh cilantro**
  Avocado, chopped or sliced, for garnish

1 Place a large baking sheet in the oven and preheat to 450°F for 10 minutes. Lightly brush the cut sides of the sweet potatoes with 1 tablespoon of the oil. Carefully remove the hot pan from the oven and arrange the oiled potatoes, cut sides down, in a single layer. Roast for 15 minutes. Use a wide spatula to turn the potatoes and roast until they are tender when pierced with the tip of a knife, about 10 minutes more. (If you cooked them ahead, reheat them in a 400°F oven for 10 minutes before proceeding.)

2 Meanwhile, heat the remaining 1 tablespoon oil and the onion in a large skillet over medium-low heat and cook, stirring, until the onion is tender and golden, about 8 minutes. Add the garlic and cook for 1 minute. Add the chili powder and cumin and cook for 20 seconds.

3 Add the black beans, tomatoes, ½ cup water, chipotle and ½ teaspoon salt and bring to a boil. Reduce the heat to low and cook, covered, for 15 minutes. Taste and add more chipotle and salt if you like. Simmer, uncovered, to thicken slightly, about 5 minutes.

4 Place a sweet potato half on each plate and mash the insides with a fork. Ladle the chili on top of the potatoes. Top each portion with a spoonful of yogurt, if using, and a sprinkling of chopped cilantro. Garnish the plates with avocado slices, or sprinkle diced avocado over the chili, and serve.

SAUTÉED CABBAGE AND CRISPY POTATO CAKE WITH MELTED CHEESE

A potato and cabbage cake is held together with some beaten eggs, topped with melted cheese and cut into wedges. Crescenza and Teleme are both soft, delicately flavored cow's-milk cheeses with a tangy taste and yeasty aroma. Crescenza is from Northern Italy, and Teleme is American-made.

Cook Time: 35 minutes
Serves: 4 to 6

- 3 tablespoons extra-virgin olive oil, plus more as needed
- 12 ounces Yukon Gold, red-skinned or round white potatoes, peeled and cut into ¼-inch dice (about 3 cups)
- 1 teaspoon coarse salt
- 1 small head (about 12 ounces) savoy cabbage, halved, cored and cut into ⅛-inch slices (about 5 cups)
- 1 garlic clove, grated
  Pinch of crushed red pepper
- 6 large eggs
  Freshly ground black pepper
- 4 ounces Crescenza, Teleme or fresh mozzarella cheese, cut into ½-inch cubes

Make a Meal
Serve with Sautéed Shredded Beets with Orange and Basil (page 168) and Steamed Spinach with Ginger and Garlic Oil (page 196).

1 Heat a large nonstick skillet over medium heat until hot. Add 2 tablespoons of the oil. When the oil is hot enough to sizzle a piece of potato, spread the potatoes in the pan. Cook, turning the potatoes occasionally with a wide spatula until they are evenly browned and crisp, about 15 minutes. Sprinkle with ½ teaspoon of the salt. Transfer to a bowl and set aside.

2 Add the remaining 1 tablespoon oil and the cabbage to the hot pan. Toss the cabbage with tongs to coat with the oil. Cover and cook over medium-low heat until the cabbage begins to wilt but is still crisp, about 5 minutes. Uncover and add the garlic and crushed red pepper. Cook, uncovered, tossing with tongs, over medium heat until the cabbage is crisp-tender but still bright green, about 5 minutes. Spread the potatoes over the top.

3 Whisk the eggs, ¼ cup water, the remaining ½ teaspoon salt and a generous grinding of black pepper in a bowl until frothy. Pour the eggs over the cabbage and potatoes. Cook over medium heat until the edges are set, about 2 minutes. Tilt the pan so that the uncooked eggs in the center run to the edges. Sprinkle the cheese evenly over the potatoes and cabbage. Cover and cook over medium-low heat until the eggs are set, 8 to 10 minutes. Let stand for 5 minutes before cutting into wedges to serve.

CANNELLINI RAGOUT WITH LEEKS, GREEN BEANS AND ORANGE Vegan

Very slightly crunchy green beans add a pleasant textural contrast to the softness of this cannellini stew. The recipe goes together quickly and makes a satisfying meal. Orange zest and a medley of fresh herbs elevate the flavor profile.

Cook Time: 25 minutes
Serves: 4 to 6

- ¼ cup extra-virgin olive oil
- 2 large leeks, dark green tops and roots trimmed, halved lengthwise, thoroughly washed and cut into ¼-inch pieces (about 2 cups)
- 1 cup sliced (½ inch) celery, plus some of the leafy tops
- 1 garlic clove, grated
  Pinch of crushed red pepper
- 1 can (14.5 ounces) diced tomatoes with juice
- 8 ounces green beans, cut into 1-inch lengths (about 2 cups)
  Coarse salt and freshly ground black pepper
- 1 strip (½ by 2½ inches) orange zest, finely chopped
- 1 tablespoon finely chopped fresh Italian parsley
- 1 tablespoon finely chopped fresh dill
- 1 tablespoon finely chopped fresh mint
- 1½ cups cooked or canned (one 15- to 16-ounce can) cannellini beans, rinsed and drained

1 Heat the oil in a large skillet until hot enough to sizzle a piece of vegetable. Add the leeks, sliced celery, celery tops, garlic and crushed red pepper and cook, stirring, over medium-low heat until the vegetables are tender but not browned, about 10 minutes.

2 Add the tomatoes, green beans, 1 teaspoon salt and a generous grinding of black pepper and bring to a boil. Simmer, stirring occasionally, over low heat until the green beans are crisp-tender, about 8 minutes. Add the orange zest, parsley, dill and mint, along with the cannellini and cook, stirring, until heated through, about 5 minutes. Season with salt and pepper to taste and serve.

Make a Meal

Serve on a bed of quinoa (see page 216) for crunch and texture, accompanied by a platter of Swiss Chard with Fragrant Garlic and Salt (page 186) and, for non-vegans, toasted bread topped with Pecorino curls.

ARTICHOKE AND POTATO STEW WITH BLACK OLIVES AND TOMATOES

This recipe is adapted from one by a friend and cookbook author Diane Kochilas. The balance of the acidic tomatoes, starchy potatoes and salty olives is perfect. A big bowl, topped with crumbled feta, generously sprinkled with chopped mint and dill and served with a green vegetable, is dinner.

Cook Time: 35 minutes
Serves: 4 to 6

- 2 packages (8 ounces each) frozen artichoke hearts, thawed, or 16 fresh baby artichokes
- ¼ cup extra-virgin olive oil
- 1 teaspoon chopped fresh oregano
  Coarse salt and freshly ground black pepper
- 1 cup coarsely chopped (½ inch) onion
- 1 can (28 ounces) Italian plum tomatoes with juice, coarsely chopped, or 2½ cups coarsely chopped peeled fresh plum tomatoes with juice
- 1½ pounds boiling potatoes, unpeeled, cubed (¾ inch)
- ½ cup pitted Kalamata olives
- 2 garlic cloves, grated
- 8 ounces crumbled mild feta cheese, preferably French (about 1 cup)
- 2 tablespoons chopped fresh mint
- 2 tablespoons chopped fresh dill

1 If using frozen thawed artichoke hearts, press between dish towels to blot excess moisture. If using fresh baby artichokes, trim off the thick outside leaves and halve lengthwise. Rinse in cold water and drain well.

2 Heat the oil in a large skillet or Dutch oven until it is hot enough to sizzle an artichoke. Add the artichoke hearts or artichokes, cut sides down, and cook over medium-low heat until golden, about 5 minutes. Turn and sprinkle with the oregano, a pinch of salt and a generous grinding of black pepper. Add the onion and cook, stirring gently, until golden, about 5 minutes.

3 Add the tomatoes, ½ cup water, the potatoes, olives and garlic, stir to blend and bring to a boil. Cook, covered, over medium-low heat, stirring occasionally, until the potatoes are very tender and beginning to fall apart, 20 to 25 minutes. Add more water, ¼ cup at a time, if the stew seems dry.

4 Taste and add more salt and pepper if needed. Both the olives and the feta are salty, so you may not need more salt. Spoon the stew into deep soup bowls and top with the feta, mint and dill.

WINTER VEGETABLE STEW WITH MOROCCAN FLAVORS Vegan

Adapt this hearty stew to what is available in the market. Substitute leeks for onions and add celery or fennel, sweet or white potatoes, green beans, peas, zucchini and/or summer squash. Stagger the addition of vegetables, adding the slow-cooking kinds at first and the quicker-cooking ones toward the end. For this stew, avoid strongly flavored vegetables like broccoli, cauliflower, Brussels sprouts and other members of the cabbage family.

Cook Time: 25 minutes
Serves: 4

- ¼ cup extra-virgin olive oil
- 2 cups diced (½ inch) onions
- 2 garlic cloves, grated
- 1½ teaspoons Moroccan spice blend (*ras el hanout*; see page 11)
  Coarse salt
- ½ teaspoon ground cumin
- ⅛ teaspoon cayenne
- 2 cups diced (½ inch) peeled butternut, acorn or other winter squash
- 1 cup diced (½ inch) carrot
- 1 cup diced (½ inch) turnip
- 1 cup diced (½ inch) parsnip
- 1 cup coarsely chopped peeled fresh tomatoes or canned plum tomatoes with juice
- ¼ cup chopped fresh cilantro, including tender stems
- 1–2 tablespoons diced preserved lemon (see page 12) or 4 fresh lemon wedges

1 Heat the oil in a large skillet over medium-low heat until it is hot enough to sizzle a piece of onion. Add the onions and cook, stirring, over medium-low heat until golden, about 10 minutes. Add the garlic, Moroccan spice blend, 1 teaspoon salt, the cumin and cayenne. Cook, stirring, for 1 minute.

2 Add the squash, carrot, turnip, parsnip, tomatoes and ½ cup water. Cover and cook over medium-low heat until the vegetables are tender, about 15 minutes. Taste and add more salt if needed

3 Add the cilantro and the preserved lemon, if using. If not, serve the stew with the lemon wedges.

Shortcuts

Look for precut winter squash, sold in many markets in plastic bags. Usually it is butternut squash, which works very well in this recipe. The skin on butternut squash softens considerably when cooked, so you may choose not to peel it.

Substitutions

Omit either the parsnip or the turnip, if desired, and substitute a cut-up large all-purpose potato.

COCONUT-VEGETABLE CURRY WITH CASHEWS Vegan

Aromatic, luscious, pretty and filled with complex flavors, this vegetable curry is wildly popular in my cooking classes. Don't be daunted by the list of ingredients to prep. Some can be omitted if your time or patience is short; read the Shortcuts below for hints.

Cook Time: 20 minutes
Serves: 4 to 6

- ¼ cup extra-virgin olive oil
- 2 teaspoons cumin seeds
- 2 cups diced (½ inch) unpeeled eggplant (about 8 ounces)
- 1 can (15–16 ounces) chickpeas, rinsed and drained
- 2 cups ½-inch cauliflower florets (from ½ small head, cored and thick stems removed)
- 1 cup diced (½ inch) onion
- 1 cup diced (½ inch) carrot
- 1 cup ½-inch lengths green beans (about 4 ounces)
- 2–3 teaspoons minced seeded jalapeño or serrano pepper, plus more to taste
- 1 tablespoon finely chopped peeled fresh ginger
- 1 tablespoon Madras curry powder
- 1 garlic clove, grated
- 1 teaspoon coarse salt
- ½ teaspoon ground turmeric
- 1 can (13.5 ounces) regular or light coconut milk
- ½ cup coarsely chopped roasted unsalted cashews
- ¼ cup finely chopped fresh cilantro

1 Heat the oil in a large skillet over medium-low heat until shimmering. Add the cumin seeds and cook, stirring, until they are a shade darker, about 2 minutes. Add the eggplant and chickpeas and cook, stirring, over medium-high heat for 5 minutes. Add the cauliflower, onion, carrot, green beans, jalapeño, ginger, curry powder, garlic, salt and turmeric. Cook, stirring, adjusting the heat to maintain a steady sizzle, for 5 minutes.

2 Add the coconut milk and bring to a boil. Cook, stirring occasionally, over medium heat until the sauce has thickened and the vegetables are tender, about 10 minutes. Spoon the curry into a serving bowl. Sprinkle with the cashews and cilantro and serve.

Shortcuts

Buy bags of cauliflower florets and trimmed green beans.

Substitutions

Vary the vegetables, adding and subtracting depending on what looks good in the market and what you have on hand. In the winter, I add potato and butternut squash. In the summer, I add tomatoes and garnish with torn fresh basil leaves.

CURRIED CHICKPEAS WITH ROASTED CAULIFLOWER AND SPINACH

Part sauté and part stew, this fragrant dish goes together quickly. The sweet, slightly peppery Madras curry powder adds punch to the chickpeas and cauliflower.

Cook Time: 30 minutes
Serves: 4

- 4 cups (1 pound) cauliflower florets (from 1 medium head)
- 3 tablespoons extra-virgin olive oil
- 3 teaspoons Madras curry powder
- Coarse salt and freshly ground black pepper
- 1 cup chopped onion
- 1 teaspoon grated peeled fresh ginger
- 1 garlic clove, grated
- 2 cans (15–16 ounces each) chickpeas, rinsed and drained
- ½ cup chopped fresh cilantro
- 2 teaspoons finely chopped seeded jalapeño pepper, or more to taste
- 1 bag (5–6 ounces) baby spinach, rinsed and drained
- 2 tablespoons fresh lime juice
- 1 cup plain low-fat or nonfat yogurt, for serving

Make a Meal

Serve with Roasted Sweet Potato Slices with Coriander and Lemon Dressing (page 203).

1 Place a large baking sheet in the oven and preheat to 450°F for 10 minutes. Toss the cauliflower, 2 tablespoons of the oil, 1 teaspoon of the curry powder, ½ teaspoon salt and a generous grinding of black pepper in a bowl. Carefully remove the hot pan from the oven and spread the cauliflower in a single layer on the pan. Roast for 15 minutes. Stir with a spatula, turning the florets and moving them around on the pan so they'll roast evenly. Roast until lightly browned and tender, about 10 minutes more.

2 Meanwhile, heat the remaining 1 tablespoon oil in a large skillet until it is hot enough to sizzle a piece of onion. Add the onion and cook, stirring, until it is golden brown, about 10 minutes. Add the remaining 2 teaspoons curry powder, the ginger and garlic and cook, stirring, over low heat for 2 minutes. Add the chickpeas, ¼ cup water, ¼ cup of the cilantro and the jalapeño and cook, stirring, until heated through, about 5 minutes.

3 Add the hot roasted cauliflower and the spinach to the chickpeas and stir to combine. Cook, covered, over medium heat until the spinach is wilted, about 2 minutes. Sprinkle with the lime juice. Spoon the stew into a serving dish and sprinkle with the remaining ¼ cup cilantro. Top each serving with a generous spoonful of yogurt.

RISOTTO-STYLE PENNE WITH TOMATOES AND RICOTTA SALATA

A photo in an Italian food magazine of tiny pasta cooked in a tomato broth until thick and creamy looked so luscious that I had to try it. The technique used—similar to making risotto—is unusual for cooking pasta. For this recipe, I use full-sized penne. The starch in the pasta gives the broth more body as it cooks. For convenience, I use canned tomatoes, but fresh tomatoes in season—they need to be peeled—are excellent.

Cook Time: 40 minutes
Serves: 4

- ¼ cup extra-virgin olive oil
- ½ cup chopped onion
- 1 garlic clove, grated
- 1 can (28 ounces) Italian plum tomatoes with juice
- 4¾ cups Easy Basic Vegetable Broth (page 46) or water
- 4 large fresh basil leaves, torn
- 12 ounces penne
- 1 cup coarsely shredded ricotta salata, Greek Kasseri, Pecorino Romano or Parmigiano-Reggiano cheese (about 4 ounces)

Make a Meal

Serve with Broiled Summer Squash with Vinaigrette, Dill and Goat Cheese (page 212).

1 Heat the oil in a large skillet or Dutch oven until it is hot enough to sizzle a piece of onion. Add the onion and cook, stirring, over medium-low heat until golden, about 5 minutes. Add the garlic and cook for 1 minute. Add the tomatoes, 2 cups of the broth and half the basil. Bring to a boil, breaking up the tomatoes with the side of a spoon, and cook over medium heat, stirring occasionally, until slightly thickened, about 15 minutes.

2 Meanwhile, pour the remaining 2¾ cups broth into a small saucepan and bring to a boil. Keep the broth hot over low heat.

3 Add the penne to the tomato-broth mixture. Adjust the heat to maintain a gentle boil and cook, stirring frequently, until the penne is al dente, gradually adding hot broth as the pasta absorbs the liquid in the pan, about 20 minutes.

4 Stir in ½ cup of the cheese and the remaining basil. Spoon the pasta into shallow bowls and top with the remaining ½ cup cheese. Serve at once.

ORECCHIETTE WITH RICOTTA, BROCCOLI RABE AND BLISTERED CHERRY TOMATOES

Orecchiette translates as "little ears," after its rounded disk shape that resembles an earlobe. Because of their thickness, they take a little longer to cook than most pasta shapes. I think they taste best when they're cooked soft with a hint of chewiness.

   Don't forget to ladle out about ½ cup of the flavorful cooking liquid before draining the pasta. You'll use it to add moisture to the pasta. Look for an artisanal ricotta that is a bit drier than the commercial supermarket kind. If using a supermarket brand, transfer it to a strainer to drain off any excess moisture before using.

Cook Time: 35 minutes
Serves: 4

- **2** tablespoons pine nuts
  Extra-virgin olive oil
- **1** pint cherry or grape tomatoes, stems removed
- **1** bunch (about 1 pound) broccoli rabe, ½ inch of stems trimmed, stalks with florets and leaves cut into 2-inch lengths
- **1** garlic clove, sliced thin
  Pinch of crushed red pepper
- **12** ounces orecchiette or other small chunky pasta shape
- **1** tablespoon coarse salt
- **8** ounces (1 cup) ricotta cheese (see headnote)
  Shavings of Pecorino Romano cheese

1 Combine the pine nuts and 1 tablespoon oil in a medium skillet over medium-low heat. Cook, stirring, until the nuts are dark golden brown, 3 to 5 minutes. Transfer to a bowl and reserve.

2 Reheat the skillet over medium-high heat until it is hot enough to sizzle a tomato. Add the tomatoes and cook, shaking the skillet, adjusting the heat between medium and medium-high, until they are blistered and softened, about 5 minutes. Remove the pan from the heat and set aside until ready to serve.

3 Bring a medium saucepan half full of water to a boil. Add the broccoli rabe and cook until tender, about 5 minutes. Drain in a colander. Wipe out the pan and add 2 tablespoons oil and the garlic. Heat over low heat until the garlic begins to sizzle, about 30 seconds. Do not brown. Stir in the crushed red pepper and the cooked broccoli rabe and toss to coat. Set aside off the heat.

Make a Meal

Serve with Chickpea Salad with
Celery, Lemon and Herbs (page 50).

4 Bring a large pot of water to a boil. Add the orecchiette and salt and cook, uncovered, stirring occasionally, until the pasta is tender, 8 to 12 minutes. When the pasta is cooked, ladle out ½ cup of the pasta cooking water and reserve. Drain the pasta in a large colander. Return the pasta to the cooking pot. Add the reserved cooking water and the ricotta and stir to blend.

5 Quickly reheat the cooked broccoli rabe and the blistered tomatoes. Add the broccoli rabe, the tomatoes with their juice, the toasted pine nuts and shavings of Pecorino Romano to taste to the pasta. Toss to combine and serve at once.

Shortcuts

Add the broccoli rabe to the boiling pasta water during the last 5 minutes of cooking. Heat the olive oil in a skillet and blister the cherry tomatoes as directed in step 2. Add the garlic and crushed red pepper to the pasta and ricotta mixture and top with the cheese shavings.

Vegan Variation

Omit the ricotta and Pecorino Romano.

GNOCCHI WITH GREEN BEANS AND WALNUT PESTO

Served hot or at room temperature, this makes a satisfying dinner. You can use almost any pasta. Vacuum-packed gnocchi made with spelt are especially delicious. Or use penne or orecchiette ("little ears"), a thick, concave pasta with lots of chew.

Cook Time: 20 minutes
Serves: 4

Pesto

- ¼ cup walnut pieces
- 1 garlic clove, grated
- ½ teaspoon coarse salt
- 2 cups loosely packed torn fresh basil leaves
- ¼ cup extra-virgin olive oil
- 3 tablespoons grated Parmigiano-Reggiano

- 12 ounces freshly made or vacuum-packed gnocchi, tortellini, orecchiette, penne or other pasta shape
- 1 tablespoon coarse salt
- 8 ounces green beans, cut into 1-inch lengths (about 2 cups)
- ¼ cup walnut pieces
- 2 tablespoons grated Parmigiano-Reggiano

Make a Meal

Serve with Chopped Tomato, Celery and Kalamata Olive Salad (page 50).

1 **To make the pesto by hand:** Combine the walnuts, garlic and salt in a large mortar and pound into a paste with the pestle. Add half of the basil leaves and pound until reduced to a coarse paste. Repeat with the remaining basil. Gradually add the oil, stirring with the pestle. Stir in the cheese. **To make the pesto in a food processor:** Combine the walnuts, garlic, salt and basil and process to a coarse puree. With the motor running, add the oil in a slow, steady stream. Transfer to a small bowl and stir in the cheese. You should have about ½ cup pesto.

2 Bring a large pot of water to a boil. Add the pasta and salt and boil, stirring, until the pasta is almost ready, 8 to 12 minutes depending on the shape. Add the green beans and boil, stirring, until crisp-tender, 3 to 5 minutes. Ladle out ½ cup cooking water and set aside. Drain the pasta and beans and return them to the hot pot. Add the pesto and half of the reserved cooking water and toss to coat. If you'd like more moisture, add the rest of the cooking water. Spoon into a serving dish and sprinkle the top with the walnuts and cheese.

Shortcuts

Making pesto is quick and easy with a big mortar and pestle, but for those who love being plugged in, use your food processor. Don't be tempted to overprocess the pesto. A coarse puree with bright green flecks is what you want.

TWICE-COOKED POLENTA GRATIN

Decadent and fabulous, this gratin begins with a batch of stovetop polenta that is layered in a baking dish with cheese, topped with half-and-half or milk and baked until golden and bubbly. The dish can be made a day ahead and then baked before serving, increasing the baking time by 10 minutes.

Cook Time: 40 minutes
Serves: 4 to 6

Extra-virgin olive oil

½ cup finely chopped onion

2 cups yellow cornmeal

1 cup half-and-half or milk

4 tablespoons grated Parmigiano-Reggiano

1 teaspoon coarse salt

8 ounces Italian fontina, Swiss raclette or mozzarella cheese, coarsely shredded (about 2 cups)

Make a Meal

Serve with the same toppings as for Easy Stovetop Polenta (page 228), or try it with Summer Stew of Zucchini, Tomatoes, Corn and Basil (page 211) or Stewed Red Bell Peppers and Tomatoes (page 173).

1 Heat 2 tablespoons olive oil in a large Dutch oven. When the oil is hot enough to sizzle a bit of onion, add the onion and cook over medium-low heat, stirring, until softened, about 5 minutes. Do not brown. Add 2½ cups water and bring to a boil.

2 Meanwhile, pour 2½ cups water into a bowl and gradually whisk in the cornmeal until blended. (This step helps to prevent lumps.)

3 Gradually stir the cornmeal mixture into the boiling water. Cook, stirring constantly, until the polenta begins to boil and pulls away from the sides of the pan, about 3 minutes. Cover the pot and let cook over very low heat, stirring occasionally, until very thick, 10 to 15 minutes.

4 Preheat the oven to 400°F. Brush a shallow 9-by-13-inch baking dish with oil.

5 Stir ½ cup of the half-and-half, 2 tablespoons of the Parmigiano-Reggiano and the salt into the polenta. Spoon half of the mixture into the baking dish. Spread with half of the shredded cheese. Add the remaining polenta, dropping spoonfuls evenly over the cheese. Spread evenly with a spatula. Sprinkle with the remaining shredded cheese. Top with the remaining ½ cup half-and-half and sprinkle with the remaining 2 tablespoons Parmigiano-Reggiano.

6 Bake until the cheese is melted and the polenta is bubbly, about 20 minutes. Serve.

THREE-MUSHROOM RAGU WITH STOVETOP POLENTA

In this savory ragu, deeply flavored porcini broth and red wine give rich, full flavor. Try it with the different varieties of mushrooms in your produce section.

Cook Time: 40 minutes
Serves: 6

Easy Stovetop Polenta (page 228)

¾ ounce dried porcini mushrooms (about 1 cup)

¼ cup extra-virgin olive oil

½ cup chopped shallots (2–3 large)

8 ounces cremini mushrooms, coarsely chopped (about 3½ cups)

6 ounces shiitake mushrooms, stems discarded, coarsely chopped (about 3 cups)

¼ cup finely chopped fresh Italian parsley

1 tablespoon chopped fresh thyme

2 garlic cloves, grated

1 cup dry red wine

2 cans (28 ounces each) Italian plum tomatoes with juice, pureed in a food processor or through a food mill

1 bay leaf

Coarse salt and freshly ground black pepper

1 Make the polenta.

2 Meanwhile, combine the dried porcini and 1½ cups water in a small saucepan and bring to a boil. Remove from the heat and let stand, covered, for 15 to 20 minutes, or until the porcini are softened. Set a fine-mesh strainer over a bowl and strain the mushrooms, reserving the porcini water. Make sure there isn't any grit in the bottom of the bowl. If there is, ladle out and reserve the clear broth and discard the grit. Chop the porcini and add to the reserved porcini broth.

3 While the polenta is cooking and the mushrooms are soaking, heat the oil in a Dutch oven over medium heat. When it is hot enough to sizzle a piece of shallot, add the shallots and cook until tender, about 5 minutes. Add the cremini and shiitake mushrooms and cook, stirring, over medium-low heat until golden and tender, 8 to 10 minutes. Stir in the parsley, thyme and garlic and cook, stirring, over low heat for 1 minute. Add the wine and bring to a boil. Cook over medium-high heat, stirring occasionally, until reduced by half, about 5 minutes.

4 Add the pureed tomatoes, bay leaf, porcini mushrooms and their broth, 1 teaspoon salt and a generous grinding of black pepper and bring to a boil. Cook, uncovered, over medium heat until the sauce is thickened, 20 to 25 minutes. Taste and add more salt and pepper, if needed. Keep the ragu warm over low heat until ready to serve.

Make a Meal

Serve with Twice-Cooked Broccoli Rabe with Red Pepper and Garlic Oil (page 179).

5 To serve, spoon a pool of ragu into shallow bowls. Top with a spoonful of the polenta and more ragu.

Vegan Variation

Omit the optional Parmigiano-Reggiano from the polenta, or serve the ragu over farro, rice, Israeli couscous, quinoa or other grains.

DOUBLE-CORN AND JALAPEÑO POLENTA GRATIN

Soft, belly-warming and tasty, this polenta gratin gets high marks from a discerning taster: my husband. Think of it as a puffy corn casserole. Refrigerate any leftovers, then cut them into thick slices and reheat them on an oiled baking sheet for breakfast.

Cook Time: 45 minutes
Serves: 6 to 8

Extra-virgin olive oil

¼ cup finely chopped onion

1 cup yellow cornmeal

1 cup whole milk or half-and-half

1 cup fresh corn kernels (from 2 ears) or thawed frozen corn

2 tablespoons grated Parmigiano-Reggiano

1 tablespoon finely chopped seeded jalapeño or serrano pepper, or more to taste

1 teaspoon coarse salt

1 cup coarsely shredded Manchego or cheddar cheese (about 4 ounces)

Make a Meal

Serve with Quick Black Bean Chili (page 130; without the sweet potatoes) or, for a lighter meal, Roasted Asparagus with Warm Cherry Tomatoes and Black Olives (page 161).

1 Preheat the oven to 400°F. Brush an 8½-by-4½-by-2½-inch loaf pan with oil.

2 Heat 1 tablespoon oil in a large Dutch oven. When the oil is hot enough to sizzle a bit of onion, add the onion and cook over medium-low heat, stirring, until softened, about 3 minutes. Do not brown. Add 1½ cups water and bring to a boil.

3 Meanwhile, pour 1½ cups water into a bowl and gradually whisk in the cornmeal until blended. (This step helps to prevent lumps.)

4 Gradually stir the cornmeal mixture into the boiling water. Cook, stirring constantly, until the polenta begins to boil and pulls away from the sides of the pan, about 3 minutes. Cover the pot and let cook over very low heat, stirring occasionally, until very thick, 10 to 15 minutes.

5 Stir in ½ cup of the milk, the corn, Parmigiano-Reggiano, jalapeño and salt. Spoon half of the mixture into the prepared loaf pan. Sprinkle with half of the shredded cheese. Add the remaining polenta, dropping spoonfuls evenly over the shredded cheese. Spread with a spatula to smooth out the surface. Pour the remaining ½ cup milk on top and sprinkle with the remaining cheese.

6 Bake until the cheese is melted and the polenta is bubbly, about 30 minutes.

SKILLET-BAKED EGGS WITH BLISTERED CHERRY TOMATOES

Quick and easy, eggs nestled in a skillet of tomatoes that have been seared in a hot pan until their skins blister make an appealing main dish for lunch or supper. If you like, serve one egg for each person on a bed of steaming hot quinoa or bulgur, mashed potatoes, a thick slice of toasted whole-grain Italian bread or a mound of polenta. You can use almost any cheese on top, such as dry Jack, Comté, cheddar, Parmigiano-Reggiano, Italian fontina, Manchego or aged Gruyère.

Cook Time: 15 minutes
Serves: 2 to 4

- 2 tablespoons extra-virgin olive oil
- 2 pints cherry or grape tomatoes, stems removed
- ½ cup thin-slivered onion
- 1 garlic clove, grated
- 2 tablespoons finely chopped fresh basil, cilantro or dill
- ½ teaspoon coarse salt
- Freshly ground black pepper
- 4 large eggs
- ¾ cup shredded cheese (see headnote)

1 Heat a large skillet until it is hot enough to sizzle and evaporate a drop of water. Add the oil and tilt the pan to coat. Add the tomatoes and cook over high heat, stirring, until blistered and softened, about 5 minutes. Add the onion and cook over medium heat, stirring, until the tomatoes are juicy, about 5 minutes. Add the garlic, basil, salt and a generous grinding of black pepper.

2 Break an egg into a small cup. Make an indentation in the sizzling tomatoes with a spoon and slip the egg into the indentation. Repeat with the remaining 3 eggs. Sprinkle the cheese on top. Cover and cook over medium-low heat until the eggs are set, about 5 minutes. Use a spatula or wide spoon to scoop out servings of eggs and tomatoes.

Make a Meal

Serve with Broccoli with Olives, Orange Zest and Parsley (page 176), Twice-Cooked Broccoli Rabe with Red Pepper and Garlic Oil (page 179) or Broccolini with Sun-Dried Tomatoes and Pine Nuts (page 178; omit the cheese).

ZUCCHINI AND RED ONION MINI OMELETS WITH ROMESCO SAUCE

A friend calls these delicate little open-faced omelets "egg babies." Technically, they're frittatas, and each cooks in a couple of minutes. Make a double batch of the versatile Romesco sauce and keep it on hand in the refrigerator to spread on toasted bread, roasted potatoes or hard-cooked eggs.

Cook Time: 10 minutes
Serves: 4

Romesco Sauce

- ½ cup coarsely chopped skin-on almonds
- ½ cup jarred piquillo peppers (see page 10) or roasted red pepper, drained, patted dry and chopped
- 4 tablespoons extra-virgin olive oil
- 1 tablespoon tomato paste
- 2 teaspoons sherry vinegar or red wine vinegar, or more to taste
- ½ teaspoon coarse salt
- ½ teaspoon smoked paprika (preferably *Pimentón de la Vera*; see page 10)
- ⅛ teaspoon cayenne

Omelets

- Extra-virgin olive oil
- 8 ounces zucchini, sliced thin (about 2 small zucchini)
- ½ cup thin lengthwise slices red onion
- 1 garlic clove, grated
- 2 tablespoons chopped fresh mint
- 2 tablespoons grated Pecorino Romano or other sharp grating cheese

- ¼ teaspoon coarse salt
- Freshly ground black pepper
- 4 large eggs

1 **To make the Romesco sauce:** Combine the almonds, peppers, 2 tablespoons of the oil, the tomato paste, vinegar, salt, smoked paprika and cayenne in a food processor and process until finely chopped. Scrape down the sides. With the motor running, gradually add the remaining 2 tablespoons oil until the mixture is smooth and creamy, stopping to scrape down the sides at least once. Transfer the sauce to a serving bowl and let stand, covered, until ready to serve. If making the sauce ahead, refrigerate and bring to room temperature before serving.

2 **To make the omelets:** Heat 1 tablespoon oil in a large skillet until it is hot enough to sizzle a piece of onion. Add the zucchini and onion and cook, stirring, over medium-low heat until the vegetables are golden, about 5 minutes. Add the garlic and cook for 1 minute. Transfer to a large bowl and stir in the mint, cheese, salt and a grinding of black pepper. In a separate bowl, whisk the eggs until frothy and stir them into the zucchini mixture.

3 Reheat the skillet used for the zucchini or heat a griddle until hot enough to sizzle and evaporate a drop of water. Lightly coat the pan with oil if needed. Add the egg mixture by ¼-cupfuls to the hot pan to make 8 to 12 round omelets about 4 inches in diameter. Use the tip of a spatula to push the runny egg back toward the center of each omelet. Cook until the eggs are set, about 1 minute. Turn with a wide spatula and cook until set on the other side, about 1 minute longer. As the omelets are done, transfer them to a platter. Serve with the Romesco sauce.

Shortcuts

- If you're in a rush or not terribly patient, use the egg mixture to make one large frittata following the directions in the recipe for Quick Supper Frittata (page 152).
- All of the mini omelets can be cooked at once on a hot griddle. If a griddle is not available, use a large skillet and cook as many as will comfortably fit at a time.

QUICK SUPPER FRITTATA

Following my mantra, "If you have an egg, you can make a meal," this frittata is an ever-changing favorite that appears on our dinner table often—always with a different flavor profile based on the ingredients on hand. Vary the number of eggs according to the appetites of your dining companions. I use 4 eggs for a small frittata, but for a heartier version, I use 6 eggs.

Cook Time: 30 minutes
Serves: 4

- ¼ cup extra-virgin olive oil
- 1 pound Yukon Gold, red-skinned or round white potatoes, unpeeled, cut into ¼-inch dice (about 2½ cups)
- ½ cup chopped red onion
- ½ teaspoon coarse salt
- ½ teaspoon smoked paprika (preferably *Pimentón de la Vera;* see page 10)
- 1 broccoli stalk, cut into 1-inch pieces (about 2 cups)
- ½ cup jarred piquillo peppers (see page 10) or roasted red pepper, drained, patted dry and chopped
- 4–6 large eggs
  Freshly ground black pepper
- ¼ cup grated Pecorino Romano, Parmigiano-Reggiano or other cheese

Make a Meal

Serve with a bowl of leftover soup, or make a Quick Hit Salad, such as Chickpea Salad with Celery, Lemon and Herbs (page 50).

1 Heat a large nonstick skillet over medium-low heat until hot. Add the oil. When the oil is hot enough to sizzle a piece of potato, spread the potatoes in the pan. Cook the potatoes, turning them occasionally with a wide spatula, until they are evenly browned and crisp, 10 to 15 minutes. Add the onion and cook, stirring, for 3 minutes. Sprinkle the potatoes with the salt and smoked paprika.

2 Meanwhile, bring a medium saucepan half full of water to a boil. Add the broccoli and cook, uncovered, for 3 minutes. Drain, rinse with cold water and shake dry. Add the broccoli and peppers to the skillet, distributing them evenly on top of the potatoes.

3 In a small bowl, whisk the eggs, 2 tablespoons water and a grinding of black pepper until frothy. Pour the eggs over the vegetables. Sprinkle the cheese on top.

4 Cook over medium to medium-low heat, tilting the pan to allow the uncooked eggs in the center to run under the set eggs around the edges, for 5 minutes. Cover and cook until the eggs are evenly set, 3 to 5 minutes more. Cut into wedges and serve directly from the pan.

Soba Noodle Salad with Snow Peas (page 60)

Skillet-Baked Eggs with Blistered
Cherry Tomatoes (page 149)

Cheese and Mushroom Melts (page 88) and Warm Green Bean and Tomato Salad with Mint (page 67)

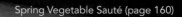
Spring Vegetable Sauté (page 160)

Tomatoes and Potatoes with
Avocado-Dill Dressing (page 56)

Vegetable Paella (page 122)

Twice-Baked Potatoes with Roasted Poblano Chiles and Queso Fresco (page 128)

Black Rice, Mango and Sugar Snap Pea Salad (page 54)

Three-Mushroom Ragu with Stovetop Polenta (page 146)

Shredded Tuscan Kale, Tomato and Avocado Salad (page 69)
with Quick Melted Comté Cheese Crisps (page 90)

Coconut-Vegetable Curry with Cashews (page 138) on jasmine rice

Pan-Seared Baby Bok Choy (page 174) and Red Rice Salad with Edamame, Tamari Walnuts and Ginger (page 52)

Carrot, Sweet Potato and Ginger Soup with Baby Bok Choy (page 33)

Roasted Asparagus with Chopped Egg, Feta and Black Olives (page 162)

White Bean and Fennel Soup (page 23) and Braised Swiss Chard with Pecorino Curls (page 84)

Stir-Fried Tofu with Oyster Mushrooms, Bell Peppers and Spinach (page 104)

Shortcut Corn Risotto with Summer
"Succotash" (page 120)

Risotto-Style Penne with Tomatoes and
Ricotta Salata (page 141)

Roasted Sweet Potatoes Topped with Quick Black Bean Chili (page 130) and Mexican Corn on the Cob (page 190)

Toasted Bulgur Pilaf with Cumin, Dried Fruit and Crispy Shallots (page 222) and Carrots with Moroccan Spices and Lemon (page 182)

Toasted Quinoa, Corn and Avocado Salad (page 62)

Vegetable Sides That Make a Meal

A popular vegetarian meal at my house is a mini buffet of vegetables served with a center-of-the-plate choice of beans, lentils, pasta, grain or another hearty dish.

I hit on this way of eating several years ago when my husband and I decided that we needed to drop a few pounds. My solution was to cut saturated fat (meat) and "white foods," including white flour, sugar, potatoes without skins, white rice and so on from our meals. Slowly, a few pounds did disappear, but perhaps the most profound difference was the change in my cooking style.

Ultimately, it was the appealing "buffet" of delicious vegetable dishes that I managed to create for each meal that won me and my discerning husband over.

BASIC VEGETABLE-COOKING TECHNIQUES

Boiling

Warned that boiling water will leach out valuable nutrients, I used to steam every vegetable. But it was Julia Child on television, plunging green beans into a large pot of boiling salted water, who liberated me from this rut. Boiling salted water softens the fibers of many vegetables, making them more succulent.

Broccoli: 3 to 5 minutes for florets; 4 to 6 minutes for broccoli with stems, depending on thickness.
Green beans: 3 to 5 minutes for young tender beans; 6 to 8 minutes for large, mature beans.

Snow peas and sugar snap peas: 1 minute. Drain and immediately rinse with cold water to "shock" or halt cooking.

High-Temperature Oven-Roasting

Almost any vegetable can be oven-roasted. To cut roasting time in half, preheat the baking sheet and the oven simultaneously. Cut the vegetables in 1-inch pieces or ½-inch-thick slices, toss with olive oil and seasonings and spread on the hot baking sheet. Turn the vegetables halfway through the roasting time and move the vegetables from the center of the pan to the hotter outside edges.

Asparagus: 10 to 12 minutes
Cauliflower (florets or "steaks"): 20 to 25 minutes
Bell pepper wedges: 30 minutes
Sweet potatoes and potatoes: ⅓- to ½-inch thickness, 30 minutes; ¼- to ½-inch dice, 20 to 25 minutes

Braising

Use the rinse water clinging to the leaves as the only moisture when cooking greens. In a large heavy pot or skillet, sauté garlic or onion in olive oil first, if desired, and add the leaves, packing them into the hot pan. Cook, covered, over medium-low heat until the leaves are wilted, 3 to 8 minutes, depending on the type of green.

Swiss chard, tender beet greens and Asian greens: 3 to 5 minutes
Tuscan (lacinato) kale, collards and mustard greens: 5 to 8 minutes
Spinach: Tender spinach leaves are best steamed in a collapsible vegetable steamer set over 1 inch of boiling water, 1 to 2 minutes

Pan-Searing

Different from sautéing in olive oil—as you would for sliced or chopped onions, carrots, zucchini, celery, mushrooms and other vegetables—pan-searing gives a blistered surface or browned color to the vegetable. This is a good way to quickly cook beets, winter squash, potatoes, red bell pepper strips or mini bell peppers or cherry or plum tomatoes. First brown or blister them on both sides in olive oil over medium-high to high heat. Next, cover and cook over low heat, turning the vegetables, until tender.

Sautéing and Stir-Frying

Whereas pan-searing concentrates flavor on the surface through browning, in sautéing, chopped or thin-sliced vegetables are stirred so that they cook evenly. To sauté, heat the olive oil in a skillet, add the vegetables and cook, stirring, over medium heat, until they reach the desired doneness. Stir-frying is similar but done over higher heat, generally to achieve crisp tenderness. To stir-fry, heat the oil in a wok, skillet or stir-fry pan until it is hot enough to evaporate a drop of water. Add the vegetables and cook, stirring, over high heat.

QUICK-COOKING ARTICHOKES WITH LEMON, MINT AND FETA

Because I've been an artichoke fan since childhood, I'm always amazed at the number of people who find them mysterious. Select small to medium artichokes instead of the big showstoppers. The smaller ones are tender, juicier and quicker to cook. The outside leaves are too precious to discard. Boil them in salted water until tender (about 10 minutes) and eat them hot or cold as a snack, dipping the tender, fleshy part of each leaf into lemon dressing, red wine vinaigrette or a garlicky mayonnaise.

Cook Time: 10 minutes
Serves: 4

- 4 medium (4–5 ounces each) artichokes
- 2 garlic cloves
- 1 leafy celery top
- 1½ teaspoons coarse salt
- 3 tablespoons extra-virgin olive oil
- 2 tablespoons fresh lemon juice
  Freshly ground black pepper
- 2 tablespoons finely chopped fresh mint
- 2 ounces feta cheese, crumbled (about ½ cup)

1 To prepare the artichokes, pull off one or two layers of the dark green outside leaves and reserve for another use (see headnote). Place each artichoke on its side and cut about ½ inch from the pointed end. Trim the end of the stem, if attached, and peel the outside of the stem with a paring knife or vegetable peeler. Halve the artichoke lengthwise. Place cut side down and halve again to make 4 quarters. Rinse with cold water.

2 Combine the artichoke quarters, 1 of the garlic cloves, bruised with the side of a knife, the celery top and 1 teaspoon of the salt in a medium pot and add enough water to cover the artichokes. Bring to a boil and cook, covered, over medium heat until the artichokes are tender when pierced with a skewer or the tip of a knife, 8 to 10 minutes. Lift the artichokes from the boiling water with a slotted spoon and drain, cut sides down, on a folded dish towel. Set aside to cool slightly.

3 Meanwhile, make the dressing. Grate the remaining garlic clove into a small bowl. Add the oil, lemon juice, the remaining ½ teaspoon salt and a generous grinding of black pepper and whisk to blend. Stir in 1 tablespoon of the mint.

Make a Meal

Serve warm with small boiled Yukon Gold or creamer potatoes. Make a double batch of Basic Vinaigrette (page 74) or Salsa Verde (page 14) and spoon over the hot potatoes. Accompany with a platter of Roasted Asparagus with Warm Cherry Tomatoes and Black Olives (page 161; omit the cherry tomatoes) or Sautéed Shredded Beets with Orange and Basil (page 168).

4 With the tip of a teaspoon, scoop out and discard the fuzzy choke from the inside of each artichoke and any small purple inner leaves that are prickly at the tips.

5 Arrange the artichokes on a serving platter, cut sides up, and spoon the lemon dressing evenly over the top. Sprinkle with the remaining 1 tablespoon chopped mint and the feta.

SPRING VEGETABLE SAUTÉ Vegan

The first asparagus and artichokes of spring inspired this simple sauté of tender young vegetables. Alas, there is nothing fast about shelling a pile of fresh peas. Bright green, sweet, frozen petite peas are a great stand-in, uncooked or cooked.

Cook Time: 20 minutes
Serves: 4

- 4 tablespoons extra-virgin olive oil
- 1 bag (12 ounces) frozen artichoke hearts, partially thawed, blotted dry
  Coarse salt and freshly ground black pepper
- ½ cup ¼-inch wedges shallots
- 1 garlic clove, sliced paper thin
- 1 cup thin diagonal slices slender carrots (from 1–2 carrots)
- 1 cup 1-inch lengths slender green beans (about 4 ounces)
- 12 ounces slender asparagus, peeled if large, cut diagonally into 1-inch lengths (about 3 cups)
- 1 cup frozen petite green peas
- 2 tablespoons chopped fresh dill or mint
  Lemon wedges

Make a Meal

Serve with boiled lentils (see page 219), Curried Lentils with Walnuts (page 125; omit the spinach and cherry tomatoes) or Lentils with Roasted Red Peppers, Dill, Mint and Feta (page 238). For a simpler meal, serve with small new potatoes boiled in their skins and tossed with olive oil and rosemary—along with Pan-Blistered Mini Bell Peppers (page 172).

1 Heat 2 tablespoons of the oil in a large skillet. When it is hot enough to sizzle a piece of artichoke heart, add the artichoke hearts, cut sides down, and cook over medium heat until golden brown, about 5 minutes. Turn, sprinkle with salt and a generous grinding of black pepper and brown the other sides, about 5 minutes. Transfer the browned artichoke hearts to a bowl.

2 Add the remaining 2 tablespoons oil, the shallots and garlic to the pan and cook, stirring, over low heat until sizzling. Add the carrots, green beans and ¼ cup water. Sprinkle with ½ teaspoon salt and a grinding of black pepper and cook, covered, until the vegetables are crisp-tender, about 5 minutes. Add the asparagus and peas and cook, stirring, uncovered, until the asparagus is crisp-tender, about 3 minutes. Add the artichokes and dill and cook, stirring, over medium-low heat until the artichokes are heated through, about 2 minutes. Serve with lemon wedges to squeeze over each serving.

Substitutions

If you can get baby artichokes, by all means use them. Trim the tough outside leaves and halve the artichokes. Cook them as directed in step 1, browning them on both sides. Then cover and cook over low heat until tender, about 5 minutes.

ROASTED ASPARAGUS WITH WARM CHERRY TOMATOES AND BLACK OLIVES Vegan

Versatile, quick-cooking and tasty, asparagus is always a welcome addition to a vegetable buffet. Drizzled with a stream of good olive oil just before serving—try one of the boutique orange, lemon or mint oils found in specialty markets—asparagus cooks quickly in a hot oven.

Cook Time: 15 minutes
Serves: 4

- 1½ pounds asparagus, peeled if large
- 4 tablespoons extra-virgin olive oil
  Coarse salt and freshly ground black pepper
- 1½ cups cherry or grape tomatoes, stems removed
- 2 tablespoons minced red onion
- 2 tablespoons coarsely chopped pitted Kalamata olives
- 1 teaspoon finely chopped fresh rosemary, plus 1 teaspoon whole leaves, for garnish

Make a Meal

Serve with Roasted Cauliflower "Steaks" (page 184) and Farro with Basil and Parsley Pesto (page 227).

1 Preheat the oven to 450°F. Spread the asparagus on a large baking sheet. Drizzle with 1 tablespoon of the oil and sprinkle lightly with salt and a grinding of black pepper. Roast until crisp-tender, stirring once, 10 to 12 minutes. Remove the asparagus from the oven and transfer to a serving platter.

2 Meanwhile, heat a medium, heavy skillet until it is hot enough to sizzle and evaporate a drop of water. Add 1 tablespoon of the oil and the tomatoes and cook over medium-high heat, shaking the pan, until the tomato skins have blistered and begun to crack, about 5 minutes. Remove from the heat. Add the remaining 2 tablespoons oil, the red onion, olives and chopped rosemary and stir to combine.

3 Spoon the tomato dressing over the asparagus. Garnish with the rosemary leaves and serve.

Variation

Roasted Asparagus with Melted Cheese Curls: Roast the asparagus for 10 minutes. Top with curls of cheese (Parmigiano-Reggiano, Pecorino Romano, Comté, Manchego, Italian fontina or other) cut from a wedge with a cheese plane and roast until the cheese is melted, about 5 minutes more.

ROASTED ASPARAGUS WITH CHOPPED EGG, FETA AND BLACK OLIVES

Half salad and half vegetable side dish, this recipe can be the centerpiece of a spring dinner, the bright green asparagus spread on a big platter and topped with the egg and feta cheese "salad," or served as one of several vegetable dishes as part of a buffet.

Cook Time: 20 minutes
Serves: 4

1¼ pounds asparagus, peeled if large

2 tablespoons extra-virgin olive oil

Coarse salt and freshly ground black pepper

2 ounces crumbled feta cheese (about ½ cup)

1 hard-cooked egg, chopped (see page 14)

¼ cup chopped pitted Kalamata olives

2 tablespoons chopped fresh dill

2 strips (½ by 2 inches each) lemon zest, cut into paper-thin lengthwise slivers

Make a Meal

Serve with Arborio Rice, Green Pea and Toasted Pine Nut Salad (page 51) and Pan-Braised Beets with Pistachio Pesto (page 166) or Pan-Blistered Mini Bell Peppers (page 172).

1 Preheat the oven to 450°F. Spread the asparagus on a large baking sheet. Drizzle with 1 tablespoon of the oil and sprinkle lightly with salt and a grinding of black pepper. Roast until crisp-tender, stirring once, 5 to 8 minutes.

2 Meanwhile stir the feta, egg, olives, 1 tablespoon of the dill and the remaining 1 tablespoon oil together in a small bowl. Sprinkle the cheese mixture over the hot asparagus and roast until warmed, about 5 minutes. With a wide spatula, transfer to a platter. Sprinkle with the remaining 1 tablespoon dill and the lemon zest and serve.

To Trim Asparagus

Hold a spear in one hand. With the other hand, bend the stem end until it snaps at the most tender spot. The spears will be of different lengths. If the stems are thick, give each one a quick swipe with a vegetable peeler.

ROASTED ASPARAGUS WITH PARMIGIANO-REGGIANO CRUMBS

As the asparagus roasts, the crumb topping turns crunchy and golden. I use fresh bread crumbs made from the interior of a day-old loaf of bread, but if you're a fan of panko—the crisp, light, large bread crumbs from Japan, now available in most supermarkets—use it, but crush them slightly for a finer consistency. Because they are dried, the panko crumbs are crispier than conventional freshly made crumbs.

Cook Time: 20 minutes
Serves: 4

- 2 tablespoons extra-virgin olive oil
- 1 cup coarse bread crumbs from day-old Italian bread, crusts removed (see headnote)
- ¼ cup grated Parmigiano-Reggiano
- 1 garlic clove, grated
- 1–1½ pounds asparagus, peeled if large
  Freshly ground black pepper

Make a Meal

Serve with Cannellini Ragout with Leeks, Green Beans and Orange (page 133), Artichoke and Potato Stew with Black Olives and Tomatoes (page 134) or Lentil and Shiitake Ragout with Green Beans (page 124).

1 Preheat the oven to 400°F. Brush a baking sheet with 1 tablespoon of the oil.

2 Toss the bread crumbs, cheese and garlic in a bowl until blended. Drizzle with the remaining 1 tablespoon oil and blend with your fingertips or a fork until the crumbs are moistened with the oil.

3 Spread the asparagus on the baking sheet. Add a generous grinding of black pepper and turn to coat with oil. Arrange the asparagus side by side in a tight line and sprinkle the crumb mixture on top, pressing it into the asparagus.

4 Roast, without disturbing, until the asparagus is tender and the crumbs are browned and crisp, 12 to 18 minutes. Serve at once.

To Make Fresh Bread Crumbs
Slice off the hard crusts from a firm, but not dry, day-old loaf of rustic bread. Cut the bread into ½-inch cubes and pulse in a food processor to medium-fine consistency. Make extra and keep in the freezer for another day.

TWICE-COOKED GREEN BEANS WITH CURRIED PECANS Vegan

Expand your green-bean repertoire with this easy and tasty twice-cooked dish. Briefly boiled in salted water and then tossed in a hot skillet with olive oil and dressed with curried pecans, the beans make a great little accompaniment.

Cook Time: 10 minutes
Serves: 4

1–1½ pounds slender green beans
    Coarse salt
 2 tablespoons extra-virgin olive oil
 1 garlic clove, grated
 ½ cup pecan pieces
 1 teaspoon Madras curry powder

Make a Meal
Serve with Curried Chickpeas with Roasted Cauliflower and Spinach (page 140).

1 Bring a large saucepan half full of water to a boil. Add the green beans and 1 teaspoon salt and boil until crisp-tender, 4 to 6 minutes, depending on the maturity of the beans. Drain and shake dry.

2 Heat a medium skillet until it is hot enough to sizzle and evaporate a drop of water. Add 1 tablespoon of the oil and heat until it is hot enough to sizzle a bean. Add the beans and cook over medium-high heat, tossing, until they blister and darken, 2 to 3 minutes. Turn off the heat, add the garlic and stir to combine. Sprinkle with a pinch of salt and transfer to a serving dish.

3 Add the remaining 1 tablespoon oil, the pecans and curry powder to the skillet and cook, stirring, over medium-low heat until the pecans are toasted and coated with the curry, about 2 minutes. Spoon the nuts over the green beans and serve.

Substitutions
Substitute walnuts for the pecans.

Variation
Roasted Asparagus with Curried Pecans: Roast the asparagus as directed for Roasted Asparagus with Warm Cherry Tomatoes and Black Olives (page 161; omit the cherry tomatoes). Prepare the curried pecans following step 3 in this recipe.

GREEN AND YELLOW WAX BEANS WITH ALMOND PESTO

Whether you use a mix of green and yellow beans or all green, this recipe is a keeper. You need just a small bunch of basil and use less olive oil and cheese than for a standard pesto.

Cook Time: 5 minutes
Serves: 4

Almond Pesto

- ¼ cup whole skin-on almonds
- 1 garlic clove, coarsely chopped
- ½ teaspoon salt
- 1½ cups loosely packed torn fresh basil leaves
- 2 tablespoons extra-virgin olive oil
- 2 tablespoons grated Parmigiano-Reggiano

- ½ cup thin lengthwise slices red onion
- 1 pound green beans, yellow wax beans or a combination, left whole If slender or cut into 1-inch lengths

Make a Meal

Serve with Whole-Roasted Tomatoes with Warm Goat Cheese (page 207) and Curried Corn with Sugar Snap Peas and Mint (page 188).

1 **To make the pesto by hand:** Combine the almonds, garlic and salt in a large mortar and pound into a paste with a pestle. Add half of the basil and pound until reduced to a coarse paste. Repeat with the remaining basil. Gradually add the oil, stirring with the pestle until blended. Stir in the cheese and set aside. **To make the pesto in a food processor:** Finely chop the almonds, garlic and salt. Gradually blend in the basil. With the motor running, add the oil in a slow, steady stream. Transfer to a small bowl and stir in the cheese. You should have about ½ cup pesto.

2 Place the onion in a small bowl of water and add a couple of ice cubes. Set aside.

3 Bring a large pot of salted water to a boil. Add the beans and boil, stirring occasionally, until tender to the bite, 4 to 6 minutes, depending on the size and maturity of the beans. Drain the beans and return to the hot pot. Drain the onion and add to the beans.

4 Add the pesto and fold until combined. Spoon into a serving dish. Serve warm or at room temperature.

Substitutions

For extra depth of flavor, make the pesto with toasted almonds. Or substitute pine nuts, walnuts or pistachios for the almonds. Vary the herbs by substituting fresh Italian parsley or mint for some of the basil.

PAN-BRAISED BEETS WITH PISTACHIO PESTO

You can use large, round beets cut into thick slices or smaller beets, quartered, for this recipe. Either way, arranged on a large platter and dotted or spread with the thick green pistachio pesto, they are beautiful to behold.

Cook Time: 15 minutes
Serves: 4

- 2 bunches medium beets, preferably with leafy green tops attached (about 1½ pounds)
- 2 tablespoons extra-virgin olive oil

Pistachio Pesto

- ¼ cup shelled and skinned pistachios, toasted
- 1 garlic clove, coarsely chopped
- ½ teaspoon coarse salt
- 1 cup loosely packed torn fresh basil leaves
- 2 tablespoons extra-virgin olive oil
- 2 tablespoons grated Parmigiano-Reggiano

  Coarse salt and freshly ground black pepper
- ¼ cup loosely packed torn fresh basil leaves, for garnish

1 Cut the leafy tops from the beets and set aside for another use (see opposite page). Peel the beets with a vegetable peeler if the skins are thick. Cut large beets into ½-inch rounds or quarter small ones. Place in a 2-quart heavy saucepan. Add 2 tablespoons water and 1 tablespoon of the oil. Cook, covered, over medium-low heat until the beets are tender when pierced with the tip of a knife, about 12 minutes, depending on the density of the beets. Check the moisture level in the pan halfway through the cooking time and add 1 to 2 tablespoons water if needed.

2 **To make the pesto by hand:** Combine the pistachios, garlic and salt in a large mortar and pound with the pestle until finely crushed. Add half of the basil and pound until reduced to a coarse paste. Repeat with the remaining basil. Gradually add the oil, stirring with the pestle. Stir in the cheese and set aside. **To make the pesto in a food processor:** Finely chop the pistachios, garlic and salt. With the motor running, gradually add the basil and process to a coarse puree. With the motor running, add the oil in a slow, steady stream. Transfer to a small bowl and stir in the cheese. You should have about ½ cup pesto.

3 When the beets are tender, uncover, drizzle with the remaining 1 tablespoon oil and lightly sprinkle with salt and black pepper. Arrange the beets on a platter and top each with a dollop of the pesto. Sprinkle with the torn basil leaves and serve.

Preparing Beets

Use a serrated vegetable peeler to remove the thick outside skin from mature beets. Young beets with thin skins need only a quick scrub with a vegetable brush and a rinse. **To shred beets:** Cut the beets into big chunks and push them through the feed tube of a food processor fitted with the wide shredding attachment or leave the beets whole and shred on the wide shredding side of a box grater. Your hands will turn purple, but if you wash them immediately with soap and hot water and rub stubborn spots with a wedge of lemon, the stains will fade.

Using Beet Greens

I always try to buy beets with greens, because they are fresher. I never discard the greens, even if I don't intend to eat them right away. I rinse and store them for a couple of days in a zip-top plastic bag until I have the 10 minutes required to braise them (see page 156). When they are cooked, I often cool and freeze them for later use. They are delicious simply sautéed with oil and garlic and served on toasted bread as a side dish, mounded in a soup bowl before ladling in the soup or placed in a tangle on top of a bowl of hot cannellini beans or lentils. I especially like the tangy taste of beet greens with a splash of balsamic or other well-aged vinegar, a spoonful of plain nonfat yogurt or a squirt of fresh lemon juice, a sprinkling of chopped fresh dill or served with a topping of crumbled feta cheese, goat cheese or shredded Parmigiano-Reggiano or Pecorino Romano.

SAUTÉED SHREDDED BEETS WITH ORANGE AND BASIL Vegan

Because they are a dense vegetable that typically requires a longer cooking time, beets present a challenge in the fast kitchen. Coarsely shredding or cutting the vegetable into small bits substantially reduces the cooking time.

Cook Time: 5 minutes
Serves: 4

1¼–1½ pounds (4–5) medium beets, preferably with leafy green tops attached

2 tablespoons extra-virgin olive oil

1 teaspoon grated orange zest

1 garlic clove, grated

Coarse salt and freshly ground black pepper

2 tablespoons finely chopped fresh basil or other herb of choice (see Substitutions)

1 Cut the tops from the beets and reserve for braising (see page 156), if desired. Peel the beets, if the skins are thick, with a vegetable peeler and coarsely shred using a box grater or the shredding blade of a food processor (see page 167).

2 Heat the oil in a large skillet until it is hot enough to sizzle a pinch of shredded beets. Add the shredded beets and orange zest and cook, stirring, adjusting the heat between medium and medium-low, until tender, about 5 minutes. Stir in the garlic, a pinch of salt and a grinding of black pepper. Sprinkle with the basil and serve.

Substitutions

Vary the herb depending on what's available. I like the taste of basil with the earthy beets, but fresh cilantro, mint, Italian parsley, dill or a combination of two or more all work.

Make a Meal

Serve with Sautéed Cabbage and Crispy Potato Cake with Melted Cheese (page 132) or Skillet-Braised Fennel with Comté Cheese (page 194) and Roasted Potato Slabs with Salsa Verde (see Substitutions, page 202).

PAN-SEARED BELGIAN ENDIVE
WITH LEMON, HONEY AND THYME

Belgian endive, those slender, short, pale green and sometimes ruby red clusters of long narrow leaves, is a revelation for those unfamiliar with this vegetable's sweet taste and juicy crispness. Although the plant originated in Belgium, it is now grown in California. Here the endive is halved lengthwise, browned in hot olive oil and then briefly boiled with a sweet, salty and sour dressing made with honey, Dijon mustard and fresh lemon juice.

Cook Time: 5 minutes
Serves: 4

4 heads Belgian endive, halved lengthwise

3 tablespoons honey

3 tablespoons fresh lemon juice

1 teaspoon Dijon mustard

1 garlic clove, grated

Coarse salt and freshly ground black pepper

1 tablespoon extra-virgin olive oil

2 teaspoons chopped fresh thyme

Make a Meal

Serve with Cumin-Scented Israeli Couscous with Caramelized Cabbage (page 116) or Vegetable Paella (page 122).

1 Place the endive in a bowl and cover with ice water. Let stand until crisped, about 10 minutes. Drain the endive, cut sides down on a folded dish towel and blot excess water.

2 Whisk the honey, lemon juice, mustard, garlic, ½ teaspoon salt and a grinding of black pepper in a small bowl and set aside.

3 Heat a skillet large enough to hold the endive in a single layer until it is hot enough to sizzle and evaporate a drop of water. Add the oil and heat until it is hot enough to sizzle the endive. Add the endive, cut sides down, and cook over medium-high heat until golden brown, 2 to 3 minutes. Turn cut sides up and sprinkle with salt and a generous grinding of black pepper.

4 Cook until crisp-tender, about 2 minutes. Pour the dressing over the endive and cook over medium-high heat, turning the endive with tongs to coat with the dressing, for about 1 minute, or until the dressing is slightly reduced. Transfer the endive to a serving dish and pour the dressing over the top. Sprinkle with the thyme and serve.

OVEN-ROASTED MINI BELL PEPPERS WITH ROSEMARY Vegan

Shaped like jalapeños, thin-skinned, sweet and flavorful mini bell peppers need little preparation or embellishment. Because they have few seeds or membranes, I sometimes roast them whole, with the stems still attached. The stems serve as little handles for dipping the peppers into a small bowl of coarse salt as they're eaten, one by one.

Cook Time: 25 minutes
Serves: 4

- 2 **boxes (8 ounces each) multicolored mini bell peppers (about 16), rinsed and dried, left whole with stems attached, or 2 small red bell peppers, cut into ½-inch wedges**
- 2 **tablespoons extra-virgin olive oil**
- 1 **teaspoon coarse salt**
  Freshly ground black pepper
- 1 **teaspoon chopped fresh rosemary**
- 1 **garlic clove, bruised with the side of a knife**

1 Place a large baking sheet in the oven and preheat to 450°F. Heat the pan in the hot oven for 10 minutes.

2 Toss the peppers and oil in a bowl. Season with ½ teaspoon of the salt and a generous grinding of black pepper. Carefully remove the hot pan from the oven and spread the oiled vegetables in a single layer on the pan. Roast for 15 minutes. Turn and stir the peppers with tongs and move them around on the pan so they'll roast evenly. Roast until blistered and tender, about 10 minutes more.

3 Place the rosemary, garlic and the remaining ½ teaspoon salt in a mortar and pound to a paste with the pestle. If you don't have a mortar and pestle, grate the garlic, combine it with the rosemary and salt on a saucer and mash together with the back of a spoon.

4 In a serving dish, stir the hot roasted peppers with the rosemary and garlic mixture until combined. Serve.

Make a Meal

Serve this versatile accompaniment hot as a garnish on pilaf, stir-fry, fried rice, beans, risotto, polenta or other starches or as a side dish with almost any buffet of vegetables.

You can serve this at room temperature or cold, splashed with balsamic vinegar.

Variation

Roasted Mini Bell Peppers with Potatoes and Rosemary: If using mini bell peppers, split each pepper in half or quarters lengthwise. Prepare small red bell peppers as directed. Toss 1 pound unpeeled Yukon Gold potatoes, cut into 1-by-¼-inch pieces, along with the peppers, in the oil, salt and black pepper. Roast on the preheated baking sheet for 15 minutes. Turn with a wide spatula and roast until the peppers are blistered and the potatoes are tender and golden, about 15 minutes more. Toss with the seasonings as described in step 4.

PAN-BLISTERED MINI BELL PEPPERS Vegan

I make these at the last minute if I need a colorful vegetable to round out a meal. The peppers are sweet, flavorful and a bit firmer than they are when oven-roasted.

Cook Time: 15 minutes
Serves: 3 to 4

- 2 **tablespoons extra-virgin olive oil**
- 2 **boxes (8 ounces each) multicolored mini bell peppers (about 16), rinsed and dried, left whole with stems attached, or 2 small red bell peppers, cut into ½-inch wedges**
- 1 **teaspoon chopped fresh rosemary**
- 1 **garlic clove, grated**

  Coarse salt and freshly ground black pepper

1 Heat a heavy skillet over medium-high heat until it is hot enough to sizzle and evaporate a drop of water. Add the oil and tilt the pan to coat evenly. Add the peppers and sear, adjusting the heat to keep the oil from splattering, turning the peppers with tongs until evenly blistered, about 5 minutes.

2 Reduce the heat to medium-low and cook, covered, until the peppers are softened, 5 to 10 minutes. Remove to a serving dish and add the rosemary, garlic, a pinch of salt and a grinding of black pepper. Stir to coat the peppers with the seasonings and serve.

Make a Meal

Serve this versatile accompaniment hot as a garnish on pilaf, stir-fry, fried rice, beans, risotto, polenta or other starches or as a side dish with almost any buffet of vegetables. Serve at room temperature or cold, splashed with balsamic vinegar. These peppers are great with white beans and broccoli, broccolini or cooked greens.

STEWED RED BELL PEPPERS AND TOMATOES Vegan

This mélange of vegetables works both as a hot side dish or as a room-temperature salad-like accompaniment. Depending on the dishes you are serving with it, decide whether you need the salty hit of the black olives or not.

Cook Time: 25 minutes
Serves: 4

- 2 **tablespoons extra-virgin olive oil**
- 2 **red bell peppers (about 8 ounces each), cut into ¼-inch-wide lengthwise slices**
- 2 **cups ¼-inch lengthwise slices onion (1 large)**
- 1 **garlic clove, grated**
- 1 **cup canned Italian plum tomatoes with juice or fresh ripe plum tomatoes, coarsely chopped**
- 1 **tablespoon chopped fresh Italian parsley**
- 1 **teaspoon dried oregano**
- ½ **teaspoon coarse salt**
  Freshly ground black pepper
  Pinch of crushed red pepper
- ¼ **cup coarsely chopped pitted Kalamata or green olives (optional; see head-note)**

1 Heat the oil in a large skillet until it is hot enough to sizzle a piece of pepper. Add the peppers and cook, stirring, over medium-high heat until they blacken, adjusting the heat as needed, 6 to 8 minutes.

2 Add the onion and stir to combine. Cover and cook over medium-low to low heat, stirring occasionally, until the onions are very tender and golden brown, about 10 minutes. Stir in the garlic and cook, uncovered, for 1 minute.

3 Add the tomatoes, parsley, oregano, salt, a grinding of black pepper and the crushed red pepper and bring to a boil. Boil, stirring occasionally, until the juices are slightly reduced and the stew is thickened, about 5 minutes. Stir in the olives, if using. Transfer to a serving dish and serve hot or at room temperature.

Make a Meal

Serve with Curried Lentils with Walnuts, Spinach and Cherry Tomatoes (page 125; omit the cherry tomatoes) and Swiss Chard Ribs Gratin (page 187).

PAN-SEARED BABY BOK CHOY WITH RED PEPPER OIL Vegan

Small heads of bok choy are available in many supermarket produce sections year-round. I love their crisp texture and mild taste. This is a basic sauté with crushed red pepper and garlic. If you prefer an Asian flavor profile, see the Variation.

Cook Time: 10 minutes
Serves: 4

6–8 small heads baby bok choy, halved lengthwise
2 tablespoons extra-virgin olive oil
1 garlic clove, grated
Pinch of crushed red pepper
Coarse salt

Make a Meal

Serve with Japanese Eggplant Stir-Fry with Shiitake, Bell Peppers and Ginger (page 191) and a bowl of Black Rice Pilaf with Edamame, Ginger and Tamari (page 232).

1 Place the bok choy in a bowl and cover with ice water. Let stand until crisped, about 10 minutes; drain well.

2 Heat the oil, garlic and crushed red pepper in a skillet large enough to hold the bok choy in a tight single layer. Cook over medium-low heat until the garlic begins to sizzle.

3 Add the bok choy, cut sides down, and cook over medium heat until the bottoms begin to brown, 4 to 5 minutes. Turn and cook until the bok choy is crisp-tender, about 2 minutes more. Season with salt to taste. Transfer to a serving dish, drizzle the oil in the skillet over the top, and serve.

Variation

Baby Bok Choy with Tamari and Ginger: Add 1 teaspoon grated peeled fresh ginger with the garlic in step 2. After turning the bok choy in step 3, drizzle with 1 tablespoon tamari and cook for 1 minute, then turn to brown the other sides of the bok choy and cook for 1 minute more. Drizzle with 1 teaspoon toasted sesame oil and sprinkle with 1 teaspoon regular or black sesame seeds, if desired.

BROCCOLI AND RED ONION STIR-FRY WITH TAMARI WALNUTS Vegan

The tamari walnuts add a pleasant twist to this simple broccoli stir-fry. Add the onion at the end of the cooking time so it stays crisp and juicy.

Cook Time: 5 minutes
Serves: 4

- ½ cup walnut pieces
- 2 tablespoons tamari
- 1 bunch (about 1 pound) broccoli, stems and florets cut into ½-inch pieces (6–8 cups)
- 2 tablespoons extra-virgin olive oil
- 1 garlic clove, grated
- ½ teaspoon grated peeled fresh ginger
- ¼ teaspoon coarse salt
- 1 medium red onion, cut into ¼-inch lengthwise slices or thin wedges (about ¾ cup)

Make a Meal

Serve with Yellow Rice and Carrot Pilaf with Mint (page 233) or Quinoa Pilaf with Apples and Curried Walnuts (page 229; omit the curried walnuts). For a second vegetable, serve Crispy Kale (page 197) or Roasted Cauliflower "Steaks" (page 184).

1 Heat the walnuts in a wok or large skillet over medium-high heat, stirring, until the walnuts are warmed and the wok is hot. Add the tamari all at once. As it sizzles, reduce the heat to medium and stir constantly until the walnuts are coated and the wok is dry, about 30 seconds. Turn the walnuts out onto a plate.

2 Add the broccoli and ¼ cup water to the wok. Cover and cook over medium heat until the broccoli is partially cooked, about 2 minutes. Drain off any water or turn the heat to high and boil until the water evaporates. Add the oil, garlic, ginger and salt and stir-fry over medium heat until the broccoli is tender and coated with the seasonings, about 2 minutes. Add the onion and toss to combine.

3 Spoon the stir-fry into a serving dish and sprinkle with the walnuts.

Substitutions

Substitute 12 ounces broccolini, cut into 1-inch lengths, for the broccoli.

BROCCOLI WITH OLIVES, ORANGE ZEST AND PARSLEY Vegan

Each week, a bunch of broccoli goes into my market basket. I consider this versatile vegetable a staple. My favorite way to cook it is to boil the trimmed stalks with the florets attached in salted water, uncovered, for long enough to render them juicy and tender but not soggy. Then all it needs is a little dressing up with chopped herbs, chopped fresh tomatoes, a sauté of mushrooms and garlic or a combo of olives, orange zest and parsley.

Cook Time: 10 minutes
Serves: 4

- 1 bunch (about 1 pound) broccoli, stems and florets cut into ½-inch pieces (about 6–8 cups)
- 1 garlic clove, coarsely grated
- ½ teaspoon coarse salt, plus more to taste
- 2 tablespoons extra-virgin olive oil
  Pinch of crushed red pepper
- ¼ cup finely chopped fresh Italian parsley
- 1 teaspoon grated orange zest
- ¼ cup coarsely chopped pitted Kalamata olives

1 Bring a large saucepan half full of water to a boil. Add the broccoli and cook until tender, 3 to 4 minutes. Drain and rinse with cold water. Set aside.

2 Mash the garlic and salt in a mortar and pestle. If you don't have a mortar and pestle, mash the grated garlic with the salt in a saucer using the back of a spoon. Heat the oil and the garlic mixture in a large skillet over medium-low heat, stirring, until the garlic begins to sizzle, 1 to 2 minutes. Stir in the crushed red pepper.

3 Add the broccoli, parsley and orange zest to the skillet and cook, stirring, over medium heat until the broccoli is hot and coated with the seasonings, about 3 minutes. Sprinkle with the olives and serve.

Make a Meal

Serve with Toasted Bulgur Pilaf with Cumin, Dried Fruit and Crispy Shallots (page 222) or Bulgur and Date Pilaf with Pecans and Parmigiano-Reggiano (page 224).

Shortcuts

Bags of broccoli florets cut down on the time needed to chop and prep a whole bunch.

Substitutions

- Substitute an equal amount of cauliflower florets for the broccoli. Add 1 cup halved cherry tomatoes or ½-inch pieces of firm, ripe plum tomatoes to the pan with the cauliflower.
- Substitute 1 teaspoon chopped fresh thyme for the parsley.

STIR-FRIED BROCCOLINI WITH SESAME AND ORANGE   Vegan

Broccolini, a cross between broccoli and Chinese broccoli (*kai lan*), has long, slender stems with clusters of small, loose florets at the top. It is a nice change of pace from broccoli. The texture is slightly crunchy and stays that way no matter how long you cook it. I like it best steamed or stir-fried. It adapts well to both Asian and Mediterranean flavors.

Cook Time: 10 minutes
Serves: 4

- 12 ounces broccolini, cut into ½- to 1-inch lengths
- 2 tablespoons extra-virgin olive oil
- 2 strips (½ by 2 inches each) orange zest, cut into paper-thin lengthwise slivers
- 1 garlic clove, grated
  Pinch of crushed red pepper
- 1 teaspoon toasted sesame oil
  Coarse salt and freshly ground black pepper

1 Combine the broccolini and ¼ cup water in a wok or large skillet and bring to a boil. Cover and cook over medium heat until the broccolini is crisp-tender, about 5 minutes. Drain the broccolini in a colander and reserve. Wipe the pan dry.

2 Add the olive oil and orange zest to the pan and stir-fry over medium heat until the zest is golden, 1 to 2 minutes. Reduce the heat to low and add the broccolini, garlic and crushed red pepper. Stir-fry until the flavors are blended, about 3 minutes. Stir in the sesame oil. Season with salt and pepper to taste. Transfer to a serving dish.

Make a Meal

Serve on a bed of red, black or brown rice (see page 217) accompanied by Cabbage, Pineapple and Peanut Salad (page 72).

BROCCOLINI WITH SUN-DRIED TOMATOES AND PINE NUTS Vegan (omit the cheese)

Broccolini is given a Mediterranean twist with the addition of sun-dried tomatoes and pine nuts that have been toasted in olive oil.

Cook Time: 10 minutes
Serves: 4

12 ounces broccolini, cut into ½- to 1-inch lengths

2 tablespoons extra-virgin olive oil

2 tablespoons pine nuts

2 tablespoons oil-packed sun-dried tomatoes, drained, blotted dry and thinly sliced

1 garlic clove, grated

Coarse salt and freshly ground black pepper

Curls of Parmigiano-Reggiano or Pecorino Romano cheese (optional)

1 Combine the broccolini and ¼ cup water in a wok or large skillet and bring to a boil. Cover and cook over medium heat until the broccolini is crisp-tender, about 5 minutes. Drain the broccolini in a colander and reserve. Wipe the pan dry.

2 Add the oil and pine nuts to the pan and toast, stirring, over medium-low heat until golden brown, 2 to 3 minutes. Remove the pine nuts from the oil with a slotted spoon or skimmer and reserve.

3 Add the broccolini, sun-dried tomatoes and garlic to the pan and stir-fry over low heat until the flavors are blended, 2 to 3 minutes. Sprinkle with salt and a generous grinding of black pepper. Spoon into a serving dish and top with the pine nuts and cheese curls, if using.

Make a Meal

Serve with Easy Stovetop Polenta (page 228) sprinkled with grated Parmigiano-Reggiano and Roasted Asparagus with Warm Cherry Tomatoes and Black Olives (page 161).

TWICE-COOKED BROCCOLI RABE WITH RED PEPPER AND GARLIC OIL Vegan

Some of us embrace the bitter taste of broccoli rabe, while others prefer the bitterness tempered. Braising broccoli rabe in water before sautéing it reduces some of the bitterness.

Cook Time: 10 minutes
Serves: 4

1 **bunch (about 1 pound) broccoli rabe**
2 **tablespoons extra-virgin olive oil**
2 **garlic cloves, cut into thin slivers**
   Pinch of crushed red pepper
   Coarse salt

Make a Meal

Serve with Farrotto with Tomatoes and Pecorino (page 115), Risotto-Style Penne with Tomatoes and Ricotta Salata (page 141) or Easy Stovetop Polenta (page 228).

1 Trim off and discard about ½ inch from the toughest part of the broccoli rabe stems. Working from the flowered ends, cut into 2-inch lengths. Swish in a large bowl of water and drain in a colander, but do not dry.

2 Place the broccoli rabe in a large skillet with about 1 inch of water. Bring to a boil over medium heat. Cover and cook until the broccoli rabe is tender, 3 to 5 minutes, depending on the thickness of the stems. Drain in a colander and wipe out the pan.

3 Add the oil, garlic and crushed red pepper to the pan and heat, stirring, over low heat, until the garlic begins to sizzle and turn golden, about 2 minutes. Add the broccoli rabe and toss with the warm oil mixture. Sprinkle with salt to taste. Transfer to a serving dish.

Variation

Broccoli Rabe with Boiled Potatoes: Bring a saucepan half full of water to a boil and add 4 to 8 unpeeled halved or quartered small Yukon Gold potatoes. Cook until tender, 10 to 20 minutes. Drain. Spread the potatoes in a shallow serving bowl and top with the cooked broccoli rabe. Pour any oil left in the skillet over the top. Pass a bottle of olive oil at the table to drizzle extra oil on the potatoes, if desired.

PAN-SEARED BRUSSELS SPROUTS
WITH HAZELNUTS   Vegan

Quickly boiling and then flash-searing in a hot skillet is the perfect preparation for these "little cabbages" with big flavor. Hazelnuts, a little nut with a distinctive taste, are the perfect match for the Brussels sprouts.

Cook Time: 10 minutes
Serves: 4

- 1 garlic clove, coarsely chopped or grated
- ½ teaspoon coarse salt
- 1 pound Brussels sprouts
- 2 tablespoons extra-virgin olive oil
- ¼ cup ground toasted and skinned hazelnuts
- Freshly ground black pepper

Make a Meal

Serve on a bed of Toasted Bulgur Pilaf with Cumin, Dried Fruit and Crispy Shallots (page 222) with a side dish of Carrots with Moroccan Spices and Lemon (page 182).

1 Mash the garlic and salt in a mortar with a pestle. If you don't have a mortar and pestle, mash the garlic with the salt in a saucer with the back of a spoon.

2 Bring 1 inch water to a boil in a large skillet. Add the Brussels sprouts and boil for 2 minutes. Drain and shake dry. Wipe out the skillet.

3 Heat the oil in the skillet until it is hot enough to sizzle a Brussels sprout. Add the Brussels sprouts and cook over medium-high heat, stirring constantly, until the sprouts begin to brown, 3 to 4 minutes.

4 Reduce the heat to low and add the garlic mixture and hazelnuts. Cook, stirring, until the garlic and ground nuts are evenly distributed, about 1 minute. Add a grinding of black pepper. Spoon into a serving dish.

Hazelnuts

Grind toasted peeled hazelnuts in a food processor or with a mortar and pestle. If only raw unpeeled hazelnuts are available, toast them in a preheated 350°F oven until lightly browned and the skins begin to crack, about 12 minutes. Pour the hot nuts onto a rough dish towel, cover and cool for 15 minutes. Rub the towel vigorously over the nuts to loosen and remove the skins. If some of the skins remain clinging to the hazelnuts, don't worry. They'll add flavor and texture.

CRISP-COOKED SAVOY CABBAGE WITH ASIAN FLAVORS Vegan

Ginger, toasted sesame oil and sesame seeds add a luscious complexity to this simple cabbage stir-fry. I prefer savoy cabbage for this dish because it is softer and has a milder flavor than the hefty, tightly packed heads of regular green cabbage.

Cook Time: 10 minutes
Serves: 4

- 2 **tablespoons extra-virgin olive oil**
- 1 **garlic clove, grated**
- 1 **teaspoon grated peeled fresh ginger**
  Pinch of crushed red pepper (optional)
- 1 **small head (about 1 pound) savoy cabbage, quartered, cored and cut into ¼-inch-wide slices (about 8 cups)**
- 1 **teaspoon toasted sesame oil**
- 1 **teaspoon sesame seeds**

Make a Meal

Serve with Stir-Fried Tofu with Oyster Mushrooms, Bell Peppers and Spinach (page 104) and white, brown, red or black rice (see page 217).

1 Heat the olive oil, garlic, ginger and crushed red pepper, if using, in a wok or large skillet over medium-low heat until the garlic begins to sizzle, 1 to 2 minutes. Immediately add the cabbage and ¼ cup water and turn the heat to medium-high.

2 Toss the cabbage with tongs and cook, adjusting the temperature to keep the cabbage sizzling but not browning, until crisp-tender, about 6 minutes. For softer cabbage, cook for 2 to 4 minutes longer.

3 Remove from the heat. Stir in the sesame oil. Transfer to a serving bowl and sprinkle with the sesame seeds.

Shortcuts

For the head of cabbage, substitute the convenient bags of shredded red and green cabbage that are now available in many markets. Before using, soak in ice water for 10 to 20 minutes to rehydrate the cabbage.

CARROTS WITH MOROCCAN SPICES AND LEMON   Vegan

Perhaps it's because we're a family who likes to snack on raw carrot sticks, but for the longest time, I neglected carrots in their cooked state. I love their bright color contrast to the green that dominates the vegetable world. This recipe features a Moroccan spice blend and preserved lemons, two of my favorite ingredients.

Cook Time: 10 minutes
Serves: 4

- 1½ teaspoons Moroccan spice blend (*ras el hanout;* see page 11)
- 1 pound long, slender carrots, cut into ¼-by-2-inch diagonal slices (about 3 cups)
- 1 garlic clove, grated
- 1 teaspoon grated peeled fresh ginger
- 1 teaspoon coarse salt
- 3 tablespoons fresh lemon juice
- 2 tablespoons extra-virgin olive oil
  Freshly ground black pepper
- 2 tablespoons finely chopped red onion
- 2 tablespoons finely chopped fresh cilantro
- 1 tablespoon minced preserved lemon rind (see page 12) or 1 teaspoon grated lemon zest

1 Sprinkle the Moroccan spice blend in a small skillet and heat, stirring, until warm and fragrant, about 2 minutes. Set aside.

2 Combine the carrots, garlic, ginger, ½ teaspoon of the salt and ¼ cup water in a medium saucepan. Bring to a boil, and cook, covered, over medium heat until the carrots are crisp-tender, 3 to 4 minutes. Uncover and cook over medium-high heat, stirring once or twice with a rubber spatula, until the water evaporates, 1 to 2 minutes. Remove from the heat.

3 Whisk the lemon juice, oil, Moroccan spice blend, the remaining ½ teaspoon salt and a grinding of black pepper in a small bowl until blended. Pour the dressing over the carrots. Stir the red onion, cilantro and preserved lemon or zest into the carrots and toss to coat. Serve at room temperature.

Make a Meal

Serve with Toasted Bulgur Pilaf with Cumin, Dried Fruit and Crispy Shallots (page 222) and Quick-Cooking Artichokes with Lemon, Mint and Feta (page 158).

MARINATED CARROTS WITH DILL AND MINT Vegan

Whole carrots, sold in bunches with the tops still on, are pretty and versatile. Here I marinate them in a mixture of rice vinegar, mint and dill. Serve warm, at room temperature or chilled.

Cook Time: 15 minutes
Serves: 4

- 2 tablespoons extra-virgin olive oil (or a flavorless oil, if preferred)
- 1 pound small, uniformly sized carrots, halved lengthwise if thick
- 1 garlic clove, grated
- ½ teaspoon coarse salt
  Freshly ground black pepper
- ⅓ cup unseasoned Japanese rice vinegar
- 1 tablespoon finely chopped fresh dill
- 1 tablespoon finely chopped fresh mint

Make a Meal
Serve with Toasted Bulgur, Tomato and Feta Salad (page 58).

1 Heat the oil in a large skillet. Add the carrots, garlic, salt and a grinding of black pepper. Cook over medium heat, turning with tongs, until the carrots are tender but still firm, 10 to 12 minutes.

2 Add the vinegar and simmer, turning the carrots, until most of the vinegar evaporates, about 5 minutes. Transfer to a serving dish and drizzle the oil in the pan on top of the carrots. Sprinkle with the dill and mint and serve warm, at room temperature or chilled.

Substitutions

Be imaginative and vary your combination of acid and spice or herb in the marinade. Try apple cider vinegar with a cinnamon stick or ½ teaspoon ground cinnamon; red wine vinegar with fresh tarragon and garlic; or white balsamic vinegar with grated orange zest, garlic and fresh rosemary.

ROASTED CAULIFLOWER "STEAKS" Vegan

Several years ago while attending a conference, I struck up a conversation with fellow cookbook author and writer Crescent Dragonwagon about our latest cooking passions. Crescent told me she had been slicing heads of cauliflower into "steaks" and roasting them in a hot oven until caramelized and tender. I couldn't wait to get home and try it. This dish is so popular in our house that a week rarely goes by when it doesn't make an appearance on our table.

Cook Time: 20 minutes
Serves: 4

- 1 medium head cauliflower (about 1½ pounds)
- 2 tablespoons extra-virgin olive oil
- ½ teaspoon coarse salt
  Freshly ground black pepper
- 1 tablespoon finely chopped fresh mint, dill or Italian parsley or a combination
- ½ lemon, seeded

Make a Meal

Serve with Curried Sweet Potato Wedges with Yogurt, Garlic and Mint Sauce (page 204) and Okra with Tomato-Ginger Sauce (page 201).

1 Place a large baking sheet in the oven and preheat to 450°F for 10 minutes.

2 Place the cauliflower, stem side down, on a cutting board and cut straight down at ½-inch intervals to make "steaks." Brush each piece on both sides with the oil. Carefully remove the hot pan from the oven and place the cauliflower steaks and any loose pieces of cauliflower florets on the pan. Sprinkle with the salt and a grinding of pepper.

3 Roast until the cauliflower is golden brown on the bottom, about 10 minutes. Turn with a wide spatula and brown the other side, about 10 minutes more. Sprinkle with the herb and squeeze a few drops of lemon juice on each slice. Transfer to a serving platter.

Substitutions

Add a generous dusting of ground cumin, smoked paprika (preferably *Pimentón de la Vera*; see page 10) or curry powder. Or prepare Orange Gremolata (page 14) or Salsa Verde (page 14) and spoon on top.

ROASTED CAULIFLOWER, RED BELL PEPPER AND RED ONION WITH ROSEMARY AND GARLIC Vegan

I often use my oven to roast a medley of vegetables, leaving the top of the stove available for cooking a second vegetable, boiling pasta, simmering grains or whatever else will make the meal. Oven-roasting at a high temperature softens and caramelizes vegetables quickly. Once you get the knack of the technique, you'll be making up your own combinations.

Cook Time: 30 minutes
Serves: 4

- ½ medium head cauliflower (about 12 ounces) or 1 bag cauliflower florets, cut into 1-inch pieces
- 1 red bell pepper, cut into 1-inch pieces
- 1 medium red onion, cut into ¼-inch lengthwise slices
- 3 tablespoons extra-virgin olive oil
- 2 teaspoons fresh rosemary
  Freshly ground black pepper
- 1 garlic clove
- ½ teaspoon coarse salt

Make a Meal

Serve with Red Quinoa with Scrambled Eggs, Asparagus and Tamari Almonds (page 118) or Sautéed Cabbage and Crispy Potato Cake with Melted Cheese (page 132).

1 Place a large baking sheet in the oven and preheat to 450°F for 10 minutes.

2 Toss the cauliflower, bell pepper and onion with the oil, 1 teaspoon of the rosemary and a generous grinding of black pepper in a large bowl. Carefully remove the hot pan from the oven and spread the oiled vegetables in a single layer on the hot pan. Roast for 15 minutes. Turn and stir the vegetables with a wide spatula, moving them around on the pan so they'll roast evenly. Roast until lightly browned and tender, 10 to 15 minutes more.

3 Place the remaining 1 teaspoon rosemary, the garlic, bruised with the side of a knife, and salt in a mortar and mash with a pestle. If you don't have a mortar and pestle, grate the garlic and mash it with the rosemary and salt on a saucer with the back of a spoon.

4 Place the hot roasted vegetables in a serving bowl and stir in the rosemary and garlic mixture until evenly distributed.

SWISS CHARD WITH FRAGRANT GARLIC AND SALT Vegan

Almost any green can be cooked using this technique. Try the outside green leaves of escarole, romaine lettuce, mustard or turnip greens, Asian stir-fry mix or Southern greens. Adjust the cooking time according to the thickness of the greens.

Cook Time: 5 minutes
Serves: 4

- 2 bunches (about 2 pounds) Swiss chard, rinsed
- 3 garlic cloves, coarsely chopped or grated
- 1 teaspoon coarse salt
- 3 tablespoons extra-virgin olive oil
- 4 lemon wedges

Make a Meal

Serve with Red Quinoa with Toasted Hazelnuts and Hazelnut Oil (page 230) and Swiss Chard Ribs Gratin (opposite page).

1 Tear the leafy parts of the chard leaves away from the ribs. Save the ribs for another use (see opposite page). Tear the leaves into 2-inch pieces.

2 Heat a large skillet until it is hot enough to sizzle and evaporate a drop of water. Add the chard with the water still clinging to the leaves. If the leaves seem dry, sprinkle with about 1 tablespoon water. Cover and cook over medium-low heat until the leaves are wilted, 3 to 5 minutes. With tongs, transfer the chard to a plate. Discard any liquid in the skillet and wipe dry.

3 Mash the garlic and salt in a mortar with a pestle. Or, if you don't have a mortar and pestle, mash the garlic and salt together on a saucer with the back of a spoon.

4 Add the oil and the garlic paste to the skillet and cook, stirring, over low heat until the garlic sizzles, about 20 seconds. Add the Swiss chard and toss with the oil mixture to coat. Serve with the lemon wedges.

Substitutions

For a hint of heat, add a pinch of crushed red pepper along with the garlic paste.

SWISS CHARD RIBS GRATIN

Friend and fellow cookbook author Linda Romanelli Leahy shared this great recipe. I'm partial to red chard because it's so pretty, but any color will do, or use a bunch of mixed colors, also known as rainbow chard.

Cook Time: 40 minutes
Serves: 4

Ribs from 1 bunch (about 1 pound) Swiss chard

Freshly ground black pepper

½ **cup shaved Parmigiano-Reggiano**

Make a Meal

Serve with Twice-Cooked Broccoli Rabe with Red Pepper and Garlic Oil (page 179) and boiled potatoes.

1 Preheat the oven to 450°F. Trim the ends from the Swiss chard ribs. If the chard is mature use a vegetable peeler to remove strings from the ribs. Trim the ribs to fit snugly into an oval or rectangular baking dish. Add about ¼ inch water and cover the dish tightly with foil.

2 Bake until the ribs are tender when pierced with the tip of a knife, 20 to 30 minutes, depending on the tenderness and size of the chard ribs. Uncover and pour off any excess juice (save it to drink or add to broth). Add a grinding of black pepper. Spread the cheese on the surface of the chard ribs and bake, uncovered, until melted, 8 to 10 minutes. Serve from the baking dish

CURRIED CORN WITH SUGAR SNAP PEAS AND MINT Vegan

Sugar snap peas and corn are so pretty together that I find myself tossing them into a skillet with whatever spice or herb I happen to have on hand. When I'm in the mood for curry, I often add it to the hot oil along with a generous dab of grated ginger and garlic.

Cook Time: 5 minutes
Serves: 4

- 12 ounces stringless sugar snap peas
- 2 tablespoons extra-virgin olive oil
- 1 teaspoon grated peeled fresh ginger
- 1 garlic clove, grated
- 2 teaspoons Madras curry powder
- 2 cups fresh corn kernels (from 3–4 ears)
- ½ cup thin-sliced scallions (white and green parts)
- ¼ cup chopped fresh mint or cilantro, including tender stems
- ½ teaspoon coarse salt

Make a Meal
Serve with Pan-Braised Beets with Pistachio Pesto (page 166) and Curried Quinoa and Apple Salad with Dried Cranberries (page 73).

1 Soak the sugar snap peas in a bowl of ice water until crisped, about 10 minutes; drain.

2 Heat the oil, ginger and garlic in a large skillet over medium-low heat until sizzling, about 20 seconds. Stir in the curry powder.

3 Add the sugar snaps, stirring until they are coated with oil. Cook, covered, over medium-low heat until the sugar snaps are crisp-tender, about 4 minutes. Add the corn and scallions and cook, stirring, for 2 minutes. Sprinkle with the mint and salt and spoon into a serving dish.

Shortcuts
- Look for stringless sugar snaps, which are tender and don't require trimming or stringing.
- Make quick work of cutting the kernels from ears of corn. Break the ear in half. Stand the corn on its end in the center of a shallow soup plate. Angle a small, sharp knife toward the cob, positioning it at the top of the ear, and slice down as close to the base of each kernel as possible. Halving the cob keeps the kernels from flying all over and ensures they land in the bowl. One ear will produce ½ to ¾ cup kernels.

Substitutions
- Use fresh basil or any other summer herb in the medley.
- Add halved cherry tomatoes before serving.

CORN SAUTÉ WITH JALAPEÑO AND CILANTRO Vegan

The heat of the jalapeño and the sweetness of the corn are perfectly balanced in this simple summer sauté.

Cook Time: 5 minutes
Serves: 4

- 2 tablespoons extra-virgin olive oil
- ¼ cup diced (¼ inch) red onion
- 1 garlic clove, grated
- 1½ teaspoons ground cumin
- 2½ cups fresh corn kernels (from 4 to 5 ears)
- 1 tablespoon coarsely chopped seeded jalapeño pepper, or to taste
- ¼ cup chopped fresh cilantro
- ½ teaspoon coarse salt

Make a Meal

Serve with Quick Black Bean Chili (page 130; with or without the roasted sweet potatoes) garnished with chopped red onion, avocado and tomato.

1 Heat the oil in a large skillet until it is hot enough to sizzle a piece of onion. Add the onion and garlic and cook, stirring, over medium-low heat for 1 minute. Stir in the cumin.

2 Add the corn and jalapeño and cook, stirring, until the corn is crisp-tender, about 3 minutes. Stir in the cilantro and salt. Spoon into a serving bowl.

Shortcuts

See the directions for cutting corn from cobs on opposite page.

Variation

Corn Sauté with Black Beans and Piquillo Peppers: Stir in ½ cup well-drained cooked or canned black beans and 2 tablespoons diced (¼ inch) jarred piquillo peppers (see page 10) or other roasted red peppers.

MEXICAN CORN ON THE COB

Corn, grilled or pan-seared, slathered with crema (a tangy thick cream, like crème fraîche) and then rolled in sharp-flavored grated cheese, is popularly called "Mexican corn." It is a real treat. Here I use a sprinkling of smoked paprika and Asiago or, if available, the sharp Mexican cheese called Cotija.

Cook Time: 15 minutes
Serves: 4

- **4 ears of corn, husked and trimmed**
- **2 tablespoons extra-virgin olive oil**
- **½ teaspoon smoked paprika (preferably *Pimentón de la Vera*; see page 10) or chili powder**
- **¼ cup sour cream, crema (Mexican sour cream; see page 9) or crème fraîche**
- **1 cup grated Asiago, Pecorino Romano, Cotija or other sharp grating cheese**
- **1 lime, cut into wedges**

1 Lightly brush the corn with a thin film of the oil. Heat a large skillet until it is hot enough to sizzle and evaporate a drop of water. Add the corn and sear over medium-high heat, turning every 2 to 3 minutes, until some of the kernels are browned and the corn is heated through, about 10 minutes. You can do the same thing on a gas grill or on a stovetop griddle.

2 Sprinkle the corn all over with the smoked paprika. Spread with a thin layer of sour cream. Place the cheese on a plate and roll the corn in the cheese. Serve with the lime wedges to squirt over the corn.

Make a Meal

Serve with Roasted Sweet Potatoes Topped with Quick Black Bean Chili (page 130) and a green vegetable such as broccolini, broccoli, green beans or a leafy green.

JAPANESE EGGPLANT STIR-FRY WITH SHIITAKE, BELL PEPPERS AND GINGER Vegan

Slender Japanese eggplants are sweeter and less moist than Italian globe eggplants, which makes them a good choice for this quick and easy stir-fry. Bright with the heat of ginger, the tang of eggplant and the richness of sesame, this side dish is especially delicious when served with other Asian-inspired dishes.

Cook Time: 5 minutes
Serves: 4

- 3 tablespoons extra-virgin olive oil
- 2 medium (about 8 ounces total) Japanese eggplants, cubed (½ inch), about 6 cups
- 5 ounces shiitake mushrooms, stems discarded, cut into ½-inch pieces (about 2 cups)
- ½ cup diced (½ inch) red bell pepper
- 2 teaspoons chopped peeled fresh ginger
- 1 garlic clove, grated
- 1 tablespoon tamari or soy sauce
- ¼ cup thin-sliced scallions (white and green parts)
- 1 teaspoon toasted sesame oil
- 1 teaspoon sesame seeds
- 1 tablespoon unseasoned Japanese rice vinegar (optional)

1 Heat a wok or large skillet until it is hot enough to sizzle and evaporate a drop of water. Add 2 tablespoons of the oil and tilt the pan to coat evenly. Add the eggplant and stir-fry over medium-high heat until it is lightly colored, about 2 minutes. Add the remaining 1 tablespoon oil and the mushrooms and stir-fry for 2 minutes. Add the bell pepper, ginger and garlic and stir-fry for 1 minute. Add the tamari and stir fry until the vegetables are browned and tender, about 1 minute.

2 Remove the pan from the heat and stir in the scallions, sesame oil and sesame seeds. Serve warm or cold. If serving cold, sprinkle the eggplant with the rice vinegar before serving.

Make a Meal
Serve with Crisp-Cooked Savoy Cabbage with Asian Flavors (page 181) and Black Rice Pilaf with Edamame, Ginger and Tamari (page 232).

BROILED EGGPLANT TOWERS WITH TOMATO, PESTO AND MOZZARELLA

Broiled eggplant holds its shape better than fried, perhaps because it doesn't absorb so much fat. Here, thick slices of eggplant and fresh ripe tomato are stacked and layered with a spoonful of pesto, topped with cheese and served like a giant vegetable sandwich.

Cook Time: 15 minutes
Serves: 4

Pesto

- 2 tablespoons pine nuts (toasted if desired; see page 15)
- 1 garlic clove, coarsely chopped
- ½ teaspoon coarse salt
- 1 cup loosely packed torn fresh basil leaves
- 2 tablespoons extra-virgin olive oil
- 2 tablespoons grated Parmigiano-Reggiano

- 4 thick (½–¾ inch) slices eggplant, cut from the widest section of a large eggplant
- 2 tablespoons extra-virgin olive oil
- 4 thick (½–¾ inch) slices ripe tomato, cut from a large tomato
- 1 teaspoon balsamic vinegar
  Coarse salt and freshly ground black pepper
- 6 ounces mozzarella cheese, cut into 4 thick (about ¼ inch) slices

1 **To make the pesto by hand:** Combine the pine nuts, garlic and salt in a large mortar and pound into a paste with the pestle. Add half of the basil leaves and pound until reduced to a coarse paste. Repeat with the remaining basil. Gradually add the oil, stirring with the pestle. Stir in the cheese. **To make the pesto in a food processor:** Finely chop the pine nuts, garlic and salt. Gradually add the basil and process to a coarse puree. With the motor running, add the oil in a slow, steady stream. Transfer to a small bowl and stir in the cheese. You should have about ¼ cup pesto.

2 Arrange the top oven rack so that the eggplant will be about 4 inches from the heat. Preheat the broiler.

3 Generously brush one side of the eggplant slices with some of the oil. Place the eggplant, oiled sides down, on a rimmed baking sheet. Brush the tops of the eggplant slices with the remaining oil. Broil until lightly browned, about 6 minutes. Turn the eggplant with a wide spatula and brown the other sides, about 5 minutes. Remove from the oven. Leave the broiler on.

4 Spread the pesto on the eggplant slices, dividing it evenly. Top with the tomato slices. Drizzle ¼ teaspoon balsamic vinegar in the center of each tomato slice and sprinkle with a pinch of salt and a grinding of black pepper. Place a slice of mozzarella on top of each tower.

Make a Meal

Serve with Warm Green Bean and Red Onion Salad with Mint (see Variations; page 67) and Warm New Potato Salad with White Wine and Scallions (page 50).

5 Broil until the cheese is melted and bubbly, about 3 minutes. Transfer to a platter and serve hot or at room temperature.

Shortcuts

Instead of making your own pesto, buy a good-quality refrigerated pesto. You will need ¼ cup for this recipe.

Substitutions

Use either mass-market mozzarella from the supermarket or fresh artisanal mozzarella. The mass-market variety is dry and rubbery when cold, but stringy and luscious when heated. Freshly made artisanal mozzarella is creamy when cold and milky and watery when heated.

SKILLET-BRAISED FENNEL WITH COMTÉ CHEESE

Braising transforms fennel's anise-like crunch into soft, mild silkiness. In this recipe, I top the fennel with shavings of a rich, nutty French cheese called Comté. Rather than turn the broiler on, I put a lid on the skillet and let the cheese melt over low heat.

Cook Time: 25 minutes
Serves: 4 to 6

- 2 medium (about 12 ounces each) fennel bulbs
- 2 tablespoons extra-virgin olive oil
- 1 garlic clove, bruised with the side of a knife
- ½ teaspoon coarse salt
  Freshly ground black pepper
- 4 ounces Comté cheese

Make a Meal
Serve with Zucchini and Red Onion Mini Omelets with Romesco Sauce (page 150).

1 Cut the stalks and most of the leafy fronds from the tops of the fennel, leaving some of the tender fronds near the center of the bulbs. Cut a thin sliver from the base of the fennel. Peel any bruises from the outside ribs with a vegetable peeler. Lay each bulb on its side and cut into quarters. (Do not trim the core; it will turn tender when cooked.) Place the fennel quarters in a large bowl, cover with ice water and let stand until crisped, about 15 minutes. Drain, but don't dry.

2 Heat the oil in a large skillet. Add the fennel, cut sides down, and cook, covered, over medium heat until lightly browned, about 10 minutes. Turn the fennel, add the garlic and sprinkle with the salt and a generous grinding of black pepper. Cook, covered, until the other sides are lightly browned and the fennel is fork-tender, about 10 minutes more.

3 With a cheese plane or vegetable peeler, cut shavings or curls of the cheese. Place 2 or 3 on top of each wedge of fennel. Cover and cook over low heat until the cheese melts, about 2 minutes. Transfer to a serving dish.

STIR-FRIED ASIAN GREENS WITH CRISP GOLDEN GARLIC Vegan

At both my farmers' market and my grocery store, I can buy gorgeous mixed greens labeled "stir-fry." These are mostly small leaves of several varieties of kale, chard, chicory and lettuces, all different colors and shapes and flavors. Sometimes a different combination is labeled "Asian," and it contains bok choy, mizuna and other Asian greens. All work well in this simple stir-fry.

Cook Time: 5 minutes
Serves: 4

- 2 **tablespoons extra-virgin olive oil**
- 2 **tablespoons thin-sliced garlic (about 4 cloves)**
   Pinch of crushed red pepper
- 1 **bag (about 1 pound) mixed Asian greens**
   Coarse salt

Make a Meal

Serve over a bowl of short-grain brown rice and sprinkle with Tamari Almonds or Walnuts (page 14). Also good served with Marinated Carrots with Dill and Mint (page 183) and Japanese Eggplant Stir-Fry with Shiitake, Bell Peppers and Ginger (page 191).

1 Heat the oil and garlic in a small skillet over medium-low heat, stirring, until the garlic is golden brown, 2 to 3 minutes. Have ready a fine-mesh strainer set over a heatproof bowl. When the garlic is dark golden brown, immediately pour the oil and garlic into the strainer. Reserve the garlic.

2 Add 1 tablespoon of the oil to a wok or a large skillet. Add the crushed red pepper and cook, stirring, over low heat for 30 seconds. Add the greens all at once and stir-fry, turning the greens with tongs until they begin to wilt, 1 to 2 minutes. Transfer the greens to a serving bowl, sprinkle with salt to taste and top with the crisp golden garlic.

Substitutions

In step 2, begin by sautéing ½ cup slivered onion or shallots in the oil until crisp-tender. Add the crushed red pepper and then the greens.

STEAMED SPINACH WITH GINGER AND GARLIC OIL   Vegan

For tender spinach leaves, I prefer the gentle steam that wafts through a vegetable steamer insert to the direct heat of the pan used for braising sturdier greens. This technique ensures the spinach cooks without becoming soggy.

Cook Time: 5 minutes
Serves: 4

- 1 tablespoon extra-virgin olive oil
- 1 garlic clove, grated
- 1 teaspoon grated peeled fresh ginger
- 1½ pounds (about 2 bunches) leaf spinach, rinsed, long stems trimmed
- Sesame seeds (optional)

1 Heat the oil, garlic and ginger in a small skillet over low heat, stirring, until sizzling, about 1 minute. Remove from the heat and reserve.

2 Place a collapsible vegetable steamer over a large pot filled with about 1 inch of water. Bring to a boil. Pack the spinach into the insert, cover and cook until wilted, 1 to 2 minutes. Lift the spinach from the steamer with tongs and place it in a serving dish. Drizzle the warm oil mixture over the spinach. Top with the sesame seeds, if using, and serve.

Make a Meal

Serve with Bulgur and Date Pilaf with Pecans and Parmigiano-Reggiano (page 224), Roasted Butternut Squash with Nutmeg and Manchego Cheese (page 210) and quinoa (see page 216) or Skillet-Baked Eggs with Blistered Cherry Tomatoes (page 149).

CRISPY KALE   Vegan

I can't take credit for inventing crispy kale, but it sure is great stuff. I often make it and leave it out for a snack, but it is also good sprinkled on stir-fried rice, grain pilaf or soup. Some recipes slowly roast the oiled kale in a 200°F oven for 30 minutes, but I crank up the oven to 400°F and get crispy kale in less than half the time. I prefer the soft, dark green pebbly-leafed Tuscan kale, which is sometimes sold as lacinato or dinosaur kale.

Cook Time: 15 minutes
Serves: 4

- 1 **small bunch (8–10 ounces) Tuscan (lacinato) kale, washed and dried**
- 2 **tablespoons extra-virgin olive oil**
  Coarse salt

Make a Meal

Eaten plain like peanuts or popcorn, crispy kale is an addictive snack. Sprinkle over a platter of fried rice, a rice or other grain pilaf or a salad of thick-sliced tomatoes.

1 Preheat the oven to 400°F. Pull the kale leaves from the tough stems. Gather the leaves together and cut into thin (⅛-inch) slivers. You should have about 6 cups packed.

2 Place the kale on a baking sheet, drizzle with the oil and toss to coat. Spread in a single layer and sprinkle lightly with a pinch or two of salt. Roast until the kale is crisp, about 12 minutes. Transfer to a serving dish.

Shortcuts

To quickly pull the ruffled kale leaf from the tough stem, fold the leaf in half over the stem, like a book. Holding the leaf firmly at the stem, use your other hand to pull the leaves down and away from the stem in one fell swoop.

OVEN-BRAISED LEEKS WITH ORANGE AND THYME   Vegan

Leeks are too often neglected when we search the produce section for a vegetable side dish. This supereasy oven-braised recipe should remedy that situation. Medium leeks are the perfect size for one per serving. You might want to double the recipe and save half for another day, sprinkling the leftovers with a bit of vinegar and turning them into a side salad for the next meal.

Cook Time: 30 minutes
Serves: 4

- 4 **medium leeks, roots, dark green tops and outside leaves trimmed**
- ¼ **cup extra-virgin olive oil**
- 1 **strip (½ by 3 inches) orange zest, cut into thin slivers**
- 1 **teaspoon chopped fresh thyme**
- ½ **teaspoon coarse salt**
  Freshly ground black pepper
- 1 **tablespoon red wine vinegar or cider vinegar (optional)**

1 Partially cut into each leek lengthwise, spread open and rinse with cold water. Place in a bowl, cover with ice water and let stand until crisped, about 10 minutes.

2 Preheat the oven to 350°F. Drain the leeks and spread them in a shallow baking dish or on a large baking sheet. Drizzle with the oil, top with the orange zest and ½ teaspoon of the thyme and sprinkle with the salt.

3 Cover with foil and bake until the leeks are tender when pierced with the tip of a knife, 20 to 25 minutes. Sprinkle with the remaining ½ teaspoon thyme and add a generous grinding of black pepper. Serve hot or add a drizzle of vinegar and serve cold.

Make a Meal

Serve with Easy Stovetop Polenta (page 228) or Cannellini with Sautéed Fennel and Blistered Cherry Tomatoes (page 235), Oven-Roasted Stuffed Portobello Mushrooms (opposite page) and Oven-Roasted Mini Bell Peppers with Rosemary (page 170).

OVEN-ROASTED STUFFED PORTOBELLO MUSHROOMS Vegan

Big and meaty, portobello mushrooms can easily be the center of the plate for an all-vegetable meal. Look for blemish-free caps with dusty brown (not moist) gills.

Cook Time: 30 minutes
Serves: 4

- 4 large (about 5 ounces each) porto-bello mushrooms, wiped clean, stems removed and reserved
- 4 tablespoons extra-virgin olive oil
- ½ cup chopped onion
- 1 cup coarse fresh bread crumbs from day-old Italian bread (see page 163) or panko (Japanese bread crumbs)
- 2 tablespoons finely chopped fresh Italian parsley
- 2 tablespoons oil-packed sun-dried tomatoes, drained, blotted dry and chopped
- 1 garlic clove, grated
- Coarse salt and freshly ground black pepper

Make a Meal

This is a perfect recipe for a vegetable buffet. Serve with Stir-Fried Asian Greens with Crisp Golden Garlic (page 195) and Roasted Potato Slabs with Romesco Sauce (page 202).

1 Preheat the oven to 400°F. Finely chop the mushroom stems.

2 Meanwhile, heat 2 tablespoons of the oil in a medium skillet until it is hot enough to sizzle a piece of onion. Add the onion and chopped mushroom stems and cook, stirring, over medium heat until golden, about 5 minutes. Add the bread crumbs, parsley, sun-dried tomatoes and garlic and cook, stirring, until the crumbs are heated through, about 2 minutes. Sprinkle with salt and pepper to taste and set aside.

3 Brush the tops and bottoms of the mushroom caps with the remaining 2 tablespoons oil. Sprinkle on both sides with salt and a grinding of black pepper. Place on a baking sheet, rounded sides up, add ¼ cup water and roast for 10 minutes.

4 Remove the pan from the oven. Turn the caps over, fill with the crumb mixture, dividing it evenly, and roast until browned and crisp, about 10 minutes more. Transfer to a platter and serve.

Variation

Oven-Roasted Portobello Mushrooms with Cheese: Top the crumbs in each portobello cap with about 1 tablespoon grated Parmigiano-Reggiano, Comté or other cheese before roasting.

OVEN-ROASTED MUSHROOMS, ONIONS AND POTATOES WITH SMOKED PAPRIKA Vegan

This versatile trio of vegetables is accented with a sprinkling of smoked paprika. If you can find them, use tiny thumbnail-sized shiitake mushrooms, which are delightfully nutty and so tender you can eat the stems. Otherwise, select the smallest shiitakes you can find.

Cook Time: 25 minutes
Serves: 4

1¼ pounds Yukon Gold potatoes, cut into ½-inch pieces

1 medium onion, cut into ½-inch pieces

5 ounces baby shiitake mushrooms, stems left on, or regular-sized shiitake mushrooms, stems discarded, caps cut into ½-inch pieces

1 small red bell pepper, cut into ½-inch pieces

3 tablespoons extra-virgin olive oil

1 teaspoon smoked paprika (preferably *Pimentón de la Vera*; see page 10)

½ teaspoon coarse salt

¼ teaspoon freshly ground black pepper

2 teaspoons finely chopped fresh rosemary

1 Place a large baking sheet in the oven and preheat to 450°F for 10 minutes.

2 Toss the potatoes, onion, mushrooms and bell pepper with the oil, smoked paprika, salt and black pepper in a large bowl. Carefully remove the hot pan from the oven and spread the oiled vegetables in a single layer on the pan. Roast for 10 minutes. Stir with a spatula, turning the vegetables and moving them around on the pan so they'll roast evenly. Roast until lightly browned and tender, 10 to 15 minutes more. Sprinkle with the rosemary. Transfer to a serving dish.

Storing Mushrooms

Never store mushrooms in plastic. Plastic traps their moisture and speeds their deterioration. If you must store them for a few days before using, refrigerate them in a paper bag or wrap them in paper towels.

Make a Meal

Serve with Pan-Blistered Mini Bell Peppers (page 172) and Roasted Butternut Squash with Nutmeg and Manchego Cheese (page 210) in the fall and winter or Swiss Chard with Fragrant Garlic and Salt (page 186) in the warmer months.

OKRA WITH TOMATO-GINGER SAUCE Vegan

This great recipe, adapted from one by my friend and culinary co-conspirator Debbie Rugh, is easy and delicious. Debbie advises buying small, slender okra for this delicate stew. When trimming the stems, be certain to snip off only the tip (don't cut into the pod and expose the seeds); that way, the texture of the okra will be less slippery.

Cook Time: 15 minutes
Serves: 4 to 6

- 1 pound small fresh okra, tips of stems trimmed, left whole (see headnote)
- 1 tablespoon extra-virgin olive oil
- 1 garlic clove, grated
- 1 can (14.5 ounces) diced tomatoes with juice or 1½ cups diced peeled fresh tomatoes
- 2 teaspoons grated peeled fresh ginger
- 1–2 teaspoons minced seeded jalapeño pepper
- ½ teaspoon coarse salt
  Freshly ground black pepper
- 2 tablespoons finely chopped fresh cilantro (optional)

1 Steam the okra in a collapsible vegetable steamer set into a saucepan with about 1 inch of boiling water, covered, until crisp-tender, 3 to 4 minutes. Lift the okra from the pan and set aside. Do not rinse in cold water.

2 Heat the oil and garlic in a medium skillet over medium-low heat until the garlic sizzles, 1 to 2 minutes. Add the tomatoes and ginger and cook, stirring, over medium heat until the sauce is thickened, about 5 minutes. Add the jalapeño, salt and a grinding of black pepper.

3 Stir the okra into the sauce and cook over medium-low heat, stirring to coat the okra with the sauce, until re-heated, about 3 minutes. Transfer to a serving bowl and sprinkle with the cilantro, if using.

Variation

Cauliflower with Curried Tomato-Ginger Sauce: Substitute 1 pound cauliflower florets for the okra. Add 1 teaspoon Madras curry powder and ½ teaspoon ground cumin to the oil and garlic in step 2.

Make a Meal

Serve with Yellow Rice and Carrot Pilaf with Mint (page 233) or Curried Quinoa and Apple Salad with Dried Cranberries (page 73) and Warm Green Bean and Tomato Salad with Mint or Warm Green Bean and Red Onion Salad with Mint (page 67).

ROASTED POTATO SLABS WITH ROMESCO SAUCE Vegan

These thick potato slices roast in half an hour or less in a hot oven. Top them with a piquant Spanish sauce made with pureed red peppers, almonds and olive oil called Romesco.

Cook Time: 30 minutes
Serves: 4

3–4 large russet potatoes, cut lengthwise
   into ⅓- to ½-inch-thick slabs

3 tablespoons extra-virgin olive oil

1 teaspoon coarse salt

1 teaspoon smoked paprika (preferably
   Pimentón de la Vera; see page 10)

¼ teaspoon freshly ground black pepper
   Romesco Sauce (page 150)

Make a Meal

Serve with Oven-Roasted Stuffed Portobello Mushrooms (page 199) and Summer Stew of Zucchini, Tomatoes, Corn and Basil (page 211) or Stir-Fried Asian Greens with Crisp Golden Garlic (page 195).

1 Place a large baking sheet in the oven and preheat to 450°F for 10 minutes.

2 Toss the potatoes, oil, salt, smoked paprika and black pepper in a large bowl. Carefully remove the hot pan from the oven and spread the oiled potatoes in a single layer on the pan. Scrape the seasoned oil from the sides of the bowl with a rubber spatula and drizzle on top of the potatoes. Roast for 15 minutes. Turn the potatoes with a wide spatula and roast until golden brown and tender, 10 to 15 minutes more.

3 While the potatoes are roasting, prepare the Romesco Sauce.

4 Serve the roasted potatoes with a spoonful of Romesco Sauce slathered on top of each slab.

Substitutions
- Substitute sweet potatoes for the russets.
- Serve with Salsa Verde (page 14) instead of the Romesco Sauce.

ROASTED SWEET POTATO SLICES WITH CORIANDER AND LEMON DRESSING   Vegan

These golden brown slabs of sweet potatoes are seasoned with ground coriander and then dressed with a zesty mixture of cilantro—coriander in its fresh form—garlic and lemon juice.

Cook Time: 30 minutes
Serves: 4

1–1½ **pounds sweet potatoes (about
2 medium), scrubbed, skins left on and
cut into ¼- to ½-inch-thick rounds**

4 **tablespoons extra-virgin olive oil**

1 **teaspoon ground coriander**

1 **teaspoon coarse salt**

Freshly ground black pepper

1 **garlic clove, chopped or grated**

2 **tablespoons fresh lemon juice**

2 **tablespoons finely chopped fresh
cilantro**

½ **teaspoon grated lemon zest**

Make a Meal

Serve with Whole-Roasted Tomatoes with Warm Goat Cheese (page 207) and Cumin Black Beans with Blistered Tomatoes and Corn (page 237).

1 Place a large baking sheet in the oven and preheat to 450°F for 10 minutes.

2 Toss the potatoes and 2 tablespoons of the oil in a large bowl. Combine the coriander and ¾ teaspoon of the salt in a small bowl. Carefully remove the hot pan from the oven and spread the oiled potatoes in a single layer on the pan. Sprinkle with half of the coriander mixture and add a generous grinding of black pepper. Roast for 15 minutes. Turn the potatoes with a wide spatula and sprinkle with the remaining coriander mixture and a generous grinding of black pepper. Roast until the potatoes are golden brown and tender, 10 to 15 minutes.

3 Pound the garlic and the remaining ¼ teaspoon salt in a mortar with the pestle. If you don't have a mortar and pestle, mash the garlic and salt in a saucer with the back of a spoon. Add the lemon juice and stir until the salt dissolves. Stir in the remaining 2 tablespoons oil until the dressing is emulsified. Stir in the cilantro and lemon zest.

4 Arrange the potatoes on a serving platter, spoon the dressing over the potatoes, turning them to coat, and serve.

CURRIED SWEET POTATO WEDGES WITH YOGURT, GARLIC AND MINT SAUCE

Warmly spiced roasted sweet potatoes topped with a cooling, tangy yogurt sauce satisfy my yearning for Indian-inspired dishes. To serve, spoon the sauce over the hot potatoes or spoon some sauce on each plate in which to dip each forkful. Double the sauce recipe for extra topping, if you like.

Cook Time: 30 minutes
Serves: 4

1–1½ pounds sweet potatoes (about 2 medium), scrubbed, skins left on, halved and cut into ½-inch wedges

2 tablespoons extra-virgin olive oil

2 teaspoons Madras curry powder

1 teaspoon coarse salt

¼ teaspoon cayenne

Yogurt, Garlic and Mint Sauce

1 cup plain low-fat or nonfat yogurt

2 tablespoons finely chopped fresh mint, or more to taste

1 garlic clove, grated

½ teaspoon grated peeled fresh ginger

1 Place a large baking sheet in the oven and preheat to 450°F for 10 minutes.

2 Toss the potatoes, oil, curry powder, salt and cayenne in a large bowl. Carefully remove the hot pan from the oven and spread the potatoes, skin sides down, in a single layer on the pan. Scrape the seasoned oil from the sides of the bowl with a rubber spatula and drizzle on top of the potatoes. Roast for 15 minutes. Turn the potatoes with a wide spatula and roast until golden brown and tender, 10 to 15 minutes more. Transfer to a shallow serving bowl.

3 Meanwhile, make the sauce: Combine the yogurt, mint, garlic and ginger in a small bowl and stir to blend. Spoon the sauce over the hot potatoes or serve a mound of sauce on each plate and dip the potatoes into the sauce with every bite.

Variations

Another way to serve this dish is to halve the potatoes lengthwise and roast, cut sides down, until tender, about 30 minutes. Serve 1 potato per person as a center-of-the-plate entrée or serve ½ potato per person as a side dish. Spoon the sauce on top.

Substitutions

Substitute ¼ cup finely chopped fresh cilantro for the mint.

BLISTERED CHERRY TOMATOES
WITH BALSAMIC Vegan

When tomatoes are out of season, I depend on these tiny gems. They are always light-years away from mealy, flavor-deprived regular winter tomatoes. This versatile recipe produces a chunky, almost saucelike mixture suitable for serving as a side dish or as a topping for roasted vegetables, potatoes, polenta, rice or pasta. Have a lid nearby when searing the tomatoes to help contain some of the splatter and keep the top of the stove fairly clean.

Cook Time: 5 minutes
Serves: 2 to 4

- 2 tablespoons extra-virgin olive oil
- 1 pint cherry or grape tomatoes, stems removed
- 1 garlic clove, grated
- 2 teaspoons balsamic vinegar, or more to taste

Make a Meal

Serve with Lentil and Shiitake Ragout with Green Beans (page 124) or Garlicky Toasted Buckwheat with Green Beans, Dill and Walnuts (page 221).

1 Heat a large heavy skillet or wok until it is hot enough to sizzle and evaporate a drop of water. Add the oil and tilt the pan to coat. Add the tomatoes and cook over medium-high heat, adjusting the heat to maintain a steady sizzle, stirring and shaking the skillet, until the tomato skins blister and crack, 3 to 5 minutes.

2 Stir in the garlic and cook for 30 seconds. Add the balsamic vinegar and remove from the heat. Spoon into a serving dish.

Variation

Curried Blistered Cherry Tomatoes: Omit the balsamic vinegar and add 1 teaspoon grated peeled fresh ginger and 1 teaspoon Madras curry powder with the garlic in step 2.

WHOLE-ROASTED TOMATOES WITH WARM GOAT CHEESE

Baked tomatoes make a pretty side dish, especially at the height of summer. This version is really easy—no stuffing, just goat cheese crumbled on top and warmed in the oven.

Cook Time: 25 minutes
Serves: 4 to 6

4–6 medium ripe tomatoes
1½ teaspoons chopped fresh thyme
   Coarse salt and freshly ground black pepper
5 ounces cold fresh goat cheese, crumbled
1 teaspoon grated orange zest
4–6 teaspoons extra-virgin olive oil

Make a Meal

Serve with Corn Sauté with Jalapeño and Cilantro (page 189) and Toasted Bulgur Pilaf with Cumin, Dried Fruit and Crispy Shallots (page 222).

1 Preheat the oven to 400°F. Cut a ¼- to ½-inch slice from the top of each of the tomatoes and reserve for another use. Hold the tomatoes, cut side down, over a fine-mesh strainer set over a small bowl and gently squeeze to remove excess juice and some of the seeds. Reserve the juice. Cut a thin sliver from the rounded bottoms so the tomatoes will stand without rolling around.

2 Arrange the tomatoes in a shallow baking dish large enough to hold them in a single layer. Sprinkle with ¾ teaspoon of the thyme, dividing it evenly, then sprinkle each with a pinch of salt and a grinding of black pepper.

3 Combine the goat cheese, the remaining ¾ teaspoon thyme, the orange zest and a generous grinding of black pepper in a small bowl and mash together with a fork. Divide the cheese mixture evenly among the tomatoes. Drizzle each with 1 teaspoon oil. Pour the reserved tomato juice into the baking dish.

4 Roast the tomatoes until they are softened and the tops are lightly browned, about 25 minutes. Serve hot or at room temperature.

Substitutions

- Use a mixture of different heirloom tomato varieties.
- Substitute a mild French feta for the goat cheese.
- Substitute fresh basil, mint or dill for the thyme.

BLISTERED PLUM TOMATOES WITH BUBBLY CHEESE

Plum tomatoes seared in a hot skillet soften and exude their juices, which caramelize into a luscious sauce. I like to serve this sumptuous dish on thick slices of toasted whole-grain bread, but it is also delicious served on a bed of lentils, rice or other grain. For best flavor, wait for ripe summer plum tomatoes. Almost any melty cheese works here, with mozzarella, Comté, Italian fontina and Manchego among my favorites.

Cook Time: 20 minutes
Serves: 4

- 2 tablespoons extra-virgin olive oil
- 2 pounds (about 8) large ripe plum tomatoes, halved lengthwise
- ½ teaspoon sugar (optional)
- ½ teaspoon coarse salt
  Freshly ground black pepper
- 2 tablespoons chopped fresh Italian parsley
- 1 garlic clove
- 4 ounces mozzarella, Comté, Gruyère, Italian fontina or Manchego cheese, shredded (about 1 cup)
- 4 thick slices whole-grain bread, toasted, grilled or broiled

Make a Meal

Serve with Green and Yellow Wax Beans with Almond Pesto (page 165) or Twice-Cooked Broccoli Rabe with Red Pepper and Garlic Oil (page 179) or Swiss Chard with Fragrant Garlic and Salt (page 186).

1 Heat a large skillet until it is hot enough to sizzle and evaporate a drop of water. Add the oil. Arrange the tomatoes, cut sides down, tightly in the pan in a single layer. Cook the tomatoes, uncovered, over medium heat until the undersides begin to brown, about 15 minutes.

2 Carefully turn the tomatoes with a wide spatula. Sprinkle each tomato with a few grains of sugar (if using), the salt and a generous grinding of black pepper. Finely chop the parsley and garlic together and sprinkle on the tomatoes.

3 Mound about 1 tablespoon of the cheese on top of each tomato. Cover the skillet and cook over medium-low heat until the cheese is melted, about 2 minutes.

4 Place the hot toasted bread on four plates and scoop the tomatoes on top of each, dividing them evenly. Spoon any juices left in the skillet over the tomatoes and serve.

Substitutions

Omit the bread and serve the cheese-topped tomatoes as a side dish.

APPLE-GLAZED ACORN SQUASH   Vegan

Perfect for fall meals, this easy-to-make skillet-cooked squash will quickly become a favorite. The skins of many varieties of winter squash soften when cooked, making them edible. No peeling is a boon for the cook in a hurry. Cooking narrow wedges in a skillet over direct heat is another time-saving technique for this typically long-cooking hard squash.

Cook Time: 15 minutes
Serves: 4

- 1   **teaspoon ground cinnamon**
- 1   **teaspoon coarse salt**
- ¼   **teaspoon freshly ground black pepper**
- 1   **tablespoon extra-virgin olive oil**
- 1   **small acorn squash (about 1½ pounds), halved, seeded and cut into 1-inch-thick wedges**
- 1   **cup unsweetened apple juice**
- 4   **lemon wedges**

Make a Meal

Serve with Chickpeas, Braised Kale and Golden Onions with Tomato, Dill and Black Olive Salsa (page 236; omit the salsa) or Bulgur with Currants, Dill, Mint and Lemon (page 214) and Broccoli and Red Onion Stir-Fry with Tamari Walnuts (page 175).

1 Combine the cinnamon, salt and pepper in a small bowl.

2 Heat a large skillet until it is hot enough to sizzle and evaporate a drop of water. Add the oil and tilt the pan to coat. Add the squash in a single layer and sprinkle with half of the spice mixture. Cook, uncovered, over medium-high heat until browned on the bottoms, about 3 minutes.

3 Turn the squash with a wide spatula and sprinkle with the remaining spice mixture. Cook until browned on the other sides, about 3 minutes.

4 Add the apple juice and cook, covered, adjusting the heat as needed, until the squash is tender and the apple juice is reduced and thickened, about 10 minutes.

5 Transfer to a serving dish. Spoon any thickened juices left in the pan over the squash. Serve with the lemon wedges.

Substitutions

- Substitute 1 teaspoon ground cumin for the cinnamon.
- Serve with lime wedges instead of lemon.
- Substitute butternut squash for the acorn, cutting it into ½-inch-thick rounds and then removing the seeds.

ROASTED BUTTERNUT SQUASH WITH NUTMEG AND MANCHEGO CHEESE

The nutty taste of butternut squash is the perfect match for Manchego, a sheep's-milk cheese for which Spain is famous.

Cook Time: 25 minutes
Serves: 4

- 1 butternut squash (about 1½ pounds), scrubbed
- 3 tablespoons extra-virgin olive oil
- ½ teaspoon ground nutmeg
- ½ teaspoon coarse salt
- ⅛ teaspoon freshly ground black pepper
- 1 cup shredded Manchego, Comté, Gruyère, cheddar or other good melting cheese

1 Place a baking sheet in the oven and preheat to 450°F for 10 minutes.

2 Cut off the stem end of the squash and halve the squash lengthwise. Remove and discard any seeds. Cut crosswise into ½-inch-thick slices.

3 Toss the squash, oil, nutmeg, salt and pepper in a large bowl.

4 Carefully remove the hot pan from the oven and spread the squash in a single layer on the pan. Roast for 10 minutes. Turn the slices over with a wide spatula and roast until browned and tender, about 10 minutes more.

5 Remove the pan from the oven and carefully sprinkle the cheese on top of the squash. Return to the oven and roast until the cheese is melted, about 3 minutes more. Transfer to a serving platter.

Make a Meal

Serve with Curried Potato, Shiitake and Broccoli Stir-Fry (page 126) or Bulgur with Garlic and Toasted Almonds (page 214) and Swiss Chard with Fragrant Garlic and Salt (page 186).

SUMMER STEW OF ZUCCHINI, TOMATOES, CORN AND BASIL   Vegan

To this version of a side dish my mother made every summer, I've added fresh corn and lots of fresh basil to capture the taste of the season.

Cook Time: 25 minutes
Serves: 4 to 6

- 2 tablespoons extra-virgin olive oil
- 2 cups diced (½ inch) onions
- ½ cup ½-inch pieces celery
- 2 garlic cloves, grated
  Pinch of crushed red pepper
- 2 cups coarsely chopped ripe fresh tomatoes or 1 can (14.5 ounces) diced tomatoes with juice
- 2 cups ½-inch pieces zucchini (about 10 ounces)
- ½ teaspoon coarse salt, or more to taste
  Freshly ground black pepper
- 1 cup fresh corn kernels (from 1–2 ears)
- 1 tablespoon red wine vinegar
- ¼ cup chopped fresh basil

1   Heat the oil in a large saucepan or Dutch oven until hot enough to sizzle a piece of onion. Add the onions and celery and cook, stirring, over medium-low heat until tender and pale golden, about 10 minutes. Do not brown.

2   Add the garlic and crushed red pepper and cook for 1 minute. Add the tomatoes, zucchini, salt and a generous grinding of black pepper. Bring to a boil. Reduce the heat to low and cook, covered, until the vegetables are very tender, about 10 minutes.

3   Add the corn and cook, stirring, over medium heat to reduce the excess juices, about 5 minutes. Add the vinegar. Taste and correct the seasonings with salt and pepper. Add the basil before serving. Serve hot, at room temperature or chilled.

Make a Meal

Serve with Roasted Potato Slabs with Romesco Sauce (page 202; omit the Romesco Sauce) and Warm Green Bean and Hard-Cooked Egg Salad with Mint (see Variations, page 67).

BROILED SUMMER SQUASH WITH VINAIGRETTE, DILL AND GOAT CHEESE

The wide variety of shapes and sizes and bright shades of yellow and green make summer squash an attractive choice. Perk up their neutral taste with a zingy vinaigrette and a sprinkling of goat cheese warmed and softened under the broiler.

Cook Time: 10 minutes
Serves: 4

- 4 young summer squash, such as green or yellow zucchini, pattypan squash, crookneck yellow or a combination, halved lengthwise
- 3 tablespoons extra-virgin olive oil
- Coarse salt and freshly ground black pepper
- 1 tablespoon red wine vinegar
- 1 garlic clove, grated
- 1 tablespoon finely chopped fresh dill
- 1 tablespoon finely chopped fresh chives or green scallion tops
- 1 ounce cold fresh goat cheese, crumbled (3–4 tablespoons)

Make a Meal

Serve with Middle Eastern Bread Salad (page 64) or Summer Tomato and Olive Bread Salad (page 71) and Warm Green Bean and Red Onion Salad with Mint (see Variations, page 67).

1 Arrange the top oven rack so that the squash will be about 4 inches from the broiler. Preheat the broiler.

2 Place the squash, cut sides up, on a baking sheet. Lightly brush both the tops and bottoms of the squash with 1 tablespoon of the oil. Sprinkle the cut sides with salt and a grinding of black pepper. Broil until lightly browned, about 3 minutes. Turn the squash over with a wide spatula and broil until the other sides are browned, about 3 minutes more. Remove the pan from the oven.

3 Meanwhile, whisk the remaining 2 tablespoons oil, the vinegar, garlic, ¼ teaspoon salt and a grinding of black pepper until blended. Arrange the squash cut sides up. Sprinkle each squash half with some of the dill and chives. Use a teaspoon to evenly drizzle the vinaigrette on top of the squash. Top each with some of the goat cheese, dividing it evenly.

4 Broil until the cheese is softened and beginning to turn golden, about 2 minutes. Serve warm or at room temperature.

Grains and Beans That Make a Meal

Every day I happily dig into a deep—and much too full—drawer in my kitchen in search of the grain or bean of the day. These staples are so versatile that I could easily come up with a different dish for every meal seven days a week, fifty-two weeks a year.

This chapter touches on the basics and offers some quick and easy recipes to pair with soups, salads and vegetable dishes to make a filling and satisfying vegetarian meal.

QUICK HITS

With a few staples on hand, a batch of basic bulgur, quinoa, farro, rice or couscous quickly becomes an interesting side dish. Here are a few ideas to get you started.

Garlic and Toasted Almonds

Cook the grain in 2 tablespoons olive oil over low heat with 2 grated garlic cloves for 1 to 2 minutes. Add the required water and a cinnamon stick and cook according to the basic instructions for the grain you are using. Top with toasted chopped or sliced almonds.

Dried Fruit and Golden Onion

Cook ½ cup chopped onion in 2 tablespoons olive oil over medium-low heat until golden, about 5 minutes. Add the grain and a handful of chopped figs, dates, dried cherries or dried apricots and cook according to the basic instructions for the grain you are using. Top with toasted chopped walnuts.

Currants with Dill, Mint and Lemon

Add a handful of dried currants to the grain when adding the required water and cook according to the basic instructions for the grain you are using. Top the cooked dish with 2 tablespoons each finely chopped fresh mint and dill and a squirt of lemon juice.

Peanut and Curry Pilaf

Cook ½ cup chopped onion in 2 tablespoons olive oil over medium-low heat until golden, about 5 minutes. Add 2 teaspoons Madras curry powder and a cinnamon stick and cook for 1 minute. Add the grain and the required water and cook according to the basic instructions for the grain you are using. Top with chopped dry-roasted unsalted peanuts.

Cranberries and Pistachios

Add a handful of dried cranberries to the grain and cook according to the basic instructions for the grain you are using. Top with a handful of toasted unsalted pistachios and 2 tablespoons thin-sliced scallion greens. Or substitute walnuts for the pistachios and drizzle the grain with 1 tablespoon walnut oil.

Pilaf with Crisp Brown Onions

Cook the grain in 1 tablespoon olive oil over medium-low heat until it becomes a shade darker. Cook according to the basic instructions for the grain you are using. Cook 1 cup thin lengthwise slices onion in ¼ cup olive oil over medium-low heat until dark golden brown, 8 to 10 minutes. Drain and spoon the onion on top of the grain.

BUCKWHEAT OR KASHA

Buckwheat, a grass related to rhubarb, is called kasha when toasted. The untoasted buckwheat groats have a mild taste, while kasha has a more pronounced flavor. Typically, buckwheat and kasha are mixed with an egg or egg white to keep the grains separate as they cook. I prefer to heat the grain in olive oil for about 5 minutes, or until lightly toasted.

Basic Preparation

Sauté 1 cup buckwheat or kasha in 2 tablespoons olive oil over medium-low heat, stirring, until lightly toasted, about 5 minutes. Add 2 cups water and 1 teaspoon coarse salt and cook, covered, over medium heat, without stirring, for 10 minutes.

BULGUR

Bulgur is among the quickest-cooking of all whole grains. It is made from boiled, dried, cracked and partially cooked whole wheat kernels. Usually sold in bulk, it is available in three textures: fine, medium and coarse. I prefer the medium or coarse grains because they retain their chewy texture and pleasant consistency when cooked.

Basic Preparation

To toast Toasting the bulgur before adding the water is optional, but intensifies its nutty taste. Preheat the oven to 350°F. Spread 1 cup medium- or coarse-grain bulgur in a 13-by-9-inch baking pan or on a rimmed baking sheet and bake, stirring once, until lightly toasted, about 10 minutes. Or heat a large skillet until it is hot enough to sizzle and evaporate a drop of water. Add 1 tablespoon extra-virgin olive oil (optional) and the bulgur. Toast, stirring frequently, adjusting the heat between medium and medium-high, until the bulgur becomes a shade darker, about 5 minutes. Then proceed with the soaking or direct-heat instructions.

To soak in boiling water Place 1 cup medium- or coarse-grain bulgur (toasted or untoasted) in a medium bowl. Add 1¼ cups boiling water for medium and 1½ cups boiling water for coarse, 1 tablespoon extra-virgin olive oil (optional) and ½ teaspoon coarse salt; stir. Let stand, tightly covered, until the water is absorbed and the bulgur is fluffy, about 20 minutes. Coarse-grain bulgur may take up to 10 minutes longer. Taste the bulgur. If the consistency and chew is to your liking, it is ready. If you prefer a softer texture, let stand for 10 minutes longer. If the bulgur has not absorbed all the water, transfer it to a fine-mesh strainer and press down with the back of a spoon to extract the excess moisture. (Fine-grain bulgur needs equal parts bulgur to water and softens in 10 minutes.)

Bulgur	Boiling Water	Soaking Time (minutes)
1 cup coarse-grain	1½ cups	30
1 cup medium-grain	1¼ cups	20
1 cup fine-grain	1 cup	10

To cook over direct heat Combine 2 cups water and ½ teaspoon coarse salt in a saucepan and bring to a boil. Stir in 1½ cups medium- or coarse-grain bulgur (toasted or untoasted). Cook, covered, over medium-low heat until the water is absorbed, about 10 minutes. Let stand off the heat for 5 minutes. If the bulgur is cooked to your liking but still watery, drain in a fine-mesh strainer and press down with the back of a spoon to extract the excess moisture.

To cook pilaf-style Heat 2 tablespoons extra-virgin olive oil in a medium skillet. Add ½ to 1 cup chopped onion and cook over medium heat, stirring, until the onion is golden, about 5 minutes. Add 1½ cups medium- or coarse-grain bulgur and 1 grated garlic clove (optional) and stir to heat and coat the bulgur with the oil. Add 2 cups water and ½ to 1 teaspoon coarse salt and bring to a boil. Cook, covered, over low heat until the water is absorbed, about 10 minutes. Let stand, covered, off the heat for 5 minutes.

COUSCOUS

Although we think of couscous as a grain, it is a pasta made from durum wheat semolina mixed with water and salt and rubbed into tiny pellets. (The larger pellets are called Israeli couscous.) Traditionally, couscous, a Moroccan specialty, is steamed over boiling water in a specially designed pot called a couscousière. The package directions on the couscous available in our markets tell us to simply soak it in boiling water until all the water is absorbed. The problem with this method is that it reconstitutes the couscous but doesn't really cook it. The result is raw-tasting. My solution is to heat the couscous in boiling water for a few minutes and then let it stand in the boiling water until all the water is absorbed. This brief cooking creates a slightly lighter, fluffier couscous.

Basic Preparation

Couscous Stir 1 cup whole wheat couscous and ½ teaspoon coarse salt into 2 cups boiling water and cook for 2 minutes. Let stand, covered, off the heat for 10 minutes, or until all the water is absorbed. Fluff with a fork. Do not stir.

Israeli Couscous Cook in a specific measurement of water (see the package directions). Or cook

it like pasta in plenty of boiling salted water until tender, 10 to 15 minutes. Drain and toss with olive oil that has been heated with 1 grated garlic clove until sizzling or with chopped onion that has been slowly cooked in olive oil until golden. For Sources, see page 239.

FARRO

Farro, or emmer wheat, is a round, chewy fat grain with a mild flavor reminiscent of barley. It is excellent in soup or salads, as a side dish or as a main and is especially satisfying with a vegetable or bean sauce. Imported from Italy, farro is available in many upscale markets, specialty markets and health food stores and is more expensive than other grains. For Sources, see page 239.

Basic Preparation

Cook farro in plenty of boiling salted water, like pasta. If the label reads "semi perlato," or pearled, most of the bran has been removed, and the grain will cook in 20 to 30 minutes. To be on the safe side, begin tasting after 15 minutes of cooking. 1 cup dry farro yields about 3 cups cooked.

QUINOA

Quinoa (pronounced "keen-wah") is often lumped in with grains, but botanically it's more closely related to beets and spinach than to wheat or other grains. Native to South America, quinoa was considered the "mother grain" by the Incas. An excellent source of protein, these tiny beads are quick-cooking and a boon to the vegetarian kitchen. They are tasty, with a pleasant, nutty flavor and a great little crunch. Quinoa comes in tan, red and black varieties, with the tan and red being most prevalent.

Red quinoa is the same as the tan except for its rusty brown outer layer and slightly earthier taste. Preparation—rinsing and cooking—is the same as for the tan. You can use the two colors interchangeably in recipes or use half tan and half red for an interesting contrast. Found mostly in upscale markets and health food stores, red quinoa is sold either in bulk or in 12-ounce boxes.

For Sources, see page 239.

Basic Preparation

To rinse Unlike other grains, quinoa must be rinsed to remove saponin, the naturally occurring bitter-tasting compound that protects it from being devoured by birds. Place the quinoa in a fine-mesh strainer and rinse under cold running water for at least 45 seconds. (To save water, swish the quinoa in a bowl of water instead of using the running water. Shake in a strainer to remove as much water as possible.) Do not skip this step.

To toast (optional) The nutty taste of quinoa is intensified by toasting it before cooking. Preheat the oven to 350°F. Spread a thin layer of the rinsed and drained quinoa (it's OK if it's damp) in a 13-by-9-inch baking pan or on a rimmed baking sheet and bake, stirring once to encourage even toasting, 15 to 20 minutes. Alternatively, the quinoa can be toasted in a hot skillet: Heat 1 tablespoon olive oil (optional) in a large skillet. Add the quinoa and heat, stirring, over medium to medium-low heat until it becomes a shade darker, about 10 minutes. I often rinse and toast

a big batch so it is ready to go whenever I'm ready to cook it. Stored in a zip-top plastic bag, it keeps for 3 months or more.

To cook Cook the rinsed and drained (and toasted, if desired) quinoa much like rice, in a large skillet using 1 part quinoa to 2 parts water. For a crunchier texture, you can use less water, but I prefer quinoa soft and fluffy. Like rice, quinoa should never be stirred during cooking, or it will turn gummy. Add the water and salt to taste to the quinoa and bring to a boil. Cook, covered, over medium-low to low heat until all the water is absorbed and the quinoa is translucent and appears to be uncoiling, 18 to 20 minutes. (As it cooks, the germ spirals away from the endosperm and makes a ring around the grain, giving it a coiled look.)

RICE

Once upon a time, our rice choices were limited to either white or brown, but today we are fortunate to find a wide selection of rice varieties in all colors and shapes from around the world.

Chinese black rice, sold as Forbidden Rice (a registered trademark of Lotus Foods), is widely distributed in supermarkets, specialty food stores and health food stores. It is my rice of choice in recipes calling for black rice, because the slender black grains contain less sticky starch than other black rices. Cooked Forbidden Rice retains its shiny ebony color and is tender and nonsticky, making it perfect for pilafs and salads. If it is unavailable, substitute brown or red rice. For Sources, see page 239.

Bhutanese red rice, also from Lotus Foods, is a specialty grain with a red bran and a distinctive herbal taste that sets it apart from other red rice in the market. If it is not available, you can substitute other types of red or brown rice. For Sources, see page 239.

Cooking Tips

* Cook rice in a large skillet instead of a deep saucepan. The greater surface area yields more evenly cooked rice.

* A rice cooker is an excellent option. Because of the lack of standardization of models, it is best to follow the manufacturer's cooking directions.

* For soft, tender grains, cook 1 cup rice in 2 cups water.

* For grains that are separate and slightly chewy, cook 1 cup rice in 1¾ cups water.

* Never stir rice while cooking (with the exception of risotto), or it will become soft and sticky.

* For salad, rinse cooked rice to remove the sticky starch from the surface. Always use freshly cooked room-temperature or warm rice. Refrigerated rice turns hard and chewy.

* The bran on brown rice creates a barrier to the water, so it requires additional water and a longer cooking time, 45 to 55 minutes.

* Cook 1 cup long-grain brown rice in 2½ to 2¾ cups water.

* Cook 1 cup short- or medium-grain brown, black or red rice in a large pot of water (like pasta) and drain when cooked to the desired consistency.

To Shorten the Cooking Time of Brown Rice

* Place the brown rice in a deep bowl, add water to cover by about 2 inches and refrigerate for 1 to 3 days. The cooking time will be reduced by about 20 minutes. Use the water the rice is soaked in, plus more as needed, for cooking.

* Look for the excellent-quality microwaveable and vacuum-sealed packages of precooked brown rice available at select stores. Although they are expensive, some cook in less than 5 minutes—a real time-saver.

* Because their bran is more porous, some black or red rices cook in less time than brown rice.

BEANS

Although slow-cooking dried beans present a challenge when time is of the essence, I try not to let that deter me. When I have more time, I often soak and cook a large batch, keeping half for a quick dinner and putting the other half in the freezer for my next pot of soup. When I don't have this stash, I depend on good-quality canned beans or, in the case of black-eyed peas, bags of commercially frozen cooked beans.

Bean Basics

Canned Beans When it comes to beans, I'm not a purist. While canned beans are not more delicious than oven-baked dried beans (see below), they are quick and superconvenient. They are available in 15- to 16-ounce cans with a volume of about 1¾ cups. Try different brands to find the one with the texture and flavor you prefer. Beans are best when they are firm and whole, not mushy and broken. Before using canned beans, empty the can into a fine-mesh strainer and rinse with water to get rid of the brine. For me, it is too salty and tastes "canned."

Oven-Baked Dried Beans   When you have more time and you're game for an excellent, if slow technique, this oven-bake method is the way to go. The low heat of the oven allows the beans to cook slowly in gently simmering, never aggressively boiling, liquid that coaxes the beans to a creamy softness. This method avoids the fluctuation in temperature encountered when a pot sits on top of the stove and the rough stirring that can mash the delicate beans as they cook. Oven-baked beans emerge firm on the outside and smooth and creamy within. They can be refrigerated for up to 5 days or frozen for later use.

Place 2 to 3 cups (about 1 pound) dried beans in a large bowl and cover with water. Soak for about 4 hours or overnight in a cool kitchen or the refrigerator. Discard the soaking liquid. Preheat the oven to 350°F. Place the beans in a deep casserole with a lid or in an enameled cast-iron pot. Add 2 or 3 garlic cloves that have been slightly crushed by pressing down on them with the side of a knife, 2 tablespoons extra-virgin olive oil, a thick slice of onion and a bay leaf or a sprig of your fresh herb of choice. Cover the beans with water or unsalted vegetable broth. (The question of when to salt beans is often debated. I prefer adding salt after the beans are cooked, but while they are still hot.) Cover the pot and place in the oven. Bake for 1 to 2 hours, checking on their progress after 1 hour. Depending on the source, some beans cook in 1 hour, while others can take up to 2 hours. You must be flexible. If the water is absorbed, add a small amount of boiling water to keep the beans moist. Do not stir, which will mash the beans.

When the beans are tender, remove them from the oven and let stand for about 30 minutes. Some of the excess liquid surrounding the beans will be absorbed as the beans cool. Any remaining cooking liquid can be strained off and reserved for soup. Add coarse salt and freshly ground black pepper to taste.

LENTILS

Tender, earthy and sweet, lentils are by far the fastest-cooking member of the legume family, making them a practical choice when you're in a hurry. No soaking is necessary. Cook lentils in twice their volume of gently boiling water (a rapid boil can turn delicate lentils mushy) until tender to the bite, usually between 15 and 25 minutes. Salt after cooking.

Lentils come in a variety of colors and sizes. I mostly cook with the dull brown lentils sold in most supermarkets, but for some dishes, I enjoy the peppery-tasting, small army-green French lentils sometimes called du Puy or the dramatic black lentils called "caviar" lentils. Because the cooking time varies with each batch, it is best to begin tasting after 15 minutes and then taste at 5-minute intervals. If the lentils become mushy, you can turn them into soup. Some markets sell vacuum-packed cooked lentils that are firm, tender and flavorful.

1 cup dried lentils yields about 3 cups cooked.

QUICK HITS FOR LENTILS

Cook a whole bag (1 pound) of lentils at once and save half for another meal, or use vacuum-packed precooked lentils if available. Here are some ideas to get you started.

Lentils and Peas Vinaigrette

Whisk ¼ cup each extra-virgin olive oil and sherry vinegar with ½ teaspoon salt and a grinding of black pepper. Toss the vinaigrette with 2 to 3 cups cooked lentils, 1 cup thawed frozen baby peas, ½ cup chopped red onion and 2 tablespoons chopped fresh mint. Serve with hard-cooked eggs (see page 14).

Tamari Lentils with Spinach

Stir 2 to 3 packed cups rinsed and drained baby spinach into 3 cups hot cooked lentils. Season with 1 to 2 tablespoons tamari or soy sauce. Garnish with Tamari Walnuts (page 14). Serve warm.

Lentils with Mushrooms and Gremolata

Cook 8 ounces (about 3 cups) chopped mushrooms (any kind) in ¼ cup extra-virgin olive oil over medium heat until golden. Add 1 grated garlic clove. Stir into 2 to 3 cups hot cooked lentils. Finely chop ¼ cup fresh Italian parsley, 1 strip (½ by 2 inches) orange zest and 1 garlic clove together and add.

Curried Lentils

Cook ½ cup chopped onion in 2 tablespoons extra-virgin olive oil over medium heat until golden. Add 2 teaspoons grated peeled fresh ginger, 2 to 3 teaspoons Madras curry powder and 1 grated garlic clove and cook for 1 minute. Stir in 3 cups hot cooked lentils and cook for 3 minutes, until warmed. Serve with plain low-fat yogurt and chopped fresh cilantro on top.

GARLICKY TOASTED BUCKWHEAT WITH GREEN BEANS, DILL AND WALNUTS Vegan

Because of its distinctive taste, kasha, or toasted buckwheat, calls out for big-flavored ingredients like olive oil, garlic and fresh dill. The green beans in this dish give it a fresh look and taste.

Cook Time: 20 minutes
Serves: 4 to 6

6 ounces green beans, cut into 1-inch pieces (about 1½ cups)

1 teaspoon coarse salt

1 tablespoon plus ¼ cup extra-virgin olive oil

1 cup kasha (toasted buckwheat) or untoasted buckwheat (see page 214)

2 garlic cloves, grated
Pinch of crushed red pepper

½ cup walnut pieces

¼ cup oil-packed sun-dried tomatoes, drained, blotted dry and slivered (about 8)

¼ cup chopped fresh dill

Make a Meal
Serve with Roasted Cauliflower, Red Bell Pepper and Red Onion with Rosemary and Garlic (page 185).

1 Bring 3 cups water to a boil in a large skillet. Add the green beans and salt and cook, uncovered, over medium heat until crisp-tender, about 5 minutes.

2 Meanwhile, heat 1 tablespoon of the oil in a small skillet. Add the buckwheat and cook, stirring, over medium-low heat until coated with oil and warmed, 2 to 3 minutes. Add the sautéed buckwheat to the pan with the beans and stir once. (Overstirring will turn the buckwheat mushy.) Cover and cook over low heat until the water is absorbed, about 10 minutes. Do not stir.

3 Meanwhile, combine the remaining ¼ cup oil, the garlic and crushed red pepper in the small skillet and cook, stirring, over low heat until the garlic begins to sizzle, 1 to 2 minutes. Add the walnuts and sun-dried tomatoes and cook until the walnuts are lightly toasted, about 2 minutes. Remove from the heat.

4 Drizzle the walnut mixture over the cooked buckwheat. Sprinkle with the dill and fluff gently with a fork; do not stir. Serve.

TOASTED BULGUR PILAF WITH CUMIN, DRIED FRUIT AND CRISPY SHALLOTS Vegan

Toasting the bulgur first in olive oil intensifies its addictive, nutty taste. The toasted flavor pairs well with the concentrated sweetness of the dried fruit.

Cook Time: 25 minutes
Serves: 4 to 6

- 1 **tablespoon plus ¼ cup extra-virgin olive oil**
- 1½ **cups medium- or coarse-grain bulgur (see page 215)**
- 2 **teaspoons ground cumin**
- ½ **cup chopped or snipped (¼ inch) dried figs or apricots**
- 1 **teaspoon coarse salt**
- 1 **cup thin-sliced shallots or small onions**
- 2 **tablespoons chopped fresh dill**
- 2 **tablespoons chopped fresh mint**
- 2 **tablespoons fresh lemon juice**

1 Heat 1 tablespoon of the oil in a large skillet. Add the bulgur and cook, stirring frequently, over medium heat until the bulgur is a shade darker, about 10 minutes. Add the cumin and cook, stirring, for 1 minute.

2 Add 2 cups water, the dried fruit and salt and bring to a boil. Cook, covered, over medium-low heat until the liquid is absorbed, about 10 minutes. Remove from the heat. Let stand, covered, for 5 minutes.

3 Meanwhile, heat the remaining ¼ cup oil in a medium skillet until it is hot enough to sizzle a slice of shallot. Add the shallots and cook, stirring, adjusting the heat to maintain a steady sizzle, until they are crisp and a deep golden brown, 6 to 8 minutes. Set a fine-mesh strainer over a heatproof bowl and strain the oil from the shallots. Reserve the oil for another use.

4 Spoon the cooked bulgur into a serving bowl. Sprinkle with the dill, mint and lemon juice and fluff with a fork. Spoon the shallots on top and serve at once.

Shortcut

Cutting dried fruits can be a sticky business, but not when you oil the cutting implement. Spray or brush kitchen scissors or the blade of your food processor with vegetable oil and snip or chop the fruit into small pieces.

Substitutions

If you don't have dried figs or apricots on hand, substitute raisins.

BULGUR AND DATE PILAF WITH PECANS AND PARMIGIANO-REGGIANO

Nutty bulgur is well balanced here by the sweetness of the dried dates and the salty, rich taste of Parmigiano-Reggiano.

Cook Time: 30 minutes
Serves: 4

- ½ cup pecan pieces
- 2 tablespoons extra-virgin olive oil
- ½ cup chopped onion
- 1½ cups medium- or coarse-grain bulgur (see page 215)
- ½ cup chopped or snipped (¼ inch) pitted dates
- 1 garlic clove, grated
- ½ teaspoon coarse salt
- ¼ cup grated Parmigiano-Reggiano, or more to taste

Make a Meal

Serve with Twice-Cooked Broccoli Rabe with Red Pepper and Garlic Oil (page 179) and Apple-Glazed Acorn Squash (page 209) or Carrots with Moroccan Spices and Lemon (page 182).

1 Spread the pecans in a small skillet and toast, stirring, over medium heat until slightly darker in color, about 5 minutes. Set aside.

2 Heat the oil in a large skillet until it is hot enough to sizzle a bit of onion. Add the onion and cook, stirring, over medium-low heat until golden, about 5 minutes. Add the bulgur and cook, stirring, until toasted, about 5 minutes. Add the dates and garlic and cook, stirring, for 1 minute.

3 Add 2 cups water and the salt and bring to a boil. Cover and cook over medium-low heat until all the water is absorbed, about 10 minutes. Remove from the heat. Let stand, covered, for 5 minutes. Add half of the cheese, fluff with a fork and transfer to a serving dish. Sprinkle the pecans and the remaining grated cheese on top.

ISRAELI COUSCOUS WITH WILTED SPINACH, TOASTED PINE NUTS AND PARMIGIANO-REGGIANO

Pine nuts, toasted to a rich golden brown, give this dish a distinctive taste. Make the couscous with or without the spinach. It works well simply as couscous with pine nuts and cheese.

Cook Time: 25 minutes
Serves: 4

   2 tablespoons extra-virgin olive oil
   ¼ cup pine nuts
   1½ cups Israeli couscous (see page 216)
   1 garlic clove, grated
   1 teaspoon coarse salt
   6 ounces spinach, coarsely chopped (about 4 cups packed)
   ¼ cup grated Parmigiano-Reggiano
   1 tablespoon fresh lemon juice

Make a Meal

Serve with Leek and Potato Soup with Roasted Cauliflower (page 34) and Stewed Red Bell Peppers and Tomatoes (page 173).

1 Heat the oil in a large skillet. Add the pine nuts and cook, stirring, over medium-low heat until golden brown, about 2 minutes. With a slotted spoon, remove the pine nuts to a small bowl and set aside.

2 Add the couscous to the oil left in the pan and cook, stirring, until golden brown, 2 to 3 minutes. Add the garlic and stir to combine. Add 2 cups water and the salt and cook, covered, over medium-low heat until the water is absorbed, about 15 minutes.

3 Add the spinach and stir to combine. Cover and cook until the spinach is wilted, about 3 minutes. Add the cheese and toss with a fork. Sprinkle with the lemon juice and toasted pine nuts and serve.

TOMATO COUSCOUS WITH CINNAMON AND RAISINS Vegan

This couscous is cooked in olive oil and seasoned with garlic, pilaf-style, before a tomato broth is added. The acid in the tomato broth slows down the cooking and adds a few extra minutes to the typical cooking time. Cinnamon and raisins add a slightly exotic flavor profile reminiscent of the Moroccan stew called tagine.

Cook Time: 25 minutes
Serves: 4

- ½ cup raisins
- 2 tablespoons tomato paste
- 1 teaspoon ground cinnamon
- 2 tablespoons extra-virgin olive oil
- 1¼ cups whole wheat couscous (see page 216)
- 1 garlic clove, grated
- 1 teaspoon coarse salt

1 Combine the raisins, tomato paste and cinnamon in a small saucepan. Add 2¼ cups water and bring to a boil, stirring. Set aside off the heat.

2 Heat the oil in a large skillet. Add the couscous and cook, stirring, over medium-low heat until the couscous is lightly toasted, about 3 minutes. Add the garlic and stir to combine.

3 Add the tomato broth and the salt to the couscous and cook, covered, over low heat until all the water is absorbed and the couscous is softened, about 15 minutes. Remove from the heat. Let stand, covered, for 5 minutes. Fluff with a fork and serve.

Make a Meal
Serve with Winter Vegetable Stew with Moroccan Flavors (page 136).

FARRO WITH BASIL AND PARSLEY PESTO

The mild, sweet taste and slight chewiness of farro make it the perfect companion to the zesty flavors in this pesto made with half parsley and half basil.

Cook Time: 20 minutes
Serves: 4 to 6

- 1 cup farro (see page 216)
- 2 teaspoons coarse salt

Basil and Parsley Pesto

- ¼ cup walnut pieces
- 1 garlic clove, coarsely chopped
- ½ teaspoon coarse salt
- 1 cup loosely packed torn fresh basil leaves
- 1 cup loosely packed fresh Italian parsley leaves, including tender stems
- ¼ cup extra-virgin olive oil
- 2 tablespoons grated Parmigiano-Reggiano

- ¼ cup walnut pieces
- 2 tablespoons grated Parmigiano-Reggiano

Make a Meal

Serve with Blistered Plum Tomatoes with Bubbly Cheese (page 208) or Blistered Cherry Tomatoes with Balsamic (page 206) and Swiss Chard with Fragrant Garlic and Salt (page 186).

1 Bring a large pot of water to a boil. Add the farro and salt and cook, stirring, until the farro is tender but still has a slight bite, 15 to 20 minutes. Drain and return the farro to the cooking pot, off the heat.

2 Meanwhile, to make the pesto by hand: Combine the walnuts, garlic and salt in a mortar and pound into a paste with the pestle. Add the basil and parsley about ½ cup at a time, pounding until reduced to a coarse paste after each addition. Gradually add the oil, 1 tablespoon at a time, stirring with the pestle after each addition. Stir in the cheese. To make the pesto in a food processor: Combine the walnuts, garlic, salt, basil and parsley and finely chop. With the motor running, add the oil in a slow, steady stream until blended to a rough puree. Transfer to a bowl and stir in the cheese. You should have ½ cup pesto.

3 Add the pesto to the hot farro and stir to blend. Spoon into a serving dish and sprinkle with the walnuts and grated cheese.

Substitutions

Substitute orzo or another small pasta or short-grain brown rice for the farro.

EASY STOVETOP POLENTA Vegan (omit the cheese)

Polenta—comforting and warming—is a terrific winter food. I especially like it as the focal point of our Sunday evening suppers, when I entertain friends. I make polenta in a variety of ways (see pages 145, 146 and 148), but this method from my friend Kathleen O'Neill is the one I use most often. For best results, cook the polenta on the lowest possible heat (a heat diffuser or "flame tamer" is useful) in a heavy enameled cast-iron Dutch oven or other heavy pot.

Cook Time: 25 minutes
Serves: 4

- 1½ cups coarse-ground polenta or cornmeal
- 2 teaspoons coarse salt
- 2 tablespoons extra-virgin olive oil
- ¼ cup grated Parmigiano-Reggiano (optional)
- Freshly ground black pepper

Make a Meal

Top with Twice-Cooked Broccoli Rabe with Red Pepper and Garlic Oil (page 179) or Three-Mushroom Ragu (page 146).

1 Bring 3 cups water to a boil in a heavy 5- to 8-quart pot. Meanwhile, whisk the polenta with 2 cups water in a bowl. When the water boils, whisk in the wet polenta mixture. (This step helps to prevent lumps.) Add the salt.

2 Using a slotted spoon or a heavy wire whisk, stir the polenta over medium-low heat until it boils. Reduce the heat to very low, cover and cook, stirring occasionally and adjusting the heat to prevent scorching or sticking, until the polenta is very thick and smooth, 20 to 25 minutes. Keep some hot water handy and whisk small amounts into the polenta if it becomes too thick before the cooking time has elapsed. The desired thickness is a matter of your personal taste—some people like it loose, while others like it thick. Either way, it is important that the polenta is thoroughly cooked.

3 Whisk in the oil and the Parmigiano-Reggiano, if using. Taste and add a generous grinding of black pepper. Keep warm until ready to serve.

QUINOA PILAF WITH APPLES AND CURRIED WALNUTS Vegan

Quinoa is the perfect canvas for the spicy sweetness of Madras curry powder. For optimal taste and texture, I use both dried and fresh apples and top the finished pilaf with a sprinkling of toasted curried walnuts.

Cook Time: 35 minutes
Serves: 4 to 6

- 1½ cups quinoa (see page 216)
- 2 tablespoons extra-virgin olive oil
- ½ cup chopped onion
- 2 teaspoons Madras curry powder
- 1 garlic clove, grated
- 1 teaspoon grated peeled fresh ginger
- ½ cup snipped (¼ inch) dried apple
- ½ cup chopped peeled apple (from 1 small apple)
- ¼ cup golden or dark raisins (optional)
- 1 cinnamon stick
- 1 teaspoon coarse salt
- ½ cup walnut pieces
- 1 tablespoon chopped fresh cilantro
- 1 tablespoon fresh lemon juice

Make a Meal

Serve with Okra with Tomato-Ginger Sauce (page 201) and Roasted Cauliflower "Steaks" (page 184) and/or Roasted Sweet Potato Slices with Coriander and Lemon Dressing (page 203).

1 Place the quinoa in a fine-mesh strainer and rinse under cold running water for at least 45 seconds. Shake the strainer to remove as much water as possible.

2 Heat 1 tablespoon of the oil in a large skillet until it is hot enough to sizzle a piece of onion. Add the onion and cook, stirring, over medium heat until softened, about 5 minutes. Add the damp quinoa and cook, stirring, over medium heat until the onion and quinoa are golden, 8 to 10 minutes.

3 Add 1 teaspoon of the curry powder, the garlic and ginger and cook, stirring, for 1 minute. Add 3 cups water, the dried and fresh apples, the raisins (if using), cinnamon stick and salt and bring to a boil. Reduce the heat to medium-low and cook, covered, until the water is absorbed and the quinoa is fluffy and has begun to uncoil, 18 to 20 minutes.

4 Meanwhile, heat the remaining 1 tablespoon oil, the remaining 1 teaspoon curry powder and the walnuts in a small skillet over medium-low heat, stirring, until the nuts are coated with curry and turn a shade darker, about 5 minutes.

5 Sprinkle the curried nuts, cilantro and lemon juice over the quinoa and fluff with a fork. Serve.

RED QUINOA WITH TOASTED HAZELNUTS AND HAZELNUT OIL Vegan

Rich and fragrant, hazelnuts and hazelnut oil are a perfect match for earthy-tasting red quinoa. The red hull on the tiny quinoa beads adds a pleasant chewiness to each spoonful.

Cook Time: 30 minutes
Serves: 4

1 cup red or tan quinoa (see page 216)

1 tablespoon extra-virgin olive oil

1 garlic clove, grated

¼ cup dried currants or raisins

1 teaspoon coarse salt

2 tablespoons hazelnut oil

½ cup chopped toasted and peeled hazelnuts

2 scallions (white and green parts), cut into thin slices

1 tablespoon fresh lime or lemon juice

1 Place the quinoa in a fine-mesh strainer and rinse under cold running water for at least 45 seconds. Shake the strainer to remove as much water as possible.

2 Heat the oil in a large skillet. Add the damp quinoa and cook, stirring, over medium heat until it dries out and smells toasted, 6 to 8 minutes. Add the garlic and cook for 1 minute.

3 Add 2 cups water, the currants and salt and bring to a boil. Cook, covered, until the water is absorbed and the quinoa is fluffy and has begun to uncoil, about 20 minutes. If there is still some moisture in the pan, cook, uncovered, over medium heat to evaporate. Do not stir.

4 When the quinoa is cooked, drizzle with the hazelnut oil and fluff with a fork to combine. Spoon into a serving dish and sprinkle with the hazelnuts, scallions and lime juice.

Make a Meal

This simple pilaf is delicious served with Twice-Cooked Green Beans with Curried Pecans (page 164; omit the curried pecans) or Roasted Asparagus with Parmigiano-Reggiano Crumbs (page 163) and Curried Corn with Sugar Snap Peas and Mint (page 188).

Shortcuts

- For speed and convenience, look for hazelnuts that are sold already toasted and peeled. If peeled but untoasted hazelnuts are available, toast them in a 350°F oven for 10 to 12 minutes or spread them in a small skillet and toast over medium heat, shaking the pan, until lightly browned, about 5 minutes.

- If only unpeeled hazelnuts are available, preheat the oven to 350°F. Spread the hazelnuts in a shallow baking pan and bake until the skins begin to crack, 10 to 12 minutes. Pour the hot nuts into a clean dish towel and rub them vigorously with the towel to remove the loosened skins. Toast and peel a double or triple batch and keep the nuts frozen for next time.

Variation

Red Quinoa with Walnuts and Walnut Oil or Almonds and Almond Oil: Substitute chopped toasted walnuts and walnut oil or toasted skin-on almonds and almond oil for the hazelnuts and hazelnut oil.

BLACK RICE PILAF WITH EDAMAME, GINGER AND TAMARI Vegan

This pretty mélange of shiny black rice, pale green edamame and carrot seasoned with fresh ginger, garlic and tamari is as pretty as it is tasty. Forbidden Rice from China (see page 217) is unique in the world of rice, and I prefer it for this recipe. If it is unavailable, substitute Bhutanese red rice (see page 218) or brown jasmine rice.

Cook Time: 25 minutes
Serves: 4

- 1 **cup Forbidden Rice (see headnote)**
- 2 **tablespoons flavorless vegetable oil**
- 2 **teaspoons grated peeled fresh ginger**
- 2 **garlic cloves, grated**
- 1 **cup frozen edamame (green soybeans)**
- ½ **cup finely chopped carrot**
- ½ **teaspoon coarse salt**
- 3 **tablespoons tamari or soy sauce**
- 2 **tablespoons finely chopped fresh cilantro**
- 1 **scallion (white and green parts), thinly sliced**

1 Bring a large saucepan three-fourths full of water to a boil. Add the rice and cook, uncovered, until the rice is tender, 20 to 25 minutes. Drain well.

2 Meanwhile, heat the oil, ginger and garlic in a large skillet over medium-low heat until they begin to sizzle, 1 to 2 minutes. Stir in the edamame, carrot and salt and cook, covered, over low heat until the vegetables are tender, about 5 minutes.

3 Add the cooked rice and tamari to the edamame mixture and cook, stirring, over low heat until heated through, about 5 minutes. Stir in 1 tablespoon of the cilantro. Spoon the rice mixture into a serving dish and top with the remaining 1 tablespoon cilantro and the scallion.

Make a Meal
Serve with Broccoli and Red Onion Stir-Fry with Tamari Walnuts (page 175) and Curried Corn with Sugar Snap Peas and Mint (page 188).

YELLOW RICE AND CARROT PILAF WITH MINT Vegan

Rice tinted golden yellow from the turmeric and flecked with bright orange carrots makes a pretty pilaf and a dramatic accompaniment to any number of vegetable side dishes.

Cook Time: 30 minutes
Serves: 4

- 2 tablespoons extra-virgin olive oil
- 1 cup chopped onion
- 1 garlic clove, grated
- 1 teaspoon grated peeled fresh ginger
- 1 teaspoon ground turmeric
- ½ teaspoon ground cumin
- 1½ cups long-grain white or basmati rice
- 1 cup finely chopped carrots (about 2 medium)
- 1 teaspoon coarse salt
- ½ cup sliced skin-on almonds
- 4 tablespoons chopped fresh mint
- 2 tablespoons fresh lemon juice

Make a Meal

Serve with Roasted Asparagus with Warm Cherry Tomatoes and Black Olives (page 161) and Warm Green Bean and Red Onion Salad with Mint (see Variations, page 67).

1 Heat the oil in a large skillet until it is hot enough to sizzle a piece of onion. Add the onion and cook, stirring, over medium heat until golden, about 10 minutes. Add the garlic, ginger, turmeric and cumin and cook, stirring, for 1 minute. Add the rice and carrots and cook, stirring, for 1 minute more.

2 Stir in 2½ cups water and the salt and bring to a boil. Cook, covered, over medium-low heat until all the water is absorbed and the rice is tender, about 15 minutes. Remove from the heat. Let the rice stand, covered, for 5 minutes.

3 Meanwhile, spread the almonds in a small skillet and toast, stirring, over low heat until golden, about 5 minutes.

4 Add ¼ cup of the almonds, 2 tablespoons of the mint and 1 tablespoon of the lemon juice to the rice and stir to combine. Spoon the rice into a serving dish and sprinkle with the remaining almonds, mint and lemon juice.

Shortcuts
- Chop the carrots quickly in a food processor.
- Look for toasted sliced skin-on almonds in your market.

SPICY RED RICE AND ORANGE PILAF Vegan

When shopping for red rice, I prefer the kind imported from Bhutan. Compared with others on the market, this rice has a distinctively herbaceous taste. The food of Bhutan is known for its use of chiles and wild herbs, inspiring me to add crushed red pepper and dill or cilantro. If Bhutanese red rice is unavailable, make this pilaf with long- or short-grain brown rice.

Cook Time: 40 minutes
Serves: 4

- 2 tablespoons extra-virgin olive oil
- ½ cup sliced scallion whites, plus ¼ cup thin-sliced green tops
- 1 tablespoon grated orange zest
- 2 teaspoons finely chopped peeled fresh ginger
- 1 garlic clove, grated
- ¼–⅛ teaspoon crushed red pepper
- 1½ cups Bhutanese red rice (see page 218)
- 1 teaspoon coarse salt
- ¼ cup chopped fresh dill or cilantro

1 Heat the oil in a large skillet until it is hot enough to sizzle a piece of scallion. Add the scallion whites, orange zest, ginger, garlic and crushed red pepper and cook, stirring, over medium-low heat until warmed, about 2 minutes.

2 Add the rice and cook, stirring, until it is coated with the seasonings, about 2 minutes. Add 2½ cups water and the salt and bring to a boil. Cook, covered, over medium-low heat until the water is absorbed and the rice is tender, 25 to 30 minutes. Remove from the heat. Let stand, covered, for 5 minutes. Sprinkle with the scallion greens and the dill or cilantro and serve.

Make a Meal

Serve with Stir-Fried Asian Greens with Crisp Golden Garlic (page 195) or Steamed Spinach with Ginger and Garlic Oil (page 196) and Oven-Roasted Mini Bell Peppers with Rosemary (page 170).

CANNELLINI WITH SAUTÉED FENNEL AND BLISTERED CHERRY TOMATOES

For this fragrant dish, use slow-cooked oven-baked cannellini beans, if you happen to have a batch ready, or use canned cannellini.

Cook Time: 30 minutes
Serves: 4 to 6

- 3 tablespoons extra-virgin olive oil
- 1 pint cherry or grape tomatoes, stems removed
- 1 teaspoon coarse salt
  Freshly ground black pepper
- 1 fennel bulb (about 1½ pounds)
- 1 garlic clove, grated
  Pinch of crushed red pepper
- 3–3½ cups cooked or canned drained and rinsed cannellini beans
- 4 tablespoons chopped fresh basil
- ½ cup grated Parmigiano-Reggiano

Make a Meal

Serve with Broccolini with Sun-Dried Tomatoes and Pine Nuts (page 178) and Broiled Eggplant Towers with Tomato, Pesto and Mozzarella (page 192).

1 Heat a medium skillet until it is hot enough to sizzle and evaporate a drop of water. Add 1 tablespoon of the oil and tilt the pan to coat. Add the tomatoes and cook, shaking the pan, over medium-high heat until they are blistered and beginning to brown, about 5 minutes. Add ½ teaspoon of the salt and a generous grinding of black pepper and set aside.

2 Meanwhile, cut a thin slice from the base of the fennel. Use a vegetable peeler to trim any bruises from the outside of the ribs. Cut off and discard the dark green stalks, but reserve enough fernlike tops to make ¼ cup chopped. Cut the fennel bulb and the white part of the stalks into ¼-inch-thick slices, then cut into ¼-inch pieces. You should have about 3 cups.

3 Heat the remaining 2 tablespoons oil in a large skillet until it is hot enough to sizzle a piece of fennel. Add the fennel, chopped fennel fronds, garlic, crushed red pepper and the remaining ½ teaspoon salt and cook, stirring, over medium heat for 5 minutes. Cover and cook over low heat until the fennel is very soft, about 15 minutes. Add the beans, blistered tomatoes, 2 tablespoons of the basil and a generous grinding of black pepper. Cook, gently folding to combine, over medium-low heat until heated through, about 5 minutes. Add ¼ cup of the grated cheese. Spoon the beans into a serving dish and top with the remaining basil and cheese.

CHICKPEAS, BRAISED KALE AND GOLDEN ONIONS WITH TOMATO, DILL AND BLACK OLIVE SALSA   Vegan

Beans and greens, a classic peasant dish, make a hearty, nutritious and flavorful meal. I prefer the mild-flavored Tuscan, or lacinato, variety, which is sometimes sold as dinosaur kale, but you can also use Swiss chard. Here I add a fresh twist to the beans and greens theme with a zesty salsa of chopped tomato, black olives and dill.

Cook Time: 25 minutes
Serves: 4

- **4 tablespoons extra-virgin olive oil**
- **1 cup thin lengthwise slices onion**
- **1 bunch (10–12 ounces) Tuscan (lacinato) kale or Swiss chard**
- **1 can (15–16 ounces) chickpeas, rinsed and drained**
- **3 tablespoons chopped fresh dill**
- **2 garlic cloves, grated**
- **1 teaspoon ground cumin**
- **½ teaspoon coarse salt**
- **Freshly ground black pepper**
- **½ cup diced firm ripe tomato**
- **3 tablespoons coarsely chopped pitted Kalamata olives**
- **1–2 tablespoons fresh lemon juice**

Make a Meal
Serve with a Grain Pilaf with Crisp Brown Onions (page 214).

1 Heat 3 tablespoons of the oil and the onion in a large skillet over medium-low heat, stirring, until the onion is limp and golden, about 10 minutes.

2 While the onion is cooking, pull the leafy parts of the kale or chard away from the ribs and tear the leaves into 2-inch pieces. Discard the ribs. Rinse the leaves in a big bowl of water and place in a colander to drain.

3 Add the chickpeas, 2 tablespoons of the dill, the garlic, cumin, salt and a generous grinding of black pepper to the onion and cook, stirring, over medium-low heat until heated through, about 5 minutes.

4 Add ½ cup water and the kale or chard and cook, covered, over medium-low heat, stirring once or twice, until wilted and tender, 5 to 10 minutes for kale and 5 minutes for chard. Transfer to a serving dish.

5 Combine the tomato, olives, the remaining 1 tablespoon dill and the remaining 1 tablespoon oil in a small bowl and stir. Spoon the salsa on top of the chickpeas and sprinkle with the lemon juice.

CUMIN BLACK BEANS WITH BLISTERED TOMATOES AND CORN Vegan

Superquick canned black beans become a tasty side dish with skillet-seared cherry tomatoes and fresh (or frozen or canned) corn kernels. Keep a lid nearby when searing the tomatoes to help contain some of the splatter. For a distinctively smoky aroma and taste, add smoked paprika, either along with or in place of the ground cumin.

Cook Time: 10 minutes
Serves: 4

- 2 tablespoons extra-virgin olive oil
- 1 cup cherry or grape tomatoes, stems removed
- 1 garlic clove, grated
- 1 teaspoon ground cumin
- ½ teaspoon smoked paprika (preferably *Pimentón de la Vera*; optional)
- 1 can (15–16 ounces) black beans, rinsed and drained
- 1 cup fresh corn kernels (from 1–2 ears), thawed frozen or canned corn
- 2 teaspoons finely chopped seeded jalapeño pepper
- ½ teaspoon coarse salt
- 1 tablespoon fresh lime juice
- 2 tablespoons finely chopped fresh cilantro

1 Heat a large skillet until it is hot enough to sizzle and evaporate a drop of water. Add the oil and tilt the pan to coat. Add the tomatoes and cook, shaking the pan, over medium-high heat until the tomatoes are blistered and beginning to brown, about 5 minutes. Reduce the heat to low.

2 Add the garlic, cumin and smoked paprika, if using, and cook, stirring, for 1 minute. Add the beans, corn, jalapeño and salt and cook, stirring, over medium-low heat until heated through, about 5 minutes. Sprinkle with the lime juice and cilantro and serve.

Make a Meal

Serve with Yellow Rice and Carrot Pilaf with Mint (page 233) and Broccoli and Red Onion Stir-Fry with Tamari Walnuts (page 175).

LENTILS WITH ROASTED RED PEPPERS, DILL, MINT AND FETA

Lentils make a splendid canvas for the bold flavors of the peppers, feta cheese and herbs in this simple recipe.

Cook Time: 30 minutes
Serves: 4

- 1 cup brown lentils
- ¼ cup extra-virgin olive oil
- 1 cup chopped onion
- 1 garlic clove, grated
- 1 jar (12 ounces) roasted red peppers, rinsed, drained and chopped (¼ inch), about 1½ cups
- ½ teaspoon coarse salt
- ¼ teaspoon freshly ground black pepper
- 4 tablespoons chopped fresh dill
- 2 tablespoons chopped fresh mint
- 1 tablespoon red wine vinegar
- ½ cup crumbled feta cheese

Make a Meal

Serve with warm hard-cooked eggs and Twice-Cooked Broccoli Rabe with Red Pepper and Garlic Oil (page 179), Steamed Spinach with Ginger and Garlic Oil (page 196) or Twice-Cooked Green Beans with Curried Pecans (page 164).

1 Cook the lentils in a large pot of gently boiling water until tender, 15 to 25 minutes. Drain.

2 While the lentils are cooking, heat the oil in a large skillet until it is hot enough to sizzle a piece of onion. Add the onion and cook, stirring, over medium-low heat until soft and golden, about 10 minutes. Add the garlic and cook for 1 minute. Stir in the red peppers, salt and black pepper. Keep warm over low heat.

3 Add the cooked lentils, 2 tablespoons of the dill and 1 tablespoon of the mint and cook, stirring, until heated through, about 5 minutes. Sprinkle with the vinegar and stir to combine.

4 Spoon into a serving dish and sprinkle with the feta. Top with the remaining 2 tablespoons dill and the remaining1 tablespoon mint.

Substitutions

Used jarred roasted piquillo peppers in place of the roasted red peppers.

Sources

Grains

Israeli couscous
www.chefshop.com
(800) 596-0885

Forbidden Rice and Bhutanese red rice
www.lotusfoods.com
(866) 972-6879

Red quinoa
www.worldpantry.com
(866) 972-6879

Farro
www.markethallfoods.com
(888) 952-4005

Middle Eastern Specialties

Pomegranate molasses
Moroccan spice blend (*ras el hanout*)
Preserved lemons
www.kalustyans.com
(800) 352-3451

Spices

Za'atar
Moroccan spice blend (*ras el hanout*)
Pimentón da la Vera (smoked paprika)
www.thespicehouse.com
(847) 328-3711

Pimentón de la Vera (smoked paprika)
www.markethallfoods.com
(888) 952-4005

Madras curry powder
www.aumarche.com
(877) 386-5551

Asian Ingredients

Black sesame seeds
Chinese sesame seed paste
www.asianfoodgrocer.com
(888) 482-2742

Mexican Ingredients

Chipotle peppers
www.mexgrocer.com
(877) 463-9476

Pepitas (hulled pumpkin seeds)
www.nutsonline.com
(800) 558-6887

Spanish Ingredients

Piquillo peppers
www.markethallfoods.com
(888) 952-4005

Cookware

www.surlatable.com
(800) 243-0852

www.chefsresource.com
(866) 765-2433

Index